About the Authors

Myles J. Connor grew up in Milton, Massachusetts, the son of a decorated policeman. During the 1960s and '70s, he was the leader of a successful Boston rock-and-roll band, Myles and the Wild Ones. He robbed his first museum when he was twenty years old. Shortly after, he gained notoriety for his daring escape from a Maine jail, and for his involvement in a dramatic shoot-out with Boston police. Myles has planned and executed numerous bank robberies and museum heists, several of which are told here for the first time.

Coauthor Jenny Siler, the author of six novels, first met Myles in the fall of 2007. Together, Jenny and Myles have interviewed many eyewitnesses to the events described in the book. For help in reconstructing and corroborating Myles's story, Jenny combed through numerous documents, including newspaper archives, police reports, court records, transcripts of FBI interviews, and personal correspondence.

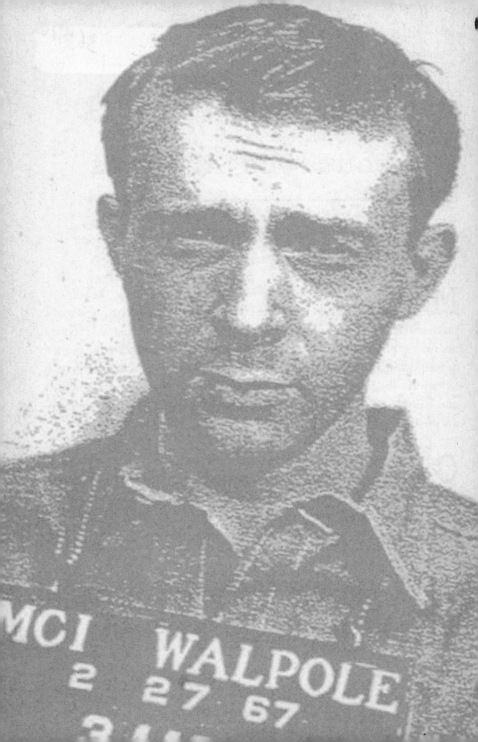

MCI WALPOLE
2 27 67

THE ART OF THE HEIST

Confessions of a Master Thief

MYLES J. CONNOR

& Jenny Siler

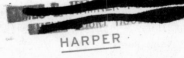

HARPER

NEW YORK • LONDON • TORONTO • SYDNEY

HARPER

A hardcover edition of this book was published in 2009 by
Collins, an imprint of HarperCollins Publishers.

HarperCollins books may be purchased for educational,
business, or sales promotional use. For information please
write: Special Markets Department, HarperCollins Publishers,
10 East 53rd Street, New York, NY 10022.

FIRST HARPER PAPER~~ ~~ ~~PUBLISHED~~ 2010.

Designed by William Ruoto

Library of Congress Cataloging-in-Publication data is
available upon request.

ISBN 978-0-06-167229-3 (pbk.)

10 11 12 13 14 OV/RRD 10 9 8 7 6 5 4 3 2 1

To my parents, Myles and Lucy
Connor, and my children Myles
J. Connor III, Kim Connor Tierney, and
my granddaughter, Taylor. Also in loving
memory of my granddaughter, Nicole.

And to my family and friends,
especially Suzanne King.

Special acknowledgment to
Martin K. Leppo, truly one of the best
trial lawyers in America, and my friend
for more than thirty years. Marty
has contributed so much to this book
that without him, it could not have
been written. And, of course, to my
longtime friend, manager, and
bandmate, Al Dotoli.

--Myles J. Connor Jr.

Prologue

By Jenny Siler

On March 18, 1990, shortly after 1:00 A.M., two men dressed in police uniforms and wearing false mustaches knocked on a side door of Boston's Isabella Stewart Gardner Museum. The night was typical of early spring in New England: foggy, with more than a bit of chill in the air. Around the city known for its Irish heart, St. Patrick's Day festivities were just winding down—in fact, revelers who were leaving a nearby party would later recall having seen the two men sitting in an unmarked car near the museum's side entrance. But for the pair waiting outside the Gardner Museum, the party was just beginning. After convincing one of the two night security guards to let them inside, the counterfeit cops quickly forced both guards down into the basement, where they duct-taped the men to support posts.

For the next hour the thieves roamed the museum unimpeded. Once in the galleries, they proceeded to unceremoniously slash priceless canvases from their frames. Though their methods were brutish, the men showed no small amount of expertise in their selection. Among the items they chose were "The Storm on the Sea of Galilee," the only seascape Rembrandt is known to have painted; "The Concert," a Vermeer masterpiece and one of only some thirty-five known paintings attributed to the Dutchman; Manet's "Chez Tortoni"; and five Degas drawings. They also took a Shang Dynasty bronze beaker and, in a gesture that has never ceased to puzzle investigators, the bronze finial from a Napoleonic flagstaff.

By 3:00 A.M. the thieves were gone, but not before they had removed the videotape from the museum's security cameras and ripped the computer printout from the motion detectors. The FBI, which soon took charge of the case, would call the heist the costliest of its kind in U.S. history. Estimates put the monetary value of the pieces taken that night at upward of $300 million. The cultural value of the masterworks, especially the one-of-a-kind Rembrandt seascape and the rare Vermeer, is, by all accounts, inestimable.

From the beginning the case proved dauntingly difficult to crack. The thieves may have been sloppy in their methods, but they left behind not a trace of evidence as to their identities. The theft of fine art differs from other crimes in that the passage of time can make these cases easier to solve rather than more difficult. Stolen artwork often surfaces years or even decades after the fact, as key players die, statutes of limitations expire, or pieces change hands. But after almost two decades, and despite a $5 million reward and global efforts to track down the missing Gardner Museum art, not a single item taken that night has been recovered.

In all that time, one name has surfaced again and again in connection with the robbery: Myles Connor.

A hometown art thief with a genius IQ and a flair for the dramatic, Connor was the man authorities immediately suspected when they were called to the Gardner Museum on the morning of March 18. When it came to museum robberies, Connor had a resume a mile long, including the 1975 theft of a Rembrandt from Boston's Museum of Fine Arts nearby. Almost every aspect of the Gardner heist carried Connor's fingerprints: the brazenness with which the theft had been carried out; the sophistication shown in the pieces chosen; even the police uniforms, which were a form of disguise Connor and his associates had used in the past.

There was only one problem with this theory: at the time of the Gardner heist, Connor was in federal custody in Illinois. Still, so strong was the FBI's suspicion that Connor was somehow involved that one of the first actions they took was to place a call to the superintendent of the jail where Connor was being held, asking him to confirm that Connor, who had a history of daring prison escapes, was still in his cell. He was.

When questioned about his involvement in the theft, Connor's reply was impudent. "You'd have known if it was me. I would have taken the Titian," he said, referring to one of the centerpieces of the Gardner Museum's collection, a large oil painting depicting the rape of Europa.

Despite his airtight alibi, Connor was and remains a prime suspect in the Gardner theft. The FBI and others claim he masterminded the heist from his prison cell, hoping to use some of the artwork as a bargaining chip to reduce his federal sentence. As with so much else in the murky world of art and antiquities theft, the truth about Connor's involvement in the events of that March evening is much more complicated than anyone might have guessed.

This account will not neatly resolve this particular case. It will show how the son of an honest cop grew up to become the country's most notorious art thief, one who is still a prime suspect in the Gardner theft. But there is more to Connor's story than the unraveling of that particular mystery. Over the course of a long career in crime, Myles Connor's passion for fine art slowly merged with his love of misadventure. He grew from a petty thief to a gun- and drug-runner, violent outlaw, and eventually art thief.

Like any true story, it is not always a pretty one. Yet Connor's charm is evident. He is a rogue at heart, a man who inspires fierce loyalty and even love in those who know him well—not through intimidation, but through the sheer force of his personality.

As incredible as it may seem, this is a work of fact, not fiction. With the exception of a small handful of incidents, to which Myles himself is the only living witness, the events described in this book have been painstakingly researched and carefully corroborated using newspaper accounts, eyewitness testimony, court records, and various other original documents. For obvious reasons, most names have been changed to protect the innocent—or guilty, as that may be. Other than that, the account you are about to read is true.

One
___

The feeling of being alone in an empty museum is always the same. There's a rush to it, an elevation of the senses that's not unlike the pleasant high of cocaine. You're not hyper, just mildly elated, drunk on the notion of having the run of the place, on the idea that all these treasures are yours to take. It's a sweet feeling, one I've never gotten tired of, not on my twentieth heist, nor my fiftieth, nor my hundredth.

I love fine art and objects of cultural significance. Over the years, I've found many ways to obtain them, some legal, some not. I'm a collector, specializing in Asian art and weaponry, especially Japanese swords. I find handcrafted pieces to be exquisite, especially those made by highly skilled craftsmen. Despite what my record might lead one to believe, I'm not particularly fond of European art. Given the option, I'd choose a Ming vase or a fourteenth-century *katana* over a Rembrandt any day. I've purchased much of my collection legitimately, at auctions or estate sales or from reputable dealers. But I've also obtained many fine works by, shall we say, less legitimate means. I've used fraud, breaking and entering, and brute force.

To be successful at not just one of these methods but all requires a certain combination of love of adventure and plain recklessness. It's what landed me in jail for the first time in my life, in 1965, and it's also what got me out.

You know the story about the guy who breaks out of jail using a fake gun? You've heard it: some con whittles a pistol out of a block of wood or a bar of soap, then blackens it with shoe polish and uses it to muscle his way past the guards. They say that's how John Dillinger broke out of Indiana's "escape-proof" Crown Point jail in 1934.

I know what you're thinking: it's a great story, but there's no way it's true. If anything, it's one of those urban legends that get more outrageous with time. For starters, no one in their right mind would have the guts to pull such a stunt. Even if someone was crazy enough to try, they sure as hell wouldn't get away with it. Maybe something like that could happen in the movies, or on TV. But in real life? No way.

Well, that's where you're wrong.

How can he be so sure? you're wondering. It's easy. See, I am that guy. In the summer of 1965 I broke out of the Hancock County jail in Ellsworth, Maine, using nothing more than a bar of soap, a razor blade, and some boot polish. It wasn't as difficult as you might think. These things never are. All you need is a plan. A plan and the balls to go through with it.

As far as lockups go, the Hancock County jail was no better or worse than similar facilities I would encounter over the years. The building, constructed in the late nineteenth century, was a large brick structure situated just back from Ellsworth's Main Street, between the courthouse and the town library, on a high embankment overlooking the Union River. The front portion of the building served as the sheriff's house. At the time of my incarceration, the sheriff's entire family, including his wife and teenage stepson, lived there. As was often the case in these small-town facilities, our meals were cooked by the sheriff's wife. The rear of the building housed the sheriff's offices, with the jail itself, a warren of damp, low-ceilinged cells, in the basement directly below.

Maine in 1965 was not exactly a hotbed of criminal activity. For the previous several years I'd been making my living singing and playing guitar in rock-and-roll clubs around the Boston area, mainly in the suburb of Revere Beach. Revere was traditionally an Italian neighborhood, and many of my acquaintances were real bad guys, mobsters who made my fellow inmates at the Hancock County jail look like kindergartners. The Ellsworth group was a motley collection of downeasters, local hicks who'd been brought in for relatively minor offenses like drunk driving or vagrancy. The worst of the bunch were there on charges of domestic assault.

I was twenty-two at the time. Though by no means a seasoned criminal, I already had two museum heists under my belt. Compared to these, the crime that landed me in the Hancock County jail was unimpressive. I'd been caught robbing a house in Sullivan, Maine, something that would have been a relatively minor offense had I not shot at the arresting officer and fled the scene. This act of brazenness had made me a celebrity among my jailmates.

As much as I enjoyed my star status, I was desperate to get home. There wasn't much to do at the little jail except play cards and read pulp paperbacks, diversions I've never really enjoyed. More important, all my possessions, including an extensive collection of art and antiques—some of which I'd procured by unconventional means—were back at my apartment in Revere. Among them were a number of Japanese swords, several Chinese vases and Japanese bronzes, some Asian watercolors, Paul Revere silver, and a particularly valuable Frederic Remington bronze statue of a cowboy on horseback that had belonged to my grandfather. These valuables represented my bank account—one I'd have to tap into if I was going to make bail and beat my current rap—and I wasn't exactly keen on the idea of leaving them unattended, especially considering the lax attitudes of many of my Revere acquaintances when it came to the issue of ownership. In short, I needed to get out, and fast.

I'd been formulating a plan for doing so almost from the beginning, paying close attention to the jailhouse rhythms, looking for an opportunity to make my escape. By my fifth day there I was pretty sure I'd found one.

Small-town lockups inevitably rely on trustees to do many of the facility's more menial tasks. Trustees are inmates, usually harmless repeat offenders, town drunks and vagrants, who tend to prefer the routine of life in lockup to the stress of fending for themselves on the street. Many of the men who become trustees are not bad people, just incapable, for whatever reason, of getting along like the rest of us. They see the jail as a kind of home and the jailers as family. The tasks they are assigned—cleaning, delivering meals—give them a much-needed sense of purpose.

Some trustees, however, enjoy what they do a little bit too much. These men generally have just enough smarts to understand power and enjoy its perks but not enough to acquire authority in the outside world. Most of them have been bullied and pushed around their whole lives and, given even the smallest amount of power, are eager to push back. The trustee in Ellsworth was such a man.

He was small of build, no taller than five foot six, somewhere in his early forties, with dark stringy hair and the clothes of a tramp. I never learned his real name, but everyone at the jail called him Bowwow, and this is what he answered to. One of his main tasks, and the one he most obviously enjoyed, was locking us into our cells in the evening. During the day we were allowed to congregate outside our cells. But at eight o'clock every night we'd hear a jangling of keys as the deputy sheriff came down the steps with Bowwow behind him.

"Okay, Bowwow," the deputy sheriff would then announce, handing the trustee his keys, "lock 'em in the cells."

And Bowwow, gleefully accepting his privilege, would lock every cell, looking us each in the eye and smiling as he did it.

My plan was not a complicated one. I'd heard the Dillinger story myself, and I figured if he could make it work, so could I. The last thing I wanted was to be involved in assaulting another peace officer, and I was banking on the fact that a fake gun would provide sufficient distraction for me to break out without causing serious physical harm to anyone.

I was not at all unfamiliar with firearms. My father and grandfather were both avid gun collectors, and I myself had been collecting firearms since I was a boy, saving my pennies to buy antique derringers instead of candy or comic books. The derringer was the gun I chose for my model, mainly because it was small enough to be realistically sculpted from a bar of soap, the only material available to me at the time.

During the afternoon of the day of my planned escape, I set to work fabricating my soap pistol. Given the crude tools and materials I had to work with, no one could have expected genius. Nonetheless, I managed to produce a reasonable facsimile of a derringer using my jail-issue razor blade. With the addition of a coat of boot polish, lent to me by a fellow prisoner, the gun looked surprisingly real.

That evening, just before the eight o'clock lockdown, I turned to my jailmates, who were gathered in the common area playing cards.

"Listen," I announced, "in about one minute I'm gonna open the door and walk out of this place. Anyone want to come along?"

The men stared at me with a mixture of awe and disbelief.

Tucking the soap derringer into the waistband of my pants, I bent down and double-knotted the laces on my boots, pulling them tight. It's details like this that can mean the difference between success and failure. I'd heard from one of the other prisoners that there was a path behind the jail that followed the river downstream. My hope was to make a run for it along this path, and I didn't want to risk getting tripped up by a loose bootlace.

As I straightened up I heard Bowwow's footsteps on the stairs and the familiar jangling of the deputy sheriff's keys. The two men reached the common area and stopped.

"Okay, Bowwow," came the deputy sheriff's familiar pronouncement. "Lock 'em in the cells."

Bowwow turned to me, leering. "Get in your cell," he snarled.

Taking a step toward the deputy sheriff, I drew my little derringer. "Look, pal," I said, waving him toward the nearest cell, "I don't want to shoot you."

Bowwow's jaw dropped.

The deputy sheriff looked at the little pistol, then back at me. He himself was unarmed, having removed his gun before coming downstairs to the cells, as is standard prison procedure. I could tell what he was thinking. I'm not a large person, and taller, bigger men like him always think they can take me. That's where I have the advantage.

"Oh no you don't," he said, grabbing my wrist with both his hands. It was the worst thing the man could have said to me.

I've always been the kind of person who hates being told what to do. A pronouncement like this is nothing more than a challenge to me, one from which I have so far never backed down.

Immediately I dropped the soap gun. I easily disengaged myself from the man's grasp and tagged him once in the chest. I didn't hit him hard—I truly didn't want to hurt him—but hard enough that he stumbled backward into the cell behind him, landing asprawl on the cement floor.

With the deputy sheriff down, I turned to Bowwow. The trustee was still standing there, his mouth wide open. I can't remember if I pushed him or tagged him, probably the latter, since I'd been entertaining this idea since my first night there. If anyone ever deserved to get hit, it was Bowwow.

In any case, down he went. And up I went, leaving the homemade derringer, which had served its purpose, behind.

"You can wash your face with that," I called out as I sprinted up the stairs to the sheriff's offices and out the side door of the jail.

I was working on blind faith, hoping that the description I'd been given of the jail grounds and the river path had been accurate. It was a good hour past sunset, the lights of the town blazing against the black of night. I headed across the small jail yard toward the short retaining wall that ran along the top of the high riverbank. Beyond the wall the ground fell away sharply to the river. Far below, phantom lights skimmed the water's black surface. Cars passing on the Route 1 bridge just a few dozen yards downstream. House windows. The lights of the jail itself and of the library next door. In the distance I could hear the roar of an upstream dam.

I turned eastward and ran, following the wall as I'd been advised to do, scanning the dark bank for the promised path and seeing nothing. I could hear footsteps behind me now, and two distinct voices, those of the deputy sheriff and the sheriff, who had no doubt been enjoying a quiet evening with his family just moments earlier.

"Halt!" A voice I recognized as the deputy sheriff's called out, far too close for comfort.

I paused for an instant on the wall, briefly considering my choices. Downstream lay the Route 1 bridge, where I could already see car lights massing in the darkness; upstream, the dam and the woods beyond. Suddenly, my options were strikingly clear: I could take my chances in the river or stay dry and end up back in my cell, presumably as a much less welcome guest than before. It took me only an instant to make my decision. Propelling myself forward into the darkness, I leaped from the wall to the embankment below. I hit the loose ground and scrambled downward, stumbling over roots and rocks, fighting the underbrush, finally making my way to a large boulder perched just above the water.

"Halt!" A second voice this time: the sheriff's.

I paused again, flexing my feet in my boots, feeling the rock against my soles. And then I jumped.

As my body arced toward the river I heard the sheriff once again, his words perfectly clear, punctuated by the darkness. "Jesus Christ!" he exclaimed. "He dove into the goddamned river!"

No kidding.

Then, in an instant, I hit the water.

To call that river cold may be the greatest understatement of my life. Frigid doesn't even cut it. January-in-the-north-woods-freeze-your-balls-off is closer to how it felt, but even that falls short. Once in the water I went down fast, rocketing into a treacherous tangle of tree limbs and other debris at the bottom of the river. Suddenly, my earlier decision to double-knot my laces, which at the time had seemed like brilliant foresight, was revealed as something less than that, as my water-logged boots pulled me down.

I struggled upward and got nowhere. I had taken a deep breath before I went under, but my lungs were already burning. Groping frantically in the darkness I located the tops of my boots. I tugged at the laces, fumbling with numb fingers at the stubborn double knots.

I'd like to say I had regrets, that my young life and all I had yet to accomplish flashed before me. I suppose it's what I should say.

But the truth is that as I lay there at the bottom of the Union River, face-to-face with the darkness around me, fighting the instinct to take a breath, my only thoughts were of the glory of what I'd just done, of what a damn fine story this whole episode would make, and what a shame it was that I wouldn't live to tell it to my friends back in Revere. Whether it was my desire to tell it firsthand or a lingering affection for all those stolen antiques in my apartment, I'll never know. But somehow I was able to find the strength to break free of the river's grasp and pull myself upward.

I came to the surface, gasping and sputtering, cold and already exhausted, but certain I had made it through the worst and was now home free. I just had to reach the opposite bank, I told myself, stretching my arms out, cutting across the powerful current toward the dark swath of woods beyond. If I could only get out of the river, they'd never catch me.

As I neared the shore, however, a light appeared in the trees, the beam of a single flashlight combing the darkness. Treading water, I stopped where I was and scanned the woods. Soon a second light appeared, then a third, then dozens more, as searchers poured into the woods from the road above. Ridiculously, I thought of all the monster movies I'd seen as a kid, the mob with their torches coming for the creature. Only this time it wasn't Dracula or Frankenstein whose blood they were after, but mine.

I turned in the water, looking back in the direction from which I'd come, once again considering my options. The question now wasn't whether I would make it back to Revere but whether the story I'd have to tell would be one of triumph or defeat. I sure as hell wasn't ready to surrender.

Two

————

It was the adrenaline rush of art and theft that landed me in that jail and in that river. If you'd known me in the years leading up to 1965, however, you never would have predicted it. A man could write a book about himself and still not solve the puzzle of who he really is.

The easy answer is that I'm Myles Connor Jr., son of Myles and Lucy Connor of Milton, Massachusetts, grandson of Charles and Ruth Johnson of Winthrop, Maine, and Bill and Mary Connor of County Galway, Ireland. I was born on February 1, 1943, during one of the biggest nor'easters of that era, at Carney Hospital in Dorchester, Massachusetts, and grew up in Milton, home to the Baker's chocolate mill and the Forbes Museum. Later in life I would become famous for robbing that museum, among others.

I would like to say my childhood was extraordinary, that acts of cruelness or deprivation made me what I am. But this is not the case. I grew up the younger of two children, in a loving home, in a town that smelled perpetually of warm cocoa and brownies. For the first thirteen years of my life we lived with my mother's parents, in a middle-class neighborhood in Milton. My maternal grandfather, though by no means wealthy (his side of the family had fallen on hard times several generations earlier), was a direct descendant of *Mayflower* passenger William Brewster. He was an avid collector of art and antiques, especially antique weapons, and it is from him that I learned much of what I know about these things.

The education I received at my grandfather's hands was not a formal one. Rather, art and the appreciation of it were constants in our home. He took great pride in his collection and loved to tell me about the individual pieces. When I was not in school I often accompanied my grandfather to the Museum of Fine Art in Boston. His encyclopedic knowledge of the pieces in the MFA's collection never ceased to amaze me.

My paternal grandparents had come to Boston from Ireland some years earlier. According to family lore, my grandfather Connor's emigration was not so much a choice as a necessity, a result of an unfortunate incident in which a local constable in County Galway was shot. If I inherited my wild nature from any one person, it would be him. During my childhood he and my grandmother lived not far from us, in South Boston, and I saw them regularly. Being good Irish Catholics, they dragged me to church every Sunday, a ritual that had little influence other than to make me forever skeptical of all organized religions. It's something I regret to this day, as I am keenly aware of the solace religion brings to some. I have often felt cheated by my own lack of faith.

My grandfather's outlaw nature had little influence on my father, who, like so many young South Boston Irishmen of his time, chose to become a police officer. I've encountered more than my share of cops in my life, and I can tell you from experience that not all of them are good men. Some are corrupt, using their power to their own benefit; some are even downright cruel. My father was neither of these things. Rather, he had an understanding of human nature and its frailties that made him deeply compassionate at heart.

If anything, he was fair to a fault, never persistent enough at getting arrests to be promoted to lieutenant. I know for a fact that there were times when he was pressured to twist the truth. I also know he never budged. Years later, when I was doing time at the state prison in Walpole, I met one of my dad's perps on the inside, and the man still remembered the integrity with which my father had conducted himself.

Ironically, much of the trouble I got into later in life may be due to my father's honest nature. I was not used to crooked cops, and in fact never imagined that the police I encountered might be any different from my father.

Like my grandfather, my father was a serious collector of guns, though he preferred modern firearms to antiques, specifically German guns manufactured after World War I. It was an interest I quickly came to share with him. Early modern guns are masterpieces in their own right. So precise are the workings of a well-made Walther or Browning that the weapon fairly floats in your hand. From an early age I accompanied my father to antique stores and flea markets.

At that time antiques collecting was not nearly as popular as it is today. There were some very good, and reasonably inexpensive, finds to be had. I spent every penny I earned doing chores and odd jobs at auctions and antique shops. By the time I was a teenager I had accumulated a substantial collection of my own.

Though I occasionally bought other pieces—I was especially fascinated by derringers—the majority of my collection consisted of antique Japanese swords, which I had come to regard not only as the finest weapons ever made but as true works of art in their own right, due to the incredibly complex process used in their creation.

Production began in the forge, where a rough blade was formed from a combination of two metals: a soft yet durable iron core, and a hard outer skin of steel that had been forged and reforged many times through a complex process of repeated heating, folding, and hammering. This ingenious method created a blade that was both incredibly strong—a result of the pliancy of the soft iron core—yet hard enough to take a razor-sharp edge thanks to the rigid steel shell.

Once the blade was finished it was subjected to a unique tempering process in which heat-resistant clay was applied to the entire blade. The clay was then scraped away only at the edge of the blade, allowing for intense tempering of the exposed area and resulting in a super-rigid edge capable of unparalleled cutting power.

Finally, the blade was painstakingly polished by hand and carefully evaluated.

As is often the case with intensely specialized crafts requiring the work of many highly skilled artisans, each step in the manufacturing process eventually evolved into its own unique art form. Perhaps the most notable of these was the *hamon,* or blade pattern. A ghostly visual effect created on the blade during the tempering process, the *hamon* marks the area of superhardened metal where the edge was exposed during tempering. Eventually, as swordsmiths realized that they could control this imprint, they created unique signature patterns to mark their work.

My fascination with these *hamon,* which are now considered art forms in themselves, not only drew me to start collecting Japanese swords as a boy but continues to inspire the collector in me today.

In addition to their common love for firearms, my father and grandfather also shared a deep interest in martial arts. My father studied jujitsu for some time. By the age of twelve I had followed in his footsteps and was taking judo classes at the Boston YMCA. I was also studying karate with a friend of my maternal grandfather, a Japanese gentleman named Watanabe. By the time I reached my early teens I had attained a modest level of proficiency and was sparring regularly with adults, a practice that no doubt contributed to my cockiness with law enforcement and other authority figures in the years to come. More interestingly, Mr. Watanabe introduced me to the fundamentals of Eastern philosophy, including the Shinto religion and the samurai code of Bushido.

Developed between the ninth and twelfth centuries from the original samurai moral code of conduct, Bushido, which literally means "way of the warrior," united the violence of samurai life with the wisdom and serenity of Confucianism and Buddhism, stressing loyalty, mastery of martial arts, and, most important, honor to the death.

Bushido is perhaps most well known for its incorporation of seppuku, a ritual in which samurais who somehow failed to uphold their honor could regain it by performing ritual suicide. But what drew me to Bushido were the seven basic virtues it espoused: rectitude, courage, benevolence, respect, honesty, honor, and loyalty. It's a code I have continued to study and adhere to all my life.

• • •

My burgeoning love of antique weapons and martial arts was matched only by my passion for rock and roll. I began singing and playing the guitar when I was twelve years old, and soon discovered that I had a real talent for making music. My first band, if you can call it that, consisted of me with a guitar and my friend Ronnie Castriano on drums. Ronnie came from Quincy, and his uncle was co-owner of the Reef, a popular nightclub in Revere. Though I would eventually go on to perform at the Reef and other clubs of its caliber, the venues Ronnie and I played in those early years were far less sophisticated.

One of the first clubs we played regularly, starting in the summer of 1957, was a place down in Nantasket called Al's Spaghetti House. Al's was little more than a boardwalk fry shack with a small stage. On summer weekends a local country band headlined there, drawing the weekend beach crowd. Ronnie had talked the owner into letting us play during the week, and we were soon drawing our own steady crowd.

Al himself was a dyed-in-the-wool Southie, a cantankerous Irishman who'd grown up just across the harbor from Boston and still had strong ties to the area, including his die-hard loyalty to the South Boston Chippewas. An amateur football team made up of off-duty Boston cops, firemen, and union tough guys, the Chippewas often came down to Al's after games or practices. As you might imagine, there was a fair amount of alcohol consumed at these gatherings. But for the most part they behaved themselves, at least to the extent that drunk Irishmen can.

One night, however, the team was especially belligerent. When Ronnie and I finished our last set, at 2:00 A.M., the footballers weren't yet ready to see the evening end. When we sat down at the bar to have our postshow Cokes (neither of us was old enough to drink at the time), things got nasty.

"You're real good," one of the Chippewas sneered, addressing Ronnie. "What are you, a faggot?"

Ronnie shook his head. "No."

"You've got long hair," the footballer commented menacingly. "You some kind of queer?"

"Yeah," one of his teammates chimed in. "You Little Richard?"

I leaned forward to get a better look at the pair. Each man had at least a foot and a hundred pounds on me. Any sane person would have known better than to take them on, but years of martial arts training and sparring with adults had left me suicidally fearless. Besides, I figured, my sobriety had to count for something.

"Yeah," I said, stepping around Ronnie. "And I'm Big Richard."

The first Chippewa took a wild swing at me and missed. I ducked, returning the punch, hitting him hard, sending him sprawling backward into the arms of his buddy.

In an instant the bar erupted. Most of the patrons hadn't witnessed the initial altercation and assumed that the beef was between the Southies and the locals. Suddenly everyone was in on the fight. One of the footballers jumped me, but I beat him off and made a break for the front door.

He followed me outside with two of his friends in tow. I managed to hold my own for a few minutes, keeping the threesome at bay, even downing one of the guys when he got close enough to hit. But soon the entire team was out on the sidewalk. Some of the Chippewas had brought their beer bottles with them and were throwing them at me. One hit me in the head and I felt myself go down. As I fell, I glanced up to see Ronnie sprinting past me, heading away from the melee. I hit the sidewalk hard, half-stunned, and felt a sharp blow to my ribs, followed by another and another, as the men gathered around to take turns kicking me.

I might have died that night, or at least been severely injured, if the cops hadn't finally pulled up. It was probably the only time in my life I was happy to see the police.

The gigs at Al's Spaghetti House provided us with steady employment during the summer months, but once the season wound down and the beach crowd went home, Ronnie and I were forced to look elsewhere for work. At the time, Milton high schoolers congregated on

Friday and Saturday nights at a place called Canteen, which was part of a clubhouse for town residents located inside Milton's Cunningham Park. It was the perfect venue for us, and we were soon playing there on a regular basis.

As our popularity grew, so did our band. By my sophomore year in high school we had gained a number of new members, mostly local kids like us who had taught themselves the rudiments of rock and roll and showed up at my house for jam sessions. Jimmy Gallagher and Chicky Goldberg were our bassists. Billy Fall and Johnny Egan played guitar. Pete Keenan and Dennis Hearn filled in on drums for Ronnie, who was less available during the school year. Trading on our onstage antics and the reputation I had earned in Nantasket, we dubbed ourselves Myles and the Wild Ones.

Our shows at Canteen were raucous affairs. At a time when the airwaves were dominated by buttoned-up instrumental groups like the Ventures, our style, which was heavy on vocals, was seen as wildly rebellious. With our sky-high pompadours and dapper smoking jackets, we put on quite a show, pounding out covers of Chuck Barry and Roy Orbison hits.

Eventually we caught the attention of Arnie "Woo Woo" Ginsburg, a well-known Boston radio personality and host of the beloved *Night Train Show* on WMEX. Myles and the Wild Ones eventually became part of Arnie's record hop retinue and began to build a following. We quickly made a name for ourselves and were soon playing at record hops and social clubs in and around the Boston area.

Every good band needs a manager. In 1959 Arnie hooked me up with Ralph Ranzo. A slick talker with a closet full of sharkskin suits, Ralph owned a local record shop in Mattapan and handled a number of bands in the Boston area. With Arnie's influence and Ralph's help, Myles and the Wild Ones graduated from Canteen to more impressive venues like the Surf Club and the Reef, both in Revere. Ralph also introduced me to a number of musicians from the Berklee College of Music in Boston, most notably a talented saxaphonist named Emmett Lowe. Emmett joined the Wild Ones onstage and also accompanied me into the studio when I cut my first single, an original song I had written titled "Someone, Somewhere." Emmett was a rare talent and eventually went on to play with James Brown.

The studio gig was a high point for me. Unfortunately, it was also the beginning of the end for Myles and the Wild Ones. By 1961 my original bandmates and I had started to go our separate ways. As we headed into the final years of high school, cars, girls, and even jobs demanded more and more of my bandmates' time.

Later that year Andy Naggi, the owner of the Revere Beach Plaza, a boardwalk resort with hotel rooms on the second floor and a restaurant and music club, the Lewis Room, on the first floor, offered me a steady gig as a single. I jumped at the chance to earn a regular paycheck, and earn it I did. I played six nights a week from eight o'clock till two in the morning, with fifteen-minute breaks between sets. Still, the pay and working conditions were better than at the local A&P. Eventually I even talked Naggi into hiring my friend Dennis Hearn to back me up on drums.

Dennis and I were a huge hit with the audiences in Revere, but despite the fact that I was earning a steady living as a musician, I was entirely on my own when it came to managing my career. With the dissolution of the Wild Ones, Ralph Ranzo had lost interest in representing me, leaving me to fend for myself. But that was about to change.

One afternoon in 1962 Dennis and I were practicing at my house when there was a knock on the door. I opened it to see a tall, gangly fourteen-year-old kid standing on the front stoop.

"You're Myles Connor," he blurted out, as if he was face-to-face with Elvis.

"I know that," I told him. "Who are you?"

"I'm Al Dotoli," he announced. "And I want to learn to play the guitar like you."

"Okay," I agreed, taking an instant liking to the kid. I ushered him inside and we started our first lesson.

I would later learn that Al had been a fan for some time before he worked up the courage to come knock on my door. He'd heard my band play on a number of occasions, at the Christopher Columbus Club in Boston's North End and at Canteen. He lived just around the corner from me in Milton, but I'd never met him because he went to the Catholic high school.

As it turned out, Al already knew how to play the guitar. His style just needed some fine-tuning. When I met him, Al was playing with a local British Wave band called the Druids. I taught him how to play my brand of rock and roll, and we quickly became friends. In return he proposed that I use the Druids as my new backup band.

I was skeptical at first. With their Beatles boots, Nehru jackets, and British musical style, the Druids seemed like a poor fit for me. But Al's plan was ingenious. The Druids, he explained, would open for me as themselves. Then they'd run backstage and change into motorcycle jackets and dungarees, transforming themselves into a rock-and-roll band.

Al's strategy worked brilliantly. Far from being a problem, the contrast in musical styles was a huge asset, broadening the appeal of both bands. On my nights off from the Lewis Room, we were soon playing shows at teen halls all over the Boston area. We eventually scored a steady gig at a place called Broadcove Teen Haven in Hingham, which was owned by a friend of my father's, a fellow Milton detective named Jimmy Cox. In addition to backing me up and playing guitar for the Druids, Al also started playing bass for my shows at the Lewis Room. It was a grueling schedule, but I loved every minute of it.

Playing music and being onstage was exhilarating. But what I really enjoyed was the opportunity my music afforded me to defy the expectations of Boston's rigid caste system. Centuries after its founding, Boston was a city that remained true to its English roots, a place where birth and breeding mattered. Boston in the 1960s was perhaps the most segregated city north of the Mason-Dixon Line. And not just in terms of race. People of different ethnicities and religions just didn't mix. The borders of class and clan were not to be crossed under any circumstances. A Southie was always a Southie and a black always a black, no matter how smart he was or how diligently he worked. Neither Andover nor Harvard was knocking on any doors in Dorchester. Similarly, the mongrel son of a Milton cop was, and always would be, just that.

But the rules of rock and roll, at least as I wrote them, had no regard for these distinctions. In those early days we couldn't afford to be picky. We would play anywhere, in any neighborhood, as long as there was a promise of a good crowd and a paycheck. Not surprisingly, our lax attitudes about social mores often got us into trouble.

Aside from being a talented musician, Al Dotoli was a natural entrepreneur. Even at fourteen, he had a head for the management side of the music business. Not content, as Ronnie and I were, to merely show up, play, and have a good time, Al had higher ambitions for the band, and was determined to start putting on shows himself.

The first concert Al put together on his own was at St. Agatha's, a Catholic parish and elementary school in Milton. Wanting to make sure the event was well attended, Al launched an all-out advertising campaign, plastering the South Shore with posters. His tactics worked. By the time I arrived for the show the auditorium at St. Agatha's was already overfull. Kids were lined up outside waiting to get in.

In those days, record hops and rock-and-roll concerts were often the scene of confrontations between rival gangs. Kids from Savin Hill in Dorchester or the East Milton townies came to a show like ours for one thing: to pay their dollar, get inside, and start a fight. Anticipating trouble, Al had hired bouncers to work the door and the floor. But despite his precautions, the atmosphere in the hall was tense from the start.

Aside from the Druids, Al had booked another local band, the Miltones, which was started by Jocko Marcellino, who would eventually go on to become the drummer for the band Sha Na Na. The Miltones opened the show for us at St. Agatha's, and the Druids played second. After their set, Al ducked into the parish hall kitchen, which we were using as a makeshift dressing room, and quickly changed out of his Beatle boots and Nehru jacket and into his signature Wild Ones motorcycle outfit.

"It's a great crowd," I said as I watched him change. "We're gonna rock 'em."

Al nodded enthusiastically, then dashed back out onstage to introduce me, as he always did.

"Give it up for Myles Connor!" I heard him yell, fighting to be heard over the roar of the crowd.

If anything can compare to the high I get from being in an empty museum, it's the feeling of stepping onstage before an audience. Any entertainer worth his salt knows exactly what I mean. As I took my place on the stage at St. Agatha's that day I was euphoric. Evidently, my condition was infectious. When I started into my first song, a cover of Roy Orbison's "Pretty Woman," the crowd went wild, dancing and cheering.

But soon enough a fight broke out. Eventually the police were called.

I was so engrossed in my music that I didn't notice what was happening until a uniformed figure strode onto the stage and grabbed the microphone from me. It was my father. Evidently he'd been trying to signal me to stop playing for some time and had finally given up and decided to take matters into his own hands.

"This is the third fight we've had here tonight," he boomed, immediately silencing the crowd. "If we have any more disturbances, we're going to shut this place down."

What could I do? Grinning, I threw my arm around him. "Oh, Dad!" I said theatrically. The place erupted in cheers.

Eventually another fight did break out, forcing my father to make good on his threat. The fight continued outside and the fire department had to be called in to hose the crowd down. Luckily, Al managed to grab the cash box and sprint out the back door with our profits before that happened. It wasn't the last time one of our shows ended in chaos, but it was certainly the most memorable.

Every rock-and-roll musician needs a persona. In constructing mine I took a cue from the name of my original band. With the money I earned playing music I bought a jet black 1955 Eldorado convertible. I quickly cultivated a reputation for wildness, drag racing or showing up to record hops and concerts riding a motorcycle Al Dotoli and I shared. One of my signature concert moves was to ride the motorcycle up onto the stage, hop off, and immediately start in on a rendition of "Good Golly Miss Molly" or "Johnny B. Goode." To further my image I took to publicly demonstrating my karate skills.

I had always loved animals and kept any number of pets at my mother's house. As the band gained popularity I took to collecting more and more exotic animals. One of my favorites was a Doberman named Gunner that I'd rescued from the experiment facility at MIT. With his sleek black coat and muscular physique, Gunner was a perfect mascot for the band.

Later, when I had moved out of my mother's house and was living in a room over the Revere Beach Plaza, I bought a baby cougar from an exotic-animal dealer in New York City. At that time the laws about keeping exotic pets were much more lax. Sinbad, as I named the little cougar, lived in my room with me. I trained him to use a litter box and took him on regular walks around Revere. Unfortunately, he eventually outgrew the confines of my small home, and I reluctantly gave him away to a fellow animal enthusiast who had more room for the cat to roam. Years later, Sinbad became quite a celebrity in his own right when he starred opposite Farrah Fawcett in a famous commercial for the Mercury Cougar.

I'd be lying if I didn't say that everything you've heard about rock and roll and women is true. It's a universal rule that women love musicians. Before my eighteenth birthday I had more girlfriends than I could handle. Soon I also had a baby on the way. Not long after, I found myself standing at the altar of St. Mary's church in Milton uttering the fateful words "I do." A few months later my son, Myles, was born.

I can tell you from experience that being eighteen, married, a father, and a rock and roller is not necessarily the best combination. Victoria was a good woman, and I had genuine feelings for her. But our marriage was doomed from the start. I was, to put it mildly, hardly a priest. Though I have yet to know a priest who could have withstood a nightly barrage of willing young women with his celibacy intact. After just a few short years together, and with a second baby already on the way, Victoria and I separated.

The wonderful world of women wasn't the only thing playing rock and roll introduced me to. It wasn't long before I found myself traveling in the same circles as some of Boston's biggest crime bosses. Today the Revere Beach oceanfront is abloom with million-dollar condominiums and espresso bars, but in the early sixties it was the Coney Island of New England, complete with an amusement park and a lively boardwalk scene. Weekend nights, kids from all over Massachusetts and beyond converged on the clubs along Revere Beach Avenue to hear local bands pay tribute to Elvis or the Everly Brothers.

Traditionally an Italian neighborhood, Revere was also where members of many of Boston's organized crime families came to party. Some even owned clubs along the Avenue. The Lewis Room was a favorite hangout of area wise guys.

It's hard to imagine a more unlikely set of friendships than those involving the son of an Irish cop and a bunch of Italian mobsters, but we had more in common than you might think.

There are four things the Italians value above all else: family, discipline, loyalty, and culture. In our shared passion for all four we were kindred spirits. The Italians were impressed by my knowledge of fine art and antiques and by my proficiency in martial arts. But more then anything, they recognized in me the kind of unwavering loyalty they demanded from their friends.

Though I am fiercely proud of my Irish heritage and deeply love my Irish family and friends, I felt more at home in the Italian clubs of Revere Beach than I ever had in the Irish bars of South Boston. Irish clubs are traditionally rowdy places. Our South Shore gigs were inevitably punctuated by name-calling and fistfights or, worse, by brawls like the one at Al's Spaghetti House. But in the Italian clubs the atmosphere was always one of order and mutual respect.

As much as I enjoyed being part of the regular crowd at the Lewis Room, I quickly became intrigued by tales of what happened away from the club, of back-alley gun battles and bank robberies in broad daylight. I have always had a sore spot for authority, and the idea of thumbing my nose at the Man (as anyone of authority was known at the time) held no small amount of allure for me.

My transition from wild-child rock and roller to career lawbreaker didn't happen all at once. My earliest crimes were on such a small scale that they didn't seem like crimes at all, like the acquisition of weapons that were not necessarily legal. It wasn't until my first successful museum robbery in 1965 that I began to think of myself as an actual criminal.

In the winter of that year the Forbes mansion in my hometown of Milton opened its doors to the public as the Captain Robert Bennet Forbes House Museum. A wealthy China trade merchant, the captain had spearheaded the expansion of U.S. trade with China during the 1800s, and he had a nice collection of Asian art to show for his efforts. Prompted by my interest in martial arts and Asian culture in general, curious to see inside the stately home I'd passed countless times as a boy, I decided to pay the museum a visit. It was an eye-opening experience, to say the least.

The Forbes collection included priceless Chinese porcelains along with precious paintings, early American silverware, and furniture of the highest quality and craftsmanship. And all of it was laid out as if the mansion was not a museum but still a private home. It was an unusual setup, the most interesting aspect of which was the obviously lax attitude about security. Unlike the collections in most other museums, the pieces in the Forbes Museum were not in glass cases or behind ropes but set out as if for daily use. The temptation was almost too much for me to bear.

I say "almost" because, despite the easy accessibility of the museum's collection, to this day I'm still not sure I would have actively set out to rob the place if it had not been for the attitudes of the museum staff. The first time I wandered into the Forbes Museum, their contempt was palpable. Though none of them knew me, they could tell just by looking that I wasn't one of them.

Milton was no different from Boston in its class snobbery. If anything, being a smaller town, it was actually worse. As the son of a policeman, I was presumed to possess neither the raw intelligence nor the breeding to appreciate something so refined as art or antiques. But unlike the majority of those who composed Milton's working class, I refused to be intimidated into believing this was actually the case. To the contrary, I knew full well I was better than those who scorned me, and set out to prove it.

Over the course of the next few months I became a regular visitor to the Forbes Museum. I quickly confirmed what I had first suspected: that security at the museum was practically nonexistent. As far as I could tell, there were no alarms. After-hours security consisted of one guard, a young man who, I observed after several evenings of casual surveillance, consistently left the premises between seven and ten every evening, presumably to visit his girlfriend.

Robbing the place, I concluded, would be a piece of cake.

In my world at the time, a robbery like the one I was planning seemed not only unremarkable but to be expected. Compared to the stories I heard nightly from my friends at the Lewis Room, the idea of sneaking into an empty building in the middle of the night and stealing a few old artifacts seemed downright tame. Certainly there was no danger of physical harm. And the theft of a few items from those who obviously had so much hardly seemed objectionable. If anything, I convinced myself, there was a Robin Hood element to the crime. I wasn't doing it for profit. I wanted the art, and I wanted the notch in my belt.

On the evening of the robbery I parked the van I normally used to haul my band's gear from gig to gig a few blocks from the museum and made my way to the premises. It was early summer, and the lush canopy of maple and oak trees on the museum property provided convenient cover as I made my way across the lawn to the back of the building. Using a small pry bar I'd brought with me, I jimmied a basement window and slipped inside.

Once upstairs I proceeded to gorge myself on precious antiques.

I took what I liked and wanted for myself, with little regard for resale value: several large Chinese vases, oil paintings, and a large silver platter that I eventually had to abandon on the lawn outside when it proved too heavy to carry. It was quite a haul. I made more than one trip out of the building, depositing my booty on the driveway, coming back later to pick it all up with the van.

The only problem was what to do next. Since the breakup of my marriage I'd been living in a small room over the Lewis Room. Realizing I couldn't possibly store everything there, I decided to leave a large portion with Vicky, who was living in Quincy with Myles III at the time. It was not the best decision I would ever make. Not long after, Vicky and her new boyfriend suffered an attack of conscience and returned their portion of the stolen goods to the front lawn of the Forbes House late one night.

But despite this minor setback, the evening was a resounding success. Elated to have pulled off my plan so easily, I vowed to follow it up with another museum heist.

It didn't take me long to make good on my promise. Soon after my success at the Forbes I set my sights on the Boston Children's Museum. The director in those days was Michael Spock, son of the famous pediatrician, and his work at the Children's Museum is credited with having revolutionized the museum experience. His hands-on philosophy, in which children were encouraged to touch priceless artifacts rather than simply view them from behind glass, seemed like a great idea to me. If they could get their hands on the stuff, surely I could too.

The first and most important lesson I learned from the Children's Museum is that there is no end to the information people will give you if you only go and ask for it. Presenting myself as a legitimate collector of Asian art (which, technically speaking, I was), I visited the museum and inquired about their collection. Impressed by my knowledge and delighted by my interest, a staff member cheerfully showed me upstairs to the museum's third-floor storage space, a treasure trove of artifacts that immediately set my heart racing.

Unlike the Forbes Museum, the Children's Museum had a substantial security system. The first- and second-floor windows were wired to a sophisticated alarm system. The third-floor windows, however, appeared to have no such safeguards. Later, standing outside the museum, I could see the reason for this: the windows were situated in such a way that only Spider-Man could have reached them. Never one to be put off by such trivial details, I decided that this was where I would make my entrance.

At the time, the Children's Museum was housed in an imposing mansion in an upscale neighborhood of equally imposing mansions in the Boston suburb of Jamaica Plain. It was a quiet part of town. On the night of the theft there wasn't a soul out to recognize me as I parked my van and made my way down the tree-lined Jamaicaway toward the museum. I was dressed in dark clothes, a trick I'd learned from Cary Grant in *To Catch a Thief*. In a bag I carried two coils of rope and the same pry bar I'd used at the Forbes Museum.

Many people are under the mistaken impression that short men are at a disadvantage in life. If anything, my stature has been one of my most important assets. A small person who has learned to use his body, as I have, is able to do things larger men find impossible. The strength and agility I've developed through years of martial arts training, combined with my naturally compact frame, have always made me an excellent climber.

On one of my earlier visits to the museum I'd scouted what I hoped would be a fairly easy route up the back of the building. Now it was time to put my skills to the test. Slinging my bag over my shoulder, I shimmied two stories up a sturdy iron drainpipe and, with considerable effort, clambered over the rooftop overhang. Once on the roof I took one of the ropes from my bag and tied one end around one of the mansion's several brick chimneys and the other end around my waist. Like a mountain climber working his way down the face of a cliff, I carefully lowered myself over the edge of the roof to the unalarmed attic window.

Spider-Man had arrived.

After snapping the latch with my pry bar and swinging my body inside, I untied myself and set to work. Unlike the Forbes Museum, where I had been able to literally drive my van right up to the front door, the Children's Museum presented a special problem. I was going to have to carry anything I took back up to the roof and then down the drainpipe. Over the course of several visits to the museum I'd made a careful selection. Most of the items I planned to take were among those in storage in the attic, but several were on exhibit in the downstairs galleries.

After pausing in the attic to get my bearings, I headed down the narrow staircase to the second floor. Still cocky from my recent success at the Forbes House, I was fairly whistling as I took the last few steps. It wasn't until I reached the downstairs hallway that I realized just how misguided my optimism was.

The scene before me was like something out of a Hollywood heist film: the dark galleries were crisscrossed with infrared beams. I stopped for a moment on the landing, trying to see a way through or around the web of red light, but there was none. I would have to satisfy myself with what I could find on the third floor.

Turning, I made my way back up to the attic to fulfill my wish list. With that accomplished, I slung my sack over my shoulder and, no doubt looking like a perverse Santa Claus, hauled myself to the rooftop. There, I tied my second rope around the bag and lowered it to the ground. Then, securing myself with the same rope I'd used to climb down to the dormer window, I clambered over the edge of the roof and shimmied down the drainpipe.

Three

As the summer of 1965 drew to a close I was in serious need of a vacation. My regular late nights at the Lewis Room, combined with the stress of marital trouble and the demands of my newfound passion for art, left me little time for relaxing. Even a Wild One needs a break from time to time.

I had spent a good portion of my childhood summers with my mother's family in Sullivan, Maine, a small community on the Atlantic coast, not far from Bar Harbor and just north of the larger town of Ellsworth. My mother's uncle was a lobsterman, and my aunt, and later my cousin, owned a campground and general store in Sullivan, from which the family made a modest living. They lived on a picturesque stretch of property overlooking Frenchman's Bay and the green hills of Mt. Desert Island. I've never known a more tranquil or beautiful place.

The summers I spent in Sullivan as a boy were some of the most magical times of my life, and I still recall them with great fondness. In the early mornings I would wander down to my great-uncle's little clapboard house by the sea and he would take me out in his lobster boat with him. In the afternoons my sister, Patsy, and my cousin Emmy Lou and I played in the woods or swam in the ice-cold waters of the bay.

Not surprisingly, these annual trips to Maine were a legacy I dearly wanted to pass on to my own children. Though Vicky and I were no longer living together, we had managed to remain friends. When I suggested that we all head north to spend a few weeks in Sullivan, she agreed.

My exploits had not gone unnoticed in Revere, where rumors of my extracurricular activities had reached the ears of the boys at the Lewis Room, contributing to their ever-growing opinion of me. Knowing my fascination with firearms, one of my Revere associates offered me a good deal on some guns he was looking to off-load, including an antique German 7.65 millimeter rifle and several army carbine-type rifles, one of which was fully automatic. Partly out of genuine interest in the firearms, and partly because of the impact I knew acquiring them would have on my reputation, I quickly agreed to the purchase.

Even back in 1965 there weren't many places in the Boston area where a man could try out these kinds of weapons without drawing unwanted attention. Thinking our trip to Maine would be the perfect opportunity to test out my new acquisitions, I loaded the guns into the trunk of my old Cadillac along with our suitcases and sleeping bags.

Like many small, rural communities, Sullivan, Maine, was a place that thrived on rumor. In July 1965 the big story making its way around the county concerned the recent death of an elderly widow and the imminent redistribution of her property. Apparently, she and her children had had a severe falling-out some years earlier. That her demise would be a source of financial gain for these ungrateful offspring was a topic of heated discussion among my relatives and their friends.

Being the altruist that I am, I immediately saw an opportunity to remedy the situation in the dead woman's favor. I would, I decided, take it upon myself to liberate any valuables the widow had left behind before her greedy children had a chance to do so. That I stood to benefit from my good deed was merely a happy consequence.

The house, which was conveniently vacant, was set back into the trees on the ocean side of Route 1, down a narrow dirt driveway bordered on one side by a steep ravine. It was a perfect setting for a burglary. Aside from the hundred-year-old locks on the windows and doors, there was nothing to stop me from walking inside and making myself at home.

On Tuesday night, the twentieth of July, Vicky and I set out for a drive along the coast. It was a beautiful evening, clear and warm, fireflies blinking like Christmas lights in the trees along the highway. Dusk had long since faded to darkness, and the moon was not yet up. The sea was a black void, glimpsed now and again through the trees, punctuated at rare intervals by the running lights of a boat or the patchwork reflection of a house window. My intent had not been to involve Vicky in my plan, but as we neared the widow's property, I found myself slowing the car. This was merely another reconnaissance mission, I reasoned as I turned off the highway and onto the narrow driveway, a chance to get the lay of the land and iron out any final details. I would take Vicky home and return the next night to carry out my plan.

I parked just up the driveway from the house, instructed Vicky to stay with the car, and made my way on foot through the darkness. As I had expected, the house offered little in the way of resistance. Within a matter of minutes I jimmied the front door lock and was inside. At this point it seemed ridiculous to let such an opportunity go to waste. I could take what I wanted and be back on the highway before anyone, including perhaps even Vicky, was the wiser.

Of particular interest to me were a pair of Tiffany lamps I had glimpsed through the living room window on my previous visit. I soon had the lamps in hand and was heading back up the driveway.

But as I came over a small rise I was disturbed to see a pair of headlights snaking down through the trees. *The rifles!* I thought, suddenly remembering the weapons in the trunk of my car. As much as I didn't want to get caught burglarizing the house, the discovery of the guns would have been far worse. The possession of automatic weapons is never something to be taken lightly, and the carbine rifles were, essentially, machine guns. The lamps might have gotten me a few months in the county lockup, but the guns could have led to a good chunk of time in a federal facility.

Abandoning the lamps, I continued up the driveway. Perhaps it was just some local kids out for a joy ride, I told myself optimistically, watching the car pull to a stop in front of the Cadillac, its headlights swarming with dust and black flies. But as I drew nearer I saw the unmistakable silhouette of a sheriff's cruiser. Abruptly, the car's engine switched off and a figure climbed out.

"Good evening," I said, immediately recognizing the man as a local deputy sheriff, Henry Hosking. Then I nodded reassuringly to Vicky, who had left the Cadillac and was walking down the driveway to meet me.

"Hello, Myles," Hosking said. "A neighbor called about your headlights. You know this is private property?"

"I heard the house was for sale," I replied, gesturing over my shoulder. "Thought we'd come take a look."

"Really," Hosking mused, plainly not buying a word of my story.

"Yeah," I persisted. "I didn't mean to cause any trouble. If you move your car, we'll be on our way."

Hosking shook his head. "I'm afraid I can't do that," he said. "In fact, I'm placing you and your wife under arrest for trespassing."

The deputy walked back to his cruiser, where he reached for his radio and began calling for backup. Realizing this might be my only chance to shift the balance of power in my favor, I lunged for the Cadillac's open passenger door and the glove compartment, where I kept a spare pistol.

Seeing me move toward my car, Hosking leaped out of the cruiser. The deputy was fast. Fortunately, I was faster. I had my pistol trained on him before he had finished unholstering his weapon.

"Listen," I told him. "I don't want to hurt you, but I'm going to get out of here."

Hosking blinked, sizing me up, silently debating my character and capabilities. For a moment I thought I had him; then he shook his head again. "Oh no you don't," he snapped, grabbing my wrists and forcing my hand, and the gun, toward the ground.

Hosking knew me to be the son of a cop and must have guessed I wouldn't intentionally shoot a man who was merely doing his job. He was right—but as we struggled the pistol went off. Surprised, as I was, by the sound of the gunshot, Hosking took an involuntary step back, moving off the shoulder of the driveway toward the edge of the ravine. Sensing an opportunity, I palmed him once in the chest, hard enough to send him sprawling backward down the hill.

"Get in the car!" I yelled to Vicky. Then, aiming into the woods well away from where Hosking had fallen, I fired a warning shot. As the crack of the pistol faded I could hear scuffling in the darkness below.

Quickly I jumped into the cruiser and pulled it to the far edge of the driveway, unblocking my escape route. Figuring I could buy myself some time, I tore the keys from the ignition and tossed them into the woods, then fired a single shot into the police radio. Confident that I had disabled the deputy's two best options for pursuit, I raced back to the Cadillac, where Vicky was already waiting for me, and barreled up the dirt drive and onto the highway.

I knew it was only a matter of time before Hosking managed to get out of the ravine and find a telephone from which to sound an all-out alert. I also knew my best hope was to be long gone by that time. But where Hosking had failed to stop me, the utter desolation of downeast Maine would soon succeed. Snaking over hills and along the rugged Atlantic coast, with few viable outlets, Route 1 was, and still is, a notoriously slow road. Though I sped south as quickly as I could in the old Cadillac, I was eventually apprehended by a state trooper and taken to the Hancock County Jail in Ellsworth. That's how I wound up treading water in the frigid Union River.

S taring at the lights on the far shore as I kicked to stay afloat, I faced the choice of swimming forward into the arms of an angry mob or backward toward the craggy riverbank and the looming brick jail from which I had just escaped.

It was not the easiest decision I've faced in my life, but exhaustion and the very real threat of hypothermia prompted me to make my choice with remarkable speed. After only a moment's hesitation I turned and began swimming back in the direction from which I had come.

I have since found out that it is widely believed that I doubled back to the jail itself and hid for some time in the attic above the sheriff's home, as candy wrappers and other debris were later discovered there. Someone else, at some other time, must have taken refuge in that attic. My actual hiding place was not far away.

After crawling out of the river and scrambling up the steep embankment, I headed for the Ellsworth public library, which was situated in a large Federal-style mansion next door to the jail. Though the brunt of the search efforts were focused on the far side of the river, there was plenty of activity on the jail side, and I was well aware of the fact that I could be discovered at any moment. Moving quickly and stealthily through the darkness, I soon reached the back of the library and found a basement window through which I could squeeze myself.

Once inside, I quickly made my way up to the second floor. I'd had a decent view of the library building from inside the jail, and I remembered seeing a cupola on the roof. My hope was to take shelter there while the frenzy over my escape died down. Up on the second floor I raced through the stacks, searching the ceiling for an access panel or trapdoor. Finally, I found what I was looking for. Clambering up onto a nearby bookshelf, I managed to hoist myself up into the rafters.

For the moment at least, I was safe.

That night I spent in the library's rafters was one of the longest of my life. Even at the height of summer, the nights in downeast Maine are uncomfortably cool. I was miserable and shivering in my wet clothes. From my perch in the rooftop cupola I was able to watch people coming and going from the jail next door. The activity continued into the wee hours of the morning. Sometime during the night a front blew in, bringing with it a stiff ocean breeze, in which the old building shifted and creaked like a ship at sea. Twice I descended from the rafters to use the telephone in hopes of reaching a friend in Revere, and both times I was convinced that there was someone else, either living or dead, in the library with me.

As the morning wore on, activity at the jail began to wane until, sometime just before dawn, it ceased almost entirely. Realizing that once the sun came up I would have no choice but to spend the remaining daylight hours in the library, I decided to leave the relative safety of my hiding place. I exited the building using the same basement window and, under the cover of darkness, made my way out of Ellsworth.

It was obvious to me that I would need some help if I was to get out of Hancock County undetected. Having been unable to reach my friend in Revere, my rough plan was to walk the thirteen miles back to Sullivan and somehow manage to contact my family without arousing the suspicions of the local authorities. Though I hadn't seen her, I'd been told by the sheriff that Vicky had been released not long after our arrest.

After leaving the library, I headed for the woods outside of town with the intent of following the railroad tracks north. As the morning wore on and the sun rose, drying my clothes and warming my body, the previous night's specters began to slowly recede. Though I was hungry and tired I felt confident that the worst was over. That afternoon my spirits were buoyed even more by the sight of a picturesque farmhouse in the distance. The farm, with its well-kept fields, red barn, and white clapboard house, was right out of a Norman Rockwell painting, conjuring in my mind images of a kindly old farmer and his wife. Certain such gentle folks would be willing to help a poor wayfarer like me, I veered from my path on the railroad tracks and began picking my way across the fields.

I hadn't gone five yards before the farmhouse door swung open and a figure in denim overalls stepped out onto the porch. The kindly old man, I told myself, come out to welcome me. The figure raised a long, thin object to his shoulder. There was an instant's delay, then the sound of a shotgun discharging reached my ears. I turned tail and ran, sticking to the cover of the woods for the rest of the afternoon.

The going was slow, and by evening I still had not reached Sullivan. As dusk fell I spotted an old railroad car diner along Route 1, and beside it a phone booth. Recognizing a possible opportunity to contact my family in Sullivan, or even my friend in Revere, I waited until dark, then crept from the woods.

As I approached the diner two young women in a car hurriedly rolled up their windows and peeled out of the parking lot. I assumed my escape from the Ellsworth jail wasn't a secret, but I had no idea the extent to which the story had been publicized in the local press. At the time I attributed the girls' reaction to my scruffy appearance.

Fishing for loose change in my pocket, I headed for the phone booth, which was occupied by a middle-aged man in lobsterman's gear. As I drew closer the man looked up and, upon seeing me, quickly hung up the phone and stepped out of the booth.

"Hey pal," I said, holding out the single quarter I'd dredged from my pocket. "You got change?" In those days, a phone call cost a nickel, and I wasn't about to waste my last twenty cents.

The man nodded. Then he reached into his pocket and, coming up with a good handful of spare change, shoved at least a dollar in coins into my hand.

By now I could see people looking out the window of the diner and I knew the cops were likely on their way. Keeping an eye on the road in either direction, I ducked into the booth and dialed my cousin's house in Sullivan. After speaking to Vicky and assuring her that I was unharmed, I hung up and tried my friend in Revere one last time. He wasn't home, but his girlfriend answered. Aware that this might be my last chance to contact him, I instructed her to convey a message: to meet me in two days at ten o'clock in the morning at the toolshed behind the red railroad car diner on Route 1 between Ellsworth and Sullivan, Maine.

As I hung up the phone and began walking back toward the woods, I heard the sound of several cars pulling into the parking lot behind me.

"Halt!" a man's voice barked. "Don't move!"

• • •

By now it should come as no surprise to you that the command didn't have its desired effect. In an instant I was off and running. I leaped from the road into an adjacent field of unmowed hay, where I immediately took cover by lying flat on the ground. I stayed like this, not moving, my body pressed against the warm earth, while the deputies passed by, their boots coming within inches of my face.

When I was confident they were gone I cautiously rose to survey my situation. I was right about the deputies: they had reached the far end of the field and were moving into the neighboring woods. In the meantime, however, backup had arrived. Route 1 was awash in headlights and flashlights. Above the din of car engines I could hear the ominous sound of rustling as dozens of volunteers swarmed into the hayfield.

Knowing just how lucky I'd been to escape detection the first time, I sprang from my hiding place and bolted across the field and into the woods, well away from where the deputies were searching. My plan was to pick the first tree I saw that looked unclimbable, shimmy up it, and spend the night in its branches. And that's what I did.

As I said before, I'd had no idea of the extent of the manhunt my escape had triggered. But from my perch I now had a perfect view of the mayhem. Dozens of flashlights flickered through the woods below, far more than had been visible that first night on the banks of the Union River. *Christ,* I thought, *they must have deputized every able-bodied man in the county.*

As I sat there contemplating this fact with no small amount of . pride, my reverie was broken by a disturbing sequence of noises from below.

"There!" came a shout, the voice pitched in my general direction. "He's up there!"

A dozen heads shifted upward, followed by a deafening boom, the sound of a shotgun discharging at close range. A moment later there was a dull thud as a small animal hit the forest floor.

"It was only a porcupine!" someone called out.

The men's willingness to shoot was disturbing; the next time, I realized, I might very well be the unlucky target. I couldn't sit and wait for that to happen.

I took a deep breath and leaped into the darkness. I hit the ground hard, landing close enough to two of the men to knock them down and scaring the daylights out of the whole crew, who immediately set off running in different directions. It was like a bad slapstick routine, and even in my anxious state I couldn't help chuckling.

In an instant I was running as well, dodging low-hanging tree limbs and fighting the underbrush as I careened through the dark woods. With my pursuers far behind me, I scrambled up another tree, shimmying a good twenty feet to the first branch, then clambering higher still. I stayed in this tree for several hours, watching the frenzied flickering of flashlight beams combing the woods.

Sometime in the very early hours of the morning I heard several voices in the darkness below. "Hey!" someone called. "He's not here, guys!"

Then a second voice, louder this time—a stage yell, clearly meant for an unseen audience of one. "There's just been a report he was spotted in Sullivan! Let's go, everyone!"

This pronouncement was followed by an exaggerated rustling and shuffling of feet. I could discern several figures moving away in the direction of the road. But clearly, many more had stayed behind. Within minutes a match flared, revealing a craggy face. Soon after, a handful of cigarettes winked on. Obviously, I would not be leaving my tree branch anytime soon.

But as the night drew to a close and the first hints of dawn appeared over Frenchman's Bay I realized I couldn't stay where I was for long. Once the sun came up I would be visible to those below.

Cautiously, I began my descent. In the early morning quiet the sounds of tree limbs creaking and snapping under my weight seemed deafening. As I neared the lowest branch I was certain the entire county had heard me. I hung for a moment, then dropped to the ground and froze, fear prickling the back of my neck.

This is it, I thought, turning slowly, feeling someone behind me. In the spare light of the gloaming a figure revealed itself: two eyes and the barrel of a gun, pointing straight at me. For a moment my stomach leaped upward, scrabbling at the back of my throat. Then, much to my relief, I realized the man was sleeping. In fact, sleeping figures littered the woods around me. Country folk used to being in bed by nine, the men had fallen asleep on their watch.

I tiptoed past them, then made my way across the hayfield, finally disappearing into the thick woods on the other side of the highway.

My second full day on the run passed uneventfully. Though I could hear the sounds of small airplanes and boats scanning the shoreline and the occasional baying of bloodhounds, I had no more close run-ins with my pursuers. I kept to the woods on the west side of Route 1. That evening, after making a supper of green apples I'd scavenged, I finally succumbed to exhaustion and fell asleep in a dense thicket of trees.

In the wee hours of the morning I was awakened by my mother's voice. Thinking I was dreaming, I sat up and rubbed my eyes, peering into the woods. A thick fog had rolled in since I'd fallen asleep, distorting the distant lights of a police roadblock on Route 1.

"Myles!" It was my mother, and definitely not a dream. It sounded like she was talking through a megaphone. "Give yourself up or you're gonna get hurt," she called, her voice breaking.

The police must have brought her up from Milton, I realized.

"We know you're in there, Myles," a cop's voice spoke up.

Through the dense undergrowth I spotted the red roof light of a cruiser—a bubble gum machine, as we liked to call it—raking the pitch dark woods as the sheriff's vehicle slowly mad its way down a dirt fire road.

"Please, Myles," my mother pleaded. "Please come out before they hurt you."

Her concern was genuine, and I felt instantly guilty. But before I could do anything I would regret, I heard a third voice over the megaphone.

"Myles!" It was Al Dotoli. "There's more cops out here than Heinz has pickles!" he called. "They'll shoot you for sure."

That was the last I heard from him, but it was enough to convince me to stay right where I was.

By dawn I was shivering and exhausted but still not ready to give up. Not long after daylight I made my way toward Route 1, intending to scope out the situation at the diner and determine whether a rendezvous with my friend was still possible.

Whether the sheriff had been tipped off to my intentions or whether the presence of law enforcement at the diner was luck, I do not know. But as I scrambled up the highway embankment on my hands and knees, I heard a familiar phrase: "Halt! Don't move!"

Fully prepared to run, I looked up to see a sheriff's deputy standing directly over me with a shotgun.

At this point I must have been slightly delusional. I made a move for the deputy, intending to take him on. He hit me squarely on the head with the butt of the gun. The blow knocked me down, but it didn't knock me out. Enraged, I struggled up again. But by this time a small crowd of law officers had gathered around us. I was hit again, and this time I went down for good.

As I lay on the ground I could hear the small-town cops standing over me, discussing what had just happened.

"What the hell did you have to do that for?" one of them asked. "He's just a little guy."

Then the deputy who had hit me first spoke up in his own defense. "He tried to take a swing at me," he said guiltily.

It was a conversation I would soon come to look back on with the same tender nostalgia with which I regarded my boyhood summers in Sullivan. Though I didn't know it at the time, it was only a matter of months before I would find myself in the same position once again, injured and on my back, surrounded by cops on all sides. Unfortunately, the conduct of the officers involved the second time would not be nearly so courteous.

Four

The outcome of my dramatic escape from the Hancock County Jail was not entirely unhappy. Once back in custody, I was taken first to the local hospital and then to a larger jail. In October I was convicted and received a two-year sentence for the jail break and Sullivan heist. But with the help of a good attorney I was soon released pending appeal.

News of what had happened in Maine, including the fact that I'd fired on a sheriff's deputy, quickly made the rounds of the Revere Beach boardwalk. I had left Revere a young rock-and-roll singer with a penchant for mischief, but I returned a known criminal with a reputation for total disrespect of the law and those sworn to uphold it. To the boys at the Lewis Room I was a hero. To the local cops I was a menace, and also a possible meal ticket for anyone with the balls to bring me in.

My exploits caught the eye of one man in particular, a Metropolitan District Commission (MDC) detective named Robert Deschamps, who soon appointed himself my unofficial shadow. Tall and beefy, Deschamps was a classic crooked cop, humorless and power-hungry, with a wicked mean streak. He often bragged openly about shooting suspects in the back after setting them up in sting operations, generally armed robberies that were engineered by informants. A womanizer with a predilection for underage girls and runaways, Deschamps fancied himself the James Bond of the MDC tactical squad. He even claimed extensive knowledge of the martial arts, boxing, long-range photography, and scuba diving. As if all this wasn't enough, his hobby was raising Dobermans.

The MDC's official job was to police the state's beaches and parks as well as certain sections of roadway, including U.S. Route 1 in Chelsea and Revere and Interstate 93 in Boston and Milton. They also shared concurrent jurisdiction with communities throughout greater Boston. Their offices were in a big brick fortress right on Revere Beach, but Deschamps, who was part of a countywide task force, spent most his time trolling the clubs along the boardwalk, harassing the patrons and the staff, just putting on a general show of making his presence known. I had nothing but contempt for the man, and I wasn't shy about making my feelings known.

I was sitting at the bar in the Lewis Room one evening when Deschamps walked in and sauntered right up to me. He quickly made it known that he'd heard some of the things I'd been saying about him, including my observations that he was a bully and a blowhard. Would I like to step outside, he asked, so we could settle this like men?

Absolutely, I told him.

The most basic laws of physics clearly favored Deschamps, who outweighed me by almost a hundred pounds. But while Deschamps held the advantage in size, I clearly held the advantage in skill.

Once outside, I easily threw the man. I tagged him two or three times, and down he went. Needless to say, he was humiliated.

I'm never one to regret my actions, and I certainly don't regret standing up to Deschamps. But if I had known the kind of trouble that would dog me as a result of our encounter, I might have thought twice about answering his challenge.

I'd made an enemy, and a powerful one at that.

Not long after the first incident with Deschamps I was again in the Lewis Room when Rolo Degrassi, the nephew of a major organized crime figure, and a Lewis Room regular, came to me with an urgent request. The cops were breathing down his neck, Degrassi explained, and he needed somewhere to stash a package for a few hours. Normally, I might have thought twice before making such an arrangement, but because of the guy's pedigree and my friendship with the Italians, I agreed to help him out.

Not long after I had secured the contraband in my apartment, Deschamps and some of his buddies from the MDC showed up at my door. I'd been set up: the cops knew exactly what they were looking for. They muscled their way inside, found the package, and placed me under arrest.

Later that night Deschamps pulled me out of my cell at the county lockup and offered me a choice: turn on my friends in Revere and agree to become a regular informant, or pack my bags for the Suffolk County jail on Deer Island. This was before the days of search and seizure laws, and even my attorney had told me jail time was a foregone conclusion. But if Deschamps thought the specter of Deer Island was enough to scare me, he was sorely mistaken. I immediately told him to get lost, in no uncertain terms.

My attorney at the time was a man named Al Farese. Farese was an old-school mob lawyer, employed and respected by some of Boston's highest-ranking organized crime figures, with the connections to prove it. After bailing me out, Farese quickly confirmed my suspicions. Degrassi, he said, was a known informant. What's more, Farese added, Deschamps had been bragging to anyone who would listen about his plans to put six bullets in me at our next encounter.

This news did not sit well with me.

After leaving Farese's office, I headed straight to the Suffolk County courthouse on Pemberton Square, where I knew the offices of Deschamps's task force were located. I quickly located Deschamps and his partner, a state police detective who was also on loan to the task force, and proceeded to tell them what I'd heard from Farese, adding that if anyone planned to put six bullets in me, they would do well to keep in mind that I would be returning fire at every step.

Then, taking a hundred-dollar bill from my wallet—which in those days was no small amount of money, especially for a public servant—I slapped it on Deschamps's desk and informed him that if he wanted to make good on his promises, I would be happy to settle our differences right there and then. The man left standing, I added, could keep the money.

By now the entire floor of detectives had gathered around us. As I finished, I saw all heads turn toward Deschamps.

I'd always known Deschamps was a coward, but even so, the next words out of his mouth surprised me.

"Y-You're listening to the wrong people, Myles," he stammered. "I never said those things, and I certainly don't want any problems with you."

Once again I had humiliated him, only this time the slap, coming on his home turf, must have stung all the worse.

Soon he would get his chance to strike back. But not before I delivered one final blow.

Back at the Lewis Room I quickly learned that I wasn't the only person in the neighborhood to have fallen victim to Degrassi. Not long before, the Italian had set up another friend of mine, Artie Doherty, with a hot pistol that had been used in a murder. Doherty had managed to slip away from the police and hide the gun, but he was sure it was Degrassi who had tipped them off, since he'd sold him the piece in the first place.

After commiserating, Artie and I quickly devised a plan to get back at both Deschamps and his informant.

A few days later I ran into Degrassi, who offered his condolences, shaking his head in poorly acted disbelief at the "bad timing" of the cops' raid on my apartment. I played along, laying the bust off as bad luck. But, I went on to inform him, I had moved the rest of my stash, including a kilo of heroin and an arsenal of automatic weapons, to a different apartment in Revere, where I had hidden the drugs in an air vent in the living room. Only he and few other trusted friends knew about this, I assured him. To add credence to my story, I then took Degrassi out to my car and showed him a kilo bag of "heroin," which was actually a mixture I'd made from flour and bitters. I even let him taste some of it on his finger.

Of course, the entire story was a lie. There was no arsenal and no drug stash. Degrassi was the only one I'd told about my new hiding place. If he was in fact a snitch, I'd soon have all the proof I needed.

To my surprise, the bastard had the balls to warn me about being too trusting.

"There's a lot of bad guys out there, Myles," he said. "You shouldn't be telling people about this stuff."

"Sure," I agreed. "But I know I can trust you."

"Of course," he answered without missing a beat.

Degrassi was such an easy mark that as I drove off, supposedly to stash the remaining heroin, I actually felt a twinge of guilt.

After leaving Degrassi, I drove to Artie's house, where my friend was waiting for me with two women, a half dozen bottles of expensive champagne, and a lavish spread of sushi and sashimi he'd ordered earlier from my favorite Japanese restaurant. Thus provisioned, we drove to a nearby hill overlooking the apartment to which I had directed Degrassi.

No sooner had we parked than a dozen marked and unmarked cars, including Deschamps's signature Lincoln, pulled up in front of the apartment. A swarm of cops then descended on the building, knocking the front door down with a battering ram before disappearing inside.

Grinning with delight, I turned to Artie and the women. "We shall now conduct a double-blind champagne-tasting contest," I announced, uncorking a bottle of Dom Pérignon, "to see who will have the honor of making the 'angry neighbor' call to the local press. I'm sure they'll be interested to see our tax dollars at work."

Seeing Deschamps and Degrassi humiliated was revenge enough for me. But Artie wasn't finished with the snitch. Several nights later Degrassi again made an appearance at the Lewis Room. Not long afterward Artie slipped out the front door, only to reappear after twenty minutes with a Cheshire cat's grin on his face.

I knew something was up, but it wasn't until an hour or so later, when Degrassi strolled out of the club, that Artie's demeanor began to make sense. As Degrassi put his hand on the door of his car he was instantly surrounded by ATF men, who leaped from parked cars and from the other side of the seawall into the street. Within seconds the officers had a gun to Degrassi's head and were pushing him down onto the ground.

Methodically, they searched Degrassi's car, slashing the seat cushions and ripping out anything that wasn't bolted in place. The search turned up a large parcel of pharmaceuticals, as well as two illegal firearms, both with particularly bad histories.

Artie had gotten his revenge. But as much as I hated Degrassi, I felt uncomfortable with what had happened. Setting a man up like that, even an asshole and a rat, is a dirty business.

Much of my dirty feeling stemmed from the fact that I knew Degrassi and Deschamps would soon trace the tip-off back to me. One of the guns, a sawed-off shotgun, was a weapon Degrassi knew I'd had access to. There's nothing more dangerous than a snitch facing jail time. Nothing, that is, except a crooked cop with an ax to grind.

Not long after the incident outside the Lewis Room, Degrassi took a fatal dive off a rooftop. Word around Revere was that it was his conscience, and his fear of what would happen to him now that it was known that he was a snitch, that had sent him over the edge. I had absolutely nothing to do with the Degrassi's death, but Deschamps was convinced I'd murdered his informant, giving him yet another reason to hate me.

Five

Over the winter of 1965–66, working on a series of tips that I have no doubt originally came from Degrassi, the police and the Suffolk County district attorney's office slowly built a case implicating me in the Forbes robbery and in a fabricated plot to steal a Rembrandt from the Fogg Museum at Harvard University. By February they had amassed sufficient "evidence" to justify a search of my apartment.

Though I hadn't committed any museum robberies since my visit to the Children's Museum, I'd continued to add to my collection of art and antiques, which by this time included a number of significant Asian porcelains and bronzes, dozens of priceless Japanese swords, and other, more unusual weapons. I'd bought many of these pieces at auction, but others had been acquired through much less legitimate means. Some, of course, were from the Forbes and the Children's Museum. Others, including a pen gun and some counterfeit money, I had purchased, though not legally. Like the weapons, the counterfeit bills were curiosity pieces, and I had no intention of trying to pass them.

On a cold evening in February my then-girlfriend, Bonnie Sue Garian, and I were sitting on the couch in my apartment in Revere, listening to music and doing what men and women do, when the door suddenly burst open and a dozen cops rushed inside, guns drawn. Garian, a Catwoman look-alike with an attitude to match, was entirely unfazed by the interruption. Rising from the couch, she stepped between me and the cops.

Never one to hesitate, I quickly took advantage of the momentary distraction to dive out the second-floor window and into a snowbank below. Barefoot, wearing only jeans and a lightweight shirt, I fled into a nearby residential neighborhood, where I eventually managed to steal a coat and boots from the mudroom of a stranger's house.

Fortunately, the bulk of my collection was stored at my mother's house in Milton. Nonetheless, I'd left behind a treasure trove of stolen artifacts in the Revere apartment, including a number of pieces I'd taken from the Forbes Museum, as well as the illegal weapons and the counterfeit money. It was enough ill-gotten gains to send me away for a good long time. Only I wasn't going, at least not without a fight.

For the next three months I lived as a ghost, sleeping on friends' couches or in drug squats, never staying in the same place for more than one night, often disguising myself. I had several close run-ins with the law, all of which received coverage in the Boston papers, who soon took to calling me the "Phantom of the North Shore." One particularly amusing incident involved Al Dotoli.

Al and I had taken to meeting up at the granite quarries behind Cunningham Park in Milton. The quarries were an ideal place to hide out from the cops. Al and I had both been going there since we were kids, and we both knew the labyrinth of fire roads, overgrown hills, and precipitous granite pits like the backs of our hands. More often than not Al would bring a picnic—generally his mother's homemade broccoli and macaroni, of which I was especially fond—and we would sit at the top of Quarry Hill and shoot the breeze.

One weekend, craving more excitement than the quarries had to offer, I proposed that we rendezvous in Boston instead. I had some business to take care of with a friend, Peter, who lived in the Back Bay neighborhood. Peter worked at MIT, but in his spare time he dabbled in making silencers. I always enjoyed talking to him about his craft.

"Let's meet at Symphony Hall," I suggested. "The back entrance."

Symphony Hall was right around the corner from Peter's place on Gainsborough Street, but logistics weren't my only reason for choosing to meet there. By this time, every cop in Boston was on the lookout for me. If I was going to go into the city, I would need a good disguise, one that would allow me to blend in with my surroundings. I'd recently acquired a Thompson submachine gun, which I'd taken to carrying in an old viola case. With the case as a prop, I figured, I could easily pass myself off as a musician, while at the same time having the comfort of knowing I could defend myself if necessary. I also figured I could have some fun with Al.

That evening, carrying the viola case in one hand and a cane in the other, my red hair concealed by an old tam-o'-shanter, my shoulders in an octogenarian's hunch, I set off for our meeting. As I approached Symphony Hall, I saw Al waiting on the sidewalk just outside the performers' entrance. He glanced my way as I made my way across the street toward him, his eyes skimming across me without the vaguest hint of recognition.

Chuckling to myself, I hobbled right up to him. "Excuse me," I said, putting on my best Irish brogue. "Could you tell me where Symphony Hall is?"

He motioned to the building behind him, still not realizing it was me. Then, slowly, his eyes widened in recognition. "You asshole!" he exclaimed. No longer able to keep a straight face, I burst out laughing.

The summer of love was still a good year away at that time, and the term *hippies* had yet to become a household word, but the crowd at Peter's apartment, a fifth-floor walk-up in one of the neighborhood's many Victorian town houses, definitely fit that description. Brotherhood was in the air, as well as the sweet odor of marijuana smoke and the tang of unwashed bodies.

Al and I were given a warm, if somewhat low-key, welcome, and more than one person offered us a joint. Several people asked me for an impromptu concert, but I quickly demurred, saying the viola was sensitive to heat and I couldn't dare expose it to the elements. It was an excuse that would have aroused suspicion anywhere else, but the freethinking hippies took it in stride. Clearly, these were my kind of people: they knew how to have a good time and didn't ask too many questions.

Not long after we arrived, however, I started to get a bad feeling. I had nothing concrete to go on, just the sense that we were in the wrong place at the wrong time.

"Let's get out of here," I told Al. "Now."

Quickly excusing ourselves, we started down the narrow staircase.

No sooner had we passed the third floor on our descent than a phalanx of Boston police officers came rushing up the stairs. I couldn't help it; as they ran past I pointed in the direction of the fourth floor. "They're up there," I said, scowling in disapproval of whatever was going on in the apartment.

After busting their way into the apartment, the cops were eventually informed by someone in the startled crowd that an old man with a viola had just left. Realizing they'd walked right past me, the men rushed down the stairs, but they were too late.

Understandably, the police were not amused by this incident, or by any of the other near misses that winter. With each close call, their frustration and, consequently, their hatred of me grew.

No one understood this more then my father. On a cold night in March I met with him in the backyard of his house in Milton. A cop himself, he knew it was only a matter of time before my luck ran out.

"They're talking about shooting you, Myles," he said, pleading with me to give myself up.

It was a heartbreaking appeal, coming from the father I loved and the cop I respected above all others, but I wasn't yet willing to admit defeat.

"They'd better be prepared to kill me," I told him. "If they do catch up with me, they're going to have a hell of a fight on their hands."

I would soon get the chance to follow through on my promise.

. . .

On the night of April 27 I was again with Bonnie Sue Garian, this time at her apartment in the Back Bay. Situated just west of the oldest part of the city, bounded on the north by the Charles River, the Back Bay neighborhood consists mainly of elegant, five- and six-story Victorian brownstones. Bonnie's apartment was in one of these buildings, not far from the Public Garden.

Just before eleven o'clock that night I left Bonnie's place to make a call from a phone booth on Beacon Street. It was chilly out, the weather typical of early spring in New England. There had been a mixture of sleet and light snow on and off all day, and the streets and sidewalks were wet with slush. As I stepped out of the phone booth and started back down Beacon Street I saw an unmarked cruiser drive by.

Seeing the cruiser slow, knowing instantly that I'd been made, I reached for my gun, a Smith and Wesson .38 I carried in a waist holster, and slipped into the doorway of a nearby building, intending to make my escape. But before I could do so I heard a voice behind me.

"Drop your weapon!"

Turning, I saw three plainclothes cops with their weapons drawn. We faced one another in a standoff.

"Not until you drop yours!" I retorted, remembering what Farese and my father had told me, certain I would be shot in cold blood if I did as I was told.

One of the cops, who I would later learn was a state police corporal named John O'Donovan, nodded in acknowledgment. He held his gun out, as did his colleagues. I returned the gesture, preparing to drop my pistol, but as I did so one of the cops who were with O'Donovan took advantage of the situation and fired, aiming right at my head.

The bullet whizzed past my ear, just barely missing its mark. Panicked, O'Donovan raised his gun to fire. Our eyes met and I looked at him as if to say, *I don't want to do this, but I have no choice.*

I fired on him, intentionally aiming to knock him down, not to kill him, then turned and fled into the building, taking the stairs down into the basement, then out a rear entrance that led to a narrow common alley between Beacon and Marlborough Streets.

After radioing for help for an ambulance for O'Donovan, the two other men, both Boston Police Department detectives, gave chase, eventually catching up with me as I clambered up a fire escape to the fifth-floor roof of a Marlborough Street brownstone.

Seeing me on the ladder, the two detectives immediately opened fire. I was hit several times in the ensuing barrage, with my shoulder sustaining the worst of the damage. Despite the excruciating pain, I managed to keep climbing, finally making my way to the rooftop, where I took shelter behind a chimney.

By now every law enforcement officer in the greater Boston area had been called to the scene. As I hunkered down on the roof, taking stock of the situation, I could hear a general commotion in the streets and buildings below: the wail of sirens and the crackling of police radios coupled with the barking of police dogs. My initial plan had been to make my escape over the adjoining rooftops, but I soon saw that this would be impossible. The buildings on either side towered a full story above the one I was on. It was a height I could not have scaled on my best day and certainly could not manage in my wounded state.

I was trapped and I knew it. I also knew it was only a matter of time before the police tracked me to my hiding spot.

Just after midnight I heard substantial activity on the adjoining rooftops. Not long after, the Emergency Service Unit's klieg lanterns snapped on, flooding the scene with light, revealing a dreamscape of crimson. My own blood provided the grisly record of my movements as I had crisscrossed the roof looking for a way off. Drainpipes, glass transoms, skylights: everything bore my smeared imprint. Up on the adjacent rooftops a hostile crowd had gathered, the silhouettes of at least a dozen cops in sharp relief.

Suddenly, a figure leaped onto the rooftop and rushed toward me. Not a man, but a police dog. I fired once, aiming just in front of the animal. The bullet found its mark, sending a geyser of gravel into the dog's face. The creature quickly turned tail and ran, slipping over the side of the roof and back down the fire escape to where his handlers were waiting.

Finally accepting the fact that there was no good way out of the situation, I contemplated my next move. I've always been a firm believer that surrender is never an option. Earlier I had spotted a car parked directly below the roof. It occurred to me that if I jumped, the vehicle might provide just enough cushioning to break the five-story fall. If not, I reasoned, I would at least die trying.

Rising from my crouch behind the chimney, I made a mad dash for the edge of the roof. Immediately, a fusillade of gunfire erupted from the buildings on either side of me. A bullet caught me in the right side of my abdomen, sending a wave of pain through my body. I would later find out that the bullet had penetrated several major organs before blowing my spleen apart, smashing into my spine, and ricocheting backward into my left kidney.

Getting shot hurts like hell, no matter where the bullet hits. But my earlier wounds were nothing compared to the agony I now felt. The liver, spleen, and kidneys are all heavily enriched with pain sensors, and I had been hit badly in all three places. Momentarily incapacitated by the searing pain, I dropped my gun, sending it skittering across the rooftop.

Fortunately, I wasn't the only casualty of the shooting barrage. The klieg lights had been disabled as well, plunging the rooftop into darkness again. Once the shooting stopped I began to hear tentative voices calling out.

"Myles? Are you okay?" They were worried not about me but about themselves, what I might still be capable of.

Taking shallow breaths so as not to exacerbate the pain in my abdomen, I rolled under the eaves of a nearby gable and waited. As my eyes adjusted to the darkness I could see figures slipping down onto the roof and creeping cautiously toward me. They didn't appear human, crabbing gingerly forward on all fours like aliens.

"Myles? Are you hit, Myles?" one of them called.

Finally, someone spotted me, and a cry went up. "Over here!"

One of the three cops from the Beacon Street shootout pulled me out from beneath the overhang and, after searching me for weapons, quickly cuffed my hands and ankles.

I rolled over onto my back to see at least a dozen cops standing over me, including the other Beacon Street officer and my old friend from Revere, Robert Deschamps. As soon as I saw Deschamps's face I knew I was in trouble, but I couldn't have possibly imagined how serious my situation was about to become.

"How's the cop I shot?" I wheezed.

"Did we hit you again?" one of the men asked, ignoring my question.

"Twice," I managed.

"Where's your girlfriend?" another cop demanded.

"Go fuck yourself," I shot back, not about to give them Bonnie's whereabouts. "I only talk to my attorney, Al Farese."

This final impudent comment pushed the men, already seething over the fact that I'd shot one of their own, over the edge. Someone kicked me hard in the groin, initiating a frenzy of rage.

Whack! Punch! Stomp! The first blow was quickly followed by another and then another as the men took turns punching and kicking me, some going so far as to rip my clothes to better target my wounds. One cop even stuck his finger into the entry wound in my side, all the while giggling and laughing in an orgy of high-spirited sadism.

As I lay on my back, shackled and unable to defend myself or even shield my body, praying for the blow that would deliver me to sweet unconsciousness, I was reminded of Dante's devils, flogging the damned in the city of Dis. Clearly, the figures who surrounded me were no longer men but wrathful and sadistic demons, their faces hideous and macabre caricatures. Gleefully they danced around me like disjointed marionettes, rotating in and out of the frenzied circle as they grew tired, stepping back so others could take over for them.

It's odd, the details the brain chooses to hold on to. I can't recall that night without remembering that someone in a nearby apartment was playing "Monday, Monday" by the Mamas and the Papas. To this day, hearing that song takes me back to that Marlborough Street rooftop.

I don't know what sustained me up there, what exactly it was that kept me alive. As I have said, I am not a religious man, but I have always been a spiritual being. I firmly believe that my survival, wounded as I was, can't be explained simply by scientific means. In my moments of deepest despair that night I felt the presence of my maternal grandmother compelling me on.

My silence must have been goading to them, especially to Deschamps, who, during a lull in the frenzy, stepped forward. Reaching down, he unzipped my pants and grabbed my genitals with one meaty hand. He lifted me off the ground like this, then threw me down again and proceeded to punch me savagely in the scrotum while the other cops looked on.

Several sets of hands grabbed me then, and I felt myself being dragged toward the edge of the roof. *This is it,* I realized. *The bastards are going to throw me off. Worse, they'll write in their reports that I fell, and no one will ever know the truth.*

Recognizing that I was about to be murdered, I suddenly came to life. "These motherfuckers are throwing me!" I yelled to the large crowd of onlookers and reporters gathered below on Marlborough Street. "I'm not falling!"

As they hesitated, a voice spoke up from the darkness. "Pull him back and kill him up here or we'll be hounded by these goddamn news people for the next decade."

With those words I was hauled back onto the roof, but not to safety. The men began to kick and beat me again, even more savagely than before. I truly believe they would have killed me had not fate, in the form of a fire captain, finally intervened.

The fire department had been working for some time to get a ladder up to the rooftop. When they at last succeeded and the fire captain saw what was going on, he became enraged.

"Knock that shit off!" he bellowed. "He's shot to shit and you don't have cause to do that."

"Go fuck yourself!" one of the cops yelled back.

The captain hesitated a moment. He was a big burly guy, his stature further exaggerated by the fireman's gear he was wearing. I could tell by the look on his face that he was seething. "I'm a captain," he announced, effectively saving my life. "I outrank you by the rules of civil service, and if you don't knock that shit off, I'll report you and have your badges." Then he stalked back to the edge of the roof and waved for a basket stretcher to be brought up.

By the time the fire department lifted me off the roof I was as close to death as the living can come. In fact, I was pronounced dead by the firemen, who were unable to discern my pulse. Still, Deschamps wasn't about to let me out of his sight. As they slid me into the back of an ambulance the detective climbed in beside me.

"Boston City?" the driver asked Deschamps, naming the charity hospital.

Deschamps thought for a moment, then shook his head. "Nah," he said. "Mass General's closer. It's been a long night and I want to get home."

It was a fateful decision for both of us. The trauma center at Massachusetts General Hospital was one of the best in the country. I am convinced that Deschamps's choice meant the difference between life and death for me.

"Christ," one of the EMTs commented as the doors were closed and we pulled away. "I've never seen anything like this. What the hell did you guys do to him?"

Deschamps looked up. "He's a bad, bad actor," he said, "and I'm going to church tonight to pray he dies."

These aren't words a man soon forgets. When we finally arrived at Massachusetts General and I was safely surrounded by hospital staff, I snapped to life.

"You'd better hope I die," I snarled from my gurney. "If not, when I get out of prison I'm coming for you and I'm gonna put a bullet right between your fucking eyes."

Six

——

I owe my life to the extraordinary staff at Massachusetts General. Without the efforts of their skilled surgical team I most certainly would have died that night. But despite their best efforts, the damage to my spine was extensive, and the doctors prepared my family for the probability that I would never walk again.

I would eventually prove them all wrong—though my condition would worsen significantly before I could do so.

On May 16, after recuperating from my initial surgery, I was transferred to the hospital at the state prison in Norfolk, Massachusetts. To call the prison hospital a cesspool of squalor is to paint a rosy picture of conditions there. The facilities were filthy and overrun with vermin of every kind. The staff, overseen by a raging alcoholic with dubious medical credentials, was not just incompetent but purposely cruel in the treatment of patients.

Because of the extensive damage to my abdomen, the surgical team at Mass General had performed a colostomy on me. But I had not recuperated sufficiently for them to close it up before my transfer. Unfortunately for me, this task fell to the doctors at Norfolk. The suffering I endured at their hands during this procedure is almost unspeakable.

Motivated by cheapness—at the time a spinal block was a much less expensive procedure than administering a general anesthetic—the head surgeon at Norfolk made the decision to forgo general anesthetic in favor of a spinal block. This decision alone might not have had such dire consequences if he hadn't also chosen to administer the neuromuscular blocker d-tubocurarine to me prior to my surgery.

Derived from the same plant native Amazonians have used for centuries as a paralytic poison, d-tubocurarine, or curare, is routinely used to immobilize patients for surgery and relax the trachea for easy intubation. But as integral as the use of curare is in major surgeries, the drug has been known to have side effects, the most serious of which occurs when the accompanying anesthetic, for whatever reason, does not take effect. In these gruesome cases, patients paralyzed by curare are unable to speak or move, and are consequently unable to communicate the fact that they are in pain. Recently, advanced systems have been instituted to better monitor whether surgery patients are fully anesthetized. Unfortunately for me, no such monitoring system existed in 1966.

As fate—or downright incompetence—would have it, the anesthesiologist chose the very spot where my spine had been struck by a bullet to insert his needle. Instead of flowing down through the spinal fluid, the anesthetic poured ineffectively into my body cavity. Of course the surgical team was entirely unaware of any of this.

For my part, I could only assume that the anesthetic had yet to take effect. As I lay there waiting for this to happen, the curare made its way down the IV tube and entered my bloodstream with the instantaneous force and power of a hard-swung baseball bat. There was a brilliant lightning flash in my brain and I could feel my mind jump within my skull. My hands went suddenly limp. My head lolled to the side. My tongue felt like a loose piece of meat in my mouth. I tried to roll my eyes but found them locked into place. I struggled to speak, but could not. To my absolute horror, I soon realized that I could not even breathe on my own.

After what I'd been through on the rooftop, my first thought was that the doctors and nurses had conspired with the police to kill me. As I struggled in vain to take a breath, I mutely cursed the men and women standing around me. *How could they do this?* I wondered, raging now, feeling myself slowly suffocating. It was a horrible sensation, much like what I'd felt the summer before when I came close to drowning in the Union River. But where bravado had buoyed me then, I was now driven purely by revenge. If I survived this, I railed, I would make Deschamps, and everyone else involved, pay dearly for what they'd done.

But the doctors were not in fact trying to kill me. What I was about to endure was much worse than death. Soon I felt a gloved hand on my mouth and the uncomfortable sensation of having a tube thrust into my throat. In an instant my lungs were filled with air. I heard the steady pumping of a ventilator and the ominous words, "He's ready!" Someone swabbed my skin with benzoin, then stretched a sterile adhesive sheet across my abdomen. *My God!* I thought, struggling to communicate the fact that I was not yet numb. *They're about to perform surgery on me!*

More than the sensation, the sound of the initial incision is something I will never forget. As the scalpel sliced through the sterile sheet and the skin below, it hissed angrily. In the instant that followed I felt nothing; then the white-hot pain hit me, the feeling of being torn open from my sternum to my pubic area. But this was nothing compared with what was to come.

After cutting me open, the surgeon proceeded to spread apart my abdominal cavity, tearing muscle and tendon. Abdominal surgery is not a delicate process, but rather requires brute force on the part of the surgeon. Think of a butcher taking apart a chicken.

It is impossible for me to accurately describe what I felt from this point on. I tried to call on my years of martial arts training to help me focus my mind away from the pain, but it was no use. The agony was so severe, so relentless, that it consumed me entirely, clattering in my head like the iron wheels of a steam locomotive. In my despair I turned to God, not for succor but out of blind rage, cursing him shamelessly for my suffering. I am not proud of the things I called him. In the years since, through extensive study of both Eastern and Western religions, I have come to believe in the essential goodness of God. But at that moment, I severed myself from him entirely.

So extreme was my agony and rage that the notion of time became utterly meaningless to me. I later learned that I endured three hours of surgery in this fully conscious state.

Pain wasn't the only result of my treatment at the prison hospital. Not only did the surgical team botch the colostomy operation, but they also made the serious mistake of feeding me solid food just days after the surgery. As a result, I contracted acute peritonitis, an extremely serious condition in which the membrane that lines the abdominal cavity becomes infected. I was in agony, my abdomen swollen like a balloon from the bacteria and gases. Still, the hospital surgeon refused to give me pain medication, saying he was concerned that I would become drug-dependent.

To make matters even worse, I required several blood transfusions, the suppliers of which were the general Norfolk prison population, many of them intravenous drug users, many of these infected with hepatitis. By late summer of 1966 I had contracted hepatitis. In September my liver suffered a complete breakdown, sending me into a coma.

After repeated requests by my family that I be moved, I was finally transferred to Boston City Hospital in late September. At the time of my arrival I weighed 66 pounds, down from my normal weight of 135 pounds. The infection was now so severe that it had eaten a hole in my diaphragm. As a result, my entire thoracic cavity was riddled with abscesses. My one remaining kidney was also badly infected, as was my circulatory system. I was in such bad shape that the chief of staff immediately called the morgue to request a body bag.

Incredibly, he would not need it. Thanks to the herculean efforts of the medical staff, which included several operations, extensive medication, and grueling aftercare, I eventually made a full recovery.

Despite the severity of my condition and the intense and almost constant pain I was in, my stay at Boston City Hospital was relatively pleasant. During the month and a half I spent there I developed personal relationships with several of the staff members, including one of the young nurses assigned to care for me, and several of the guards in my security detail.

One of the men sent to keep watch over me was a state policeman named John Regan. Regan was a close friend of my father's and had volunteered for the job as a favor to him. Though I had been introduced to Regan on several occasions, we were not especially close. But the time we spent together over the course of my long hospital stay changed that. The more I got to know Regan, the more I grew to like and admire him. My relationship with him would continue for years to come. Eventually he would become like a second father to me.

One of my other regular guards was a Suffolk County corrections officer named John Bergeron. At six foot four and nearly four hundred pounds, Bergeron looked like a cross between a sumo wrestler and an out-of-work Santa Claus. He was a naturally friendly man, with a sense of humor to match mine. We hit it off immediately and came to look forward to seeing each other. Bergeron especially loved hearing about my rock-and-roll escapades, and I happily obliged him with tales of raucous parties and crazed groupies.

As much as I wanted to, I knew I couldn't stay at Boston City Hospital forever. In mid-December my doctors finally deemed me well enough to leave. It was a bittersweet pronouncement. Though I was relieved to have survived the physical ordeal that had begun so many months earlier, my release and subsequent transfer back into the care of the Suffolk County authorities meant I would now be awaiting trial in much less pleasant surroundings.

Today, the old Charles Street Jail has been reincarnated as a luxury hotel. Anyone with four hundred dollars to spare can spend a night between luxury sheets in their own private lockup, or dine on native oysters and Wagyu beef in the hotel's cleverly named restaurant, Clink. But in 1967 the place was an unmitigated shithole.

Built in 1851 and seemingly unmaintained in the intervening years, the imposing granite structure housed more than two hundred cells, each a mere ten feet by eight feet in size, all linked to a ninety-foot central rotunda by a series of dramatic iron catwalks. At one time the jail served as a model for correctional facilities nationwide. But during my incarceration it was in a state of putrid decay, the first floor perpetually covered in several inches of standing water, the upper floors infested by giant rats and waterbugs the size of a man's fist that had made their way over from the nearby Charles River. Many of the inmates were mentally ill, and their moans and screams could be heard nonstop.

Prisoners were literally pleading to get out of Charles Street, preferring to admit guilt and move on to the state system rather than go to trial and spend a few more months at the facility. In fact, the place was so squalid that the United States Supreme Court eventually ruled imprisonment there to be a violation of a person's basic civil rights.

There was, however, one upside to my transfer to the jail. At the hospital I had been allowed visits only from close family members. At Charles Street my friends were able to come and see me as well. Those who did were shocked by what they saw. Though I had gained back some of the weight I'd lost while at Norfolk, I was still some forty pounds shy of my normal weight and nearly unrecognizable, even to those who knew me best. John Bergeron, my former guard from Boston City Hospital, occasionally dropped by my cell as well. His visits, along with my mother's daily pilgrimages, provided a huge boost to my spirits.

Fortunately, I knew I wouldn't be at Charles Street for long. My guilt in the Back Bay shooting was indisputable, and even I had to concede that a plea bargain was the best possible option. Since I wouldn't be going to trial, I no longer needed the services of Al Farese, and was now being represented by a close friend of my father's named John Irwin, who had offered to defend me for free.

Not long after arriving at the jail, I was taken to the Suffolk County Court House for my arraignment and bail hearing. The charges against me, stemming from the Back Bay shoot-out and other incidents, including the earlier police raid on my apartment in Revere, were numerous and included assault with intent to kill and several counts of assault with a dangerous weapon. After my successful escape in Maine, the guards weren't taking any chances. I was led into the courtroom in handcuffs and chains, shackled to a fellow prisoner.

From my place in the dock I spotted a contingent of family and friends, all seated together in the second row back from the front of the courtroom. My attorney, John Irwin, was there, of course, along with my mother and father, my sister, Patsy, and two longtime family friends, Pat Hunt and Jackie O'Donal.

As we waited for the proceedings to begin, Irwin approached the dock and spoke to me.

"This is just a formality, Myles," he said reassuringly. "Waive the formal reading of the indictments and plead not guilty."

After Irwin had returned to his seat, my father rose and came forward. I had not seen much of him since my arrest. The hospital visits, I knew, were unbearably painful for him. And I certainly could not blame him for being reluctant to visit me in jail. No cop wants to see his son behind bars.

"How are you doing, Myles?" he asked.

His concern was so genuine that I felt instantly guilty for what I'd put him through. He was a good man, I thought, and hardly deserved this.

"Good, Dad," I told him.

"You feelin' okay?"

I shrugged. "I've been better. But yeah, I'm okay."

"Do you see anyone you know here today?"

"Sure," I answered, motioning to the array of familiar faces in the second row. "There's Mom and Patsy, and Pat and Jackie."

"Anyone else? Down there in the front row?"

I scanned the faces, quickly recognizing two MDC cops I knew from Revere. "Yeah," I said, glaring at the men. "Nick Caselli and John Hurley."

"Anyone else?" my father prodded.

I shook my head, puzzled by his line of questioning. The only other people in the front row of seats were a handful of teenage girls who I assumed were in the custody of Caselli and Hurley and, like me, awaiting arraignment.

My father returned to his seat. Not long after, following Irwin's instructions, I entered my not guilty plea and, along with the poor fellow I was shackled to, was taken back to Charles Street. Though by all appearances it had been a routine day in court, my father's questions regarding the identities of the girls in the front row of the courtroom continued to nag at me.

It was not until a week later, when John Bergeron came to visit me, that I finally understood why my father had been so persistent with his inquiry.

I knew in my gut that something was wrong as soon as Bergeron appeared on the catwalk outside my cell. Though he made an attempt at small talk, the normally easygoing guard was subdued and standoffish. He was carrying that morning's edition of the *Boston Herald-Traveler* with him. I soon learned why.

"You made the papers again today," he said after our initial, slightly awkward exchange.

"I did?" I asked, pleased, though hardly surprised. By then I had grown used to having my escapades reported on. A natural showman, I relished every minute of fame—or infamy. "What are they saying this time?"

Bergeron shrugged, clearly uncomfortable with the subject. "I'm not really sure," he said at last.

"C'mon," I pressed. "You read the article, didn't you? What have I been up to now?"

"Something to do with a morals charge," he said reluctantly, after a moment's hesitation.

"What the hell's that supposed to mean?" I asked, feeling relieved, certain now that this was the lead-in to one of Bergeron's signature bawdy jokes. I had never seen him deadpan so well.

"I don't know," he muttered. "Something about underage girls in Revere."

I looked him in the eye, still trying to get the joke in all of this. He turned away. Plainly, he was telling a difficult truth.

My mind raced back to every woman I'd been even vaguely involved with over the past several years. I'd had a number of girlfriends and plenty of short-term flings. But I was always careful to make sure everyone I dated was of legal age. There had been one instance where a girl had lied to me and I'd found out her real age after taking her out a few times, but I seriously doubted she would have gone to the police. Our parting had been amicable, and she had even introduced me to her parents. It was possible there might have been someone else like her about whom I had been ignorant.

"Let me see the paper," I told Bergeron.

He passed it between the bars of my cell.

Reading the article, I quickly understood why Bergeron had been so reluctant to come to me. The police were claiming that I was a prime suspect for a violent rape on a young girl committed in the Revere area during the summer of 1965. In fact, I was being indicted for assault with intent to commit rape, commission of an unnatural act, and armed robbery of a minor. The article went on to say that Caselli and Hurley, the two detectives who had been at my arraignment hearing, were responsible for cracking the case, and that I had been identified by my accusers in a police lineup.

Rape is a despicable crime, rape of a young girl one of the foulest acts a person can commit. I felt physically ill at the thought of being linked to something so heinous. That I can be a stubborn son of a bitch with no fear and even less respect for authority is something to which I readily admit. But I have always lived by a strong code of ethics when it comes to civilians. I was loyal to the extreme to my family and friends, and roundtable chivalrous in my treatment of women.

My greatest fear at that moment was not the consequences these charges would have for me in prison, where being labeled a "skinner" carried severe, often deadly, penalties, but what my family and friends would think of me. How could I possibly look my mother in the eye knowing she had read this about me? I wondered desperately. I thought of all the people who would read the story and believe it: my old school chums, friends from Revere, ex-girlfriends, the young nurse at Boston City Hospital who had been so kind to me.

For a moment I was numb. Again, I tried to remember anything that might explain the horrid accusations. Finding nothing, I looked up at Bergeron.

"I've never done anything like that in my life, Mr. B.," I said. "How the hell can they say that? Besides, I was never in any lineup."

Bergeron's posture softened. He knew and liked me well enough to want to believe me. "I know you'd never do this sort of thing, Myles," he said. But I could tell he wasn't sure what to think.

As I would soon find out, it's a whole lot easier to tell a lie than to prove one wrong. That's the dirty thing about accusations: once made, they stick, no matter how much proof to the contrary is produced.

Suddenly I understood: I'd been framed. My humiliation and horror turned to smoldering anger. That had to be it. Deschamps and his buddies from Revere, not content with the prospect of a twenty-year prison sentence, were determined to see me severely punished—perhaps even killed—by my fellow inmates.

The realization that I had been deliberately set up drove me into a blind fury. I exploded in my cell, ranting like a lunatic, cursing myself for having failed to kill each and every cop on the Marlborough Street rooftop, threatening Deschamps and the other two detectives, Caselli and Hurley, with unspeakable acts of violence. I was, literally, insane with rage. Because of my weakened physical condition, I had armed myself with a variety of homemade weapons, and I was fully prepared to use them on anyone stupid enough to even imply they thought I might be capable of the heinous crimes of which I had been accused.

As a result of the atrocious conditions we were all forced to endure, and the fact that most of the guards and inmates at Charles Street shared common backgrounds—working class Irish or Italian—there was a general sense of camaraderie at the jail. My friendship with Bergeron and the fact that my father was also a cop had served to further endear me to the staff. Up to that point I'd returned their goodwill by being a model prisoner, so the guards were understandably disturbed to see me so violently agitated.

A few hours into my tirade the guard captain, an old Irishman, came to my cell to inform me that he had called my father and my attorney, John Irwin, and that both men were on their way to see me.

"Myles," he said, "for whatever it's worth, no one here believes that stuff in the paper. We all know about your battles with the police and that this is their way of getting you back. Just realize we aren't part of it. We're not your enemies."

The captain's speech had a calming effect. I knew he was right and that I was taking out my frustration on the wrong people by lashing out at the Charles Street staff. But I was still seething.

When, half an hour later, I was taken from my cell to one of the conference rooms to meet with my father and John Irwin, I erupted once again, cursing the Boston police and the MDC, voicing my regrets over having let Deschamps and the others live. Eventually my rage ebbed and I realized the pain my words were causing my father. After all, he was one of them.

"I can understand why you're so angry and upset," my father said when I finally let him speak. "But don't be. I know you didn't do these things."

"How can you say you know anything?" I asked. "It was in the goddamn paper. Even if you don't believe it, everyone else will."

My father laid his hand on my arm. I could tell he was struggling with the accusations, wanting more than anything to believe it was all a lie. "Remember when you were brought into court shackled to that other fellow?"

"Sure," I answered, recalling my arraignment hearing.

"And you remember those girls in the front row with Caselli and Hurley?"

"Yeah."

"Well, that was your lineup. That girl had been brought in to pick you out as the person who assaulted her."

Though the fact that Caselli and Hurley had conducted their lineup during my hearing was disturbing, I was nonetheless comforted by this revelation. Surely, I thought, the identifications wouldn't hold up in court. You can't just point out a shackled prisoner to a bunch of teenage girls and ask them if he's a rapist. No judge in the world would allow this kind of testimony in his or her courtroom.

My father and I talked for a while longer, and by the time I returned to my cell I was feeling better. I was innocent, after all, and still possessed the false confidence of all innocent men.

John Irwin visited me several times over the next few weeks to discuss the details of my plea agreement. On his counsel, I eventually agreed to plead guilty to the several charges of assault with intent to murder—reduced from about ninety such charges—that had been brought against me in conjunction with the Back Bay shoot-out. In addition, I would also plead guilty to a handful of charges stemming from the contraband police had discovered during the raid on my Revere apartment. The charges included possession of a silencer, a pen gun, stolen goods, and counterfeit money. By all rights, I should have also been charged with possession of the explosive C-4, which the cops had found during the raid. But amazingly, they had failed to recognize the substance.

In return for my guilty plea, Irwin surmised, I would likely face a sentence of anywhere from seven to fifteen years in state prison, this to run concurrently with the time I had yet to serve for the Maine burglary and the jail escape. It was hardly ideal, but it seemed to be the best I could hope for under the circumstances.

Just days before my final court date and transfer to the state prison at Walpole, my attorney came to see me one last time. The prosecution had approached him with yet another offer.

"If you plead guilty to the statutory rape charge and the indecent assault and battery and unnatural acts charges," Irwin informed me, "the Commonwealth will recommend a three-to-five-year sentence to run concurrent with the sentence you're already serving." He smiled enthusiastically. "It's a gift with no downside risk."

"A gift?" I was flabbergasted and insulted. "Do you really think I had anything to do with those crimes?" I asked.

"No," he replied. "But it doesn't matter what I think. The prosecution has an eyewitness now, and it's very hard to refute that kind of testimony."

"I won't do it," I said. "I won't plead guilty to a crime I know I didn't commit, especially something like this."

"Look, Myles," Irwin persisted. "The costs associated with a trial like this are astronomical, and the odds of an acquittal at this point are slim to none. My advice to you is to take the deal. It won't make any difference in your sentence."

"I don't care about my sentence or the cost," I protested. In fact, I would have gladly doubled my sentence rather than plead to the morals charge. "I'm going to fight this. You can tell the goddamn cops and prosecutors who are behind this that they can go fuck themselves. Understand?"

Irwin nodded. "I do," he said. "But I'm not so sure the same can be said for you."

Seven

On February 27, 1967, I was transferred from the Charles Street jail to the Massachusetts Correctional Institution at Walpole. My sentence was twelve to twenty years, though in our last conversation my attorney had assured me that with time credited for good behavior I could be back on the streets in as little as six. In theory, I might be back in the art business by the age of thirty. The only question was whether I would live that long.

At the time Walpole housed some of the most notorious criminals on the East Coast, including some of New England's highest-ranking mob bosses. Since opening in the mid-1950s, the prison had earned a well-deserved reputation for being one of the toughest maximum-security facilities in the country, a place where inmates of dubious character—skinners and diddlers and snitches—were routinely beaten and frequently killed.

I was barely twenty-four when I passed through Walpole's gate that first time, five foot six and 120 pounds, still recovering from the physical ordeal of the past ten months, with a rape indictment hanging perilously over my head. A betting man would not have wagered on my survival.

Despite the fact that the odds were decidedly against me, I don't remember feeling afraid. Fear is not an emotion I'm prone to, nor do I dwell on the implications of death. The intake photos from that day show this to be true. My face, almost boyish, is that of a rookie, but my expression is a convict's stony glare, a challenge and a warning to anyone foolish enough to take me on.

I was ready to fight for my life. Fortunately, I wouldn't have to.

The friendships I'd cultivated at the Lewis Room extended far beyond the geographical boundaries of Revere Beach. By the time I got to Walpole, every Italian in the place knew I was coming and welcomed me with open arms. And they weren't the only ones anticipating my arrival.

If I was a minor celebrity outside the prison walls, on the inside I was a superstar. The incredible details of that winter's manhunt and the ensuing rooftop shoot-out, along with the earlier Maine jailbreak, were well known among the Walpole population. Being a con means living constantly under someone else's thumb. The fact that I had refused to back down brought me instant respect from nearly every inmate I encountered. That I quickly proved myself to be loyal and a straight shooter firmly cemented those feelings.

Like all such places, Walpole prison is an ugly facility, mean in both intent and design. Viewed from the outside, it looks like some kind of alien fortification, a chalky monolith rising incongruously from the pastoral New England woods that surround it. The twenty-foot-high walls that form the rectangular outer perimeter are topped by coils of razor wire and electric fence, anchored at all four corners and both entrances by intimidating guard towers. Just inside the front entrance the main facility sprawls like a minicity, a series of two- and three-tiered cellblocks set at right angles off a four-hundred-foot long corridor. Beyond the cellblocks is a large exercise yard where the prison workshop is located. It's a place I've come to know intimately over the course of several stays, mastering the nuances of the structure as well as the complex culture of those who inhabit it.

At the time of my first stay the cellblocks were divided between minimum- and maximum-security wings, each set at opposite ends of the central corridor, separated by the service facility, a large one-story building that housed the mess hall, auditorium, infirmary, and library, among other things.

One of the maximum-security cellblocks, Block Nine, was reserved for those in protective custody, mainly snitches or child molesters, who would have faced near-certain death in the general population. The other, Block Ten, housed especially violent or troublesome inmates. It was a foul place. Having been denied the most basic rights, the prisoners in Block Ten retaliated by throwing garbage, food scraps, and sometimes even their own feces into the long central corridor. The stench was unbearable, the cells crawling with every kind of vermin imaginable.

On the minimum-security end were three triple-tiered cellblocks, each housing seventy-two inmates. It was here, in Block B, in a windowed cell furnished only with toilet, sink, and cot, that I would serve out my sentence.

The daily routine at Walpole allowed us plenty of time outside our cells for both work and recreation. Employment was mandatory for every prisoner. Most inmates worked in either the kitchen, the laundry, the plate shop, or the foundry, and I fully expected to do the same. But the warden had other plans for me. Not long after my arrival I was appointed to the position of entertainment director.

My first order of business was to form a band. It was not a difficult task. Walpole was home to many talented musicians, all of whom were desperate to put their skills to use. I quickly assembled a top-notch backup group for myself. Our first show was a huge success, and we were soon playing every Sunday afternoon in the auditorium.

Our concerts were religiously attended, by both inmates and staff alike. As a rule, prison society is strictly segregated; it's extremely rare to see everyone sitting down peacefully together. But on Sunday afternoons six hundred inmates of all races and religions gathered to hear us play. Not once was there an altercation.

• • •

When I wasn't playing music I spent much of my free time in the gymnasium, lifting weights and keeping up with my martial arts practice. Already a serious student of Buddhism, I took advantage of the relative lack of distractions in prison to deepen my practice, reading whatever I could get my hands on through friends on the outside or the prison library, and meditating regularly in my cell.

Of course I continued my studies of art and antiques as well. Friends from that time often recall seeing me with my nose buried in the most recent Sotheby's or Christie's catalogue. I've always been blessed with a near-photographic memory. I'm able to digest and retain significant amounts of information. After that first stay in prison I probably knew more about art than most museum curators do.

As much as I loved reading about art, I was eager to try my hand at creating it myself. I soon became a frequent visitor to the crafts room. Over time I came to master the craft of scrimshaw, a painstaking art form most often associated with native Americans and nineteenth-century whalemen, in which detailed scenes are etched onto ivory or bone.

Though the conditions at Walpole were in no way comparable to those at Charles Street, the prison housed its fair share of vermin. Understandably, these creatures were not popular with most of my fellow inmates. But I welcomed their presence in my cell. A consummate animal lover, I viewed the creatures as my pets. Using matchsticks and scrap wood from the shop, I built tiny cages in which to house my growing menagerie of insects, spiders, and even mice.

As I mentioned before, Walpole was home to many well-known convicts. But perhaps none was quite as notorious as Albert DeSalvo, the confessed Boston Strangler. DeSalvo was an odd man with a head of thick black hair and a pugilist's face. I came to know him quite well during my time at Walpole, as he often sat at the workstation next to mine in the crafts room. DeSalvo spent most of his time making chokers, the irony of which was entirely lost on him but which provided more than a few good laughs for the rest of us. When the weather was warm, DeSalvo ran a little ice cream stand in the prison yard, selling

Hoodsies and Creamsicles. It was a position that made him quite popular with his fellow inmates.

DeSalvo loved music and never missed one of our Sunday concerts. In fact, my most vivid memory of him is from one of these events. Toward the end of my stay I talked the warden into letting me put on a big show and barbecue in the prison yard. I even convinced him to let Al Dotoli come in and produce the concert. Figuring the inmates there needed a distraction as much as we did, I also arranged to have a group of folks from the local senior citizens' center bussed over for the occasion.

The show turned out to be quite a festive event, especially for DeSalvo, who spent most of the concert dancing with one or another of our gray-haired visitors. Al Dotoli still has an old home movie from that day, which he shot, that shows DeSalvo grinning like a madman, his arms thrown over the shoulders of two elderly women who, I'm certain, had no clue they were dancing with a notorious serial killer.

In person DeSalvo, who was not the sharpest con in the bunch, seemed an unlikely candidate for mass murderer. Most of us harbored serious doubts that he was the actual Boston Strangler. It's a theory that has been bolstered both by glaring inaccuracies in DeSalvo's confession and recently recovered DNA evidence from the crimes. Unfortunately, these revelations came too late for DeSalvo, who was brutally murdered not long after I left Walpole that first time.

Despite the best efforts of the prison staff to direct our attention to legitimate pursuits, the most popular class at Walpole was taught not in the workshops or the service facility but on the cellblocks and in the yard, where Criminal Arts 101 was an essential part of the core curriculum. An elite finishing school for robbers, con men, forgers, murderers, and every type of criminal in between, Walpole taught the basics and taught them well.

For my part, I was a straight-A student, constantly taking mental notes on the nuances of human interaction within the prison walls, learning as I went along. I quickly discovered the importance of allegiances and the skills necessary to cultivate these essential bonds.

Many prison gang leaders gain their authority through fear and the constant threat of violence against those who oppose them. This has never been my style. I've always found other tactics such as loyalty and kindness to be more effective. Most cons have lived lives of unimaginable deprivation. Orphaned or neglected as children, shuttled from one institution to another, a great many of the men who make up the prison population have never known love or true friendship. Offered these things for the first time, most respond with fierce devotion.

Within several months of my arrival at Walpole I had surrounded myself with a group of loyal associates. United by our youth and our reckless contempt for authority, we were a force to be reckoned with by anyone—inmate or guard—who dared to take us on. Among the group were men who would remain my lifelong friends. The friendship of one man in particular, Ralph Petrozziello, would alter the course of my life in ways none of us could have foreseen.

Ralph came to Walpole soon after I did. A tough kid from hardscrabble Roslindale, Ralph was my physical opposite in many ways. While I was fair and slight of build, Ralph was a dark-skinned Italian American with black eyes, a shock of jet black hair, and a brawny body. But our resumes were strikingly similar. Like me, Ralph had been sentenced to Walpole for shooting a cop, and had a reputation for defiance. He was also unfailingly loyal to his friends, commanding respect and affection from those around him.

Not surprisingly, we took to each other immediately. Ralph soon became like a brother to me.

Though I had carved out a place for myself in the complex world of the prison, I could not shake the specter of my upcoming rape trial. As serious as the charges were, I took solace in the fact that I would get a chance to disprove them once and for all in a court of law. Naively, I placed my faith in my actual innocence and my airtight alibi: at the time the rape was committed I'd been onstage, playing to a packed house at the Lewis Room. On the other hand, the only evidence the prosecution had linking me to the rape was the testimony of the young victim. The odds of an acquittal seemed squarely in my favor.

Unfortunately, my logic failed to take into account the power of an eyewitness identification.

An eyewitness is one of the most powerful and persuasive tools at a prosecutor's disposal, especially when that witness is the victim and a child. A young girl bravely pointing out her attacker from the stand can sway any jury. But despite their emotional appeal, these identifications have been proven time and time again to be extremely unreliable. Human memory is a flawed system, highly susceptible to suggestion. Only with the widespread use of DNA testing have we come to understand exactly how inaccurate such testimony often is. According to the Innocence Project, a national litigation and public policy organization dedicated to exonerating wrongfully convicted people through DNA testing, eyewitness misidentification is the single greatest cause of wrongful convictions nationwide, playing a role in more than 75 percent of convictions overturned through DNA testing.

It's impossible for me to say what my young accuser believed or didn't believe. By the date of my trial enough time had elapsed for her to have been convinced of almost anything regarding the events of the night she was attacked. That she was still a child and that one of the lead detectives on the case was her neighbor and a close family friend surely must have colored her memories. Given the vehemence with which he insisted upon my guilt, it's difficult to imagine her denying it.

As soon as I saw her on the stand at my trial I understood that John Irwin had been right that day at the Charles Street Jail. No juror in the world could have ruled against her. Her vulnerability was palpable, as was her pain. Clearly, she had suffered deeply. As angry as I was, I could not help feeling for her.

When asked to point me out to the jury, she was unable to look at me. Keeping her head down, she raised her hand and gestured across the courtroom toward where I was sitting. Not only did she identify me as her attacker, but she also testified that I had referred to myself by name during the attack. Bizarrely, this utterly unbelievable detail became the strongest piece of "evidence" in the case against me.

The testimony of nearly a dozen people as to my whereabouts that night was utterly meaningless in the face of that one little girl.

On February 25, 1970, having been found guilty of assault and unnatural acts on a child, I was sentenced to an additional ten to fifteen years in state custody. I can truthfully say that, aside from the deaths of my mother and father, it was the only time in my life I ever shed a tear.

The conviction was devastating. Even so, I never once regretted my decision to decline the plea offer. There was the principle of it, of course, the fact that I simply would not admit to a crime I hadn't committed. But there were other, more practical reasons to be grateful for having refused to make a deal. What John Irwin had failed to tell me during our last meeting at the Charles Street Jail was that although my prison sentence in the rape charge would have run concurrently with my other sentences, I would have faced additional time—most likely a life sentence—in a facility for sexual predators and the criminally insane upon my release from Walpole. Worse, a guilty plea on my part would have meant forfeiting any chance to appeal the jury's verdict.

At least, I told myself as the van carried me back to Walpole after the sentencing hearing, there was still a possibility, however slim, that I might eventually clear my name.

Eight

You've already heard me confess that I'm not a particularly pious man. At the best of times I'm a skeptic; at the worst I've renounced God—at least any conventional notion of God—entirely, even cursed him. But despite my lack of faith there are a handful of events in my life I can only describe as miracles. The first of these was my survival on the Back Bay rooftop; the second was the arrival of a man named John Harding at Walpole prison in the summer of 1970.

Harding came to Walpole, as I did, from the Charles Street Jail. Small and delicate of frame, with an air of profound defeat, he was the kind of man who best survives prison by flying well below the radar. "Head down and mouth shut" would have been my counsel had I met him on the way in, and "Do whatever is asked of you without flinching." Though, looking back, I'm grateful I was not there at intake to give him this advice.

There are inmates who thrive on harassing the new arrivals. But that was never my thing. If anything, I felt sorry for the guys coming in, especially those, like Harding, who obviously lacked the skills required for prison life. In fact, if it hadn't been for his big mouth and my good friend Billy Irish, I probably wouldn't have noticed Harding at all.

Billy and I were friends from way back. We'd grown up just around the corner from each other in Milton, where our fathers were both on the police force. Our lives took strikingly divergent paths, however, when Billy's father, a decorated marine who had fought in numerous battles in the Pacific during World War II and who suffered severe posttraumatic stress, was fired from the force and later sent to prison for bookmaking, leaving Billy's mother to care for seven small children. Not long after his father went away the family suffered an even worse tragedy when Billy's mother was hit by a bus. Billy, along with his brothers and sisters, was sent first to an orphanage and then to a string of bleak and abusive foster homes.

After his mother's accident I lost touch with Billy entirely. I might never have seen him again if he hadn't walked into a concert I was playing several years later. The way Billy tells it, he spent his last thirty-five cents to get in to see me, no small sacrifice considering the fact that his shoes were so worn that he'd taken to patching them with pieces of cereal boxes. As far as I'm concerned, it was money well spent. To this day he is one of my closest friends.

In the winter of 1970, while I was standing trial for the rape of the young girl in Revere, Billy was doing federal time on the top tier of the Charles Street Jail. Federal prisoners, who were housed together on the building's fifth floor, had it worse than anyone at Charles Street. The windows on the uppermost tier had no glass in them but were covered instead with thin sheets of plywood, loosely attached, which let in not only the bitter New England cold but stray pigeons as well. The entire tier was covered with bird shit. To make matters worse, federal prisoners were confined to their cells at all times, except for meals.

Billy was sitting in his cell playing solitaire one day when one of the tier sweepers, a state inmate, passed by. The man stopped and peered through the bars of Billy's cell. "You're Myles Connor, aren't you?"

The assumption wasn't completely unreasonable. Billy and I are both redheads, the same age, and about the same size and build.

Billy shook his head. "You've got me confused with someone else."

But the guy wasn't buying it. "Don't worry, Myles," he said, lowering his voice just a notch. "I know you're here under an alias. I won't tell anyone."

"Look, pal," Billy told him, "I'm not Myles Connor."

"It's okay, really," the man persisted. "I'm a big fan of yours. I saw you play up in Revere. You're real good."

Billy shrugged. Clearly there was no convincing the guy.

"In any case," he went on. "I wanted to apologize to you."

"Oh yeah? What for?"

"I feel like I might have made a mistake. I heard you got blamed for something I did a long time ago."

"What's that?" Billy asked.

The man hesitated. "That sex charge," he admitted at last. "The one up in Revere. I did that."

Billy turned and took his first good look at the sweeper, who was obviously not playing with a full deck. To admit to being a child rapist on the inside was incomprehensibly stupid. To do so to the person who'd been wrongly convicted of the crime was an act of suicide. Billy's first instinct was to reach through the bars of his cell and strangle the guy. But for my sake he stopped himself. "I appreciate you telling me this," he said, struggling to sound sincere. "By the way, you never told me your name."

The sweeper smiled, like a kid who'd done wrong and received a pardon and a pat on the head from his dad. "Harding," he replied. "John Harding."

There is no direct method of communication between prisoners in the federal lockup at Charles Street and those at Walpole. The best Billy could hope for after his conversation with Harding was that a relative or mutual friend might visit and then be persuaded to pass the news to me, a process that could have taken months. Fortunately, fate intervened in my favor.

Not long after Harding's visit to Billy's fifth-tier cell, the federal inmates at Charles Street rioted in protest of the horrific conditions there. In response to the riots, a judge ordered all federal prisoners transferred from Charles Street to Walpole.

Upon his arrival at the prison, Billy sought me out immediately. I was overjoyed to see my friend, and even more so when he told me about Harding. There was only one problem: Harding was still at Charles Street.

"Not for long," Billy said. "He's just there while his plea arrangement gets straightened out. Then he'll be coming to Walpole."

As much as I wanted to believe Harding's confession, I knew better than to be anything but cautiously optimistic. Cons will say all sorts of crazy things, either to impress their fellow inmates or because for some sick reason they crave the notoriety. Having been falsely accused of a crime myself, I had no wish to do the same to someone else. But if Harding was telling the truth, getting him to admit to what he'd done was the only hope I had of clearing my name.

My biggest concern was that Harding would come to his senses, realize the gravity of what he'd told Billy, and ask to be put into protective custody. If this happened, I'd never find out the truth.

When Harding first got to Walpole I made sure everyone treated him like royalty. I had a solid crew by then, and they all pitched in to make nice with the new kid, buying him fudge pops from Al DeSalvo's ice cream stand. In the mean time, I set to work trying to get Harding's record pulled. He was telling everyone he was in for burglary. But after what he'd told Billy, I wasn't buying this version of events.

Now that everything is computerized, pulling a fellow inmate's file isn't so easy. But back then it was routine. There was a friendly case worker with access to the records room who, with the help of an inmate trustee and the persuasion of a monetary gift, was willing to do this kind of thing for us.

"Your boy's got a thing for little girls," the trustee informed me one afternoon on the yard. "He's got a bunch of morals charges on his record. All minor children."

I had the confirmation I needed. Now it was time to act.

Considering the fact that the life I've lived has never been short on violence, I myself am not a violent man. There are people out there—and believe me, I've known plenty of them—who take pleasure in inflicting pain. Hurting another being is not something I enjoy at all. Whenever possible I've gone to great lengths to avoid bloodshed. But a lifetime spent in the company of criminals has taught me that there are people in the world who respond only to violence, and that force is sometimes a necessary evil.

As I said before, convicted sex offenders are reviled by their fellow prisoners. There were plenty of men in Walpole prison who would have loved nothing more than to get their hands on John Harding and torture him mercilessly. Even knowing what Harding had done, I had no wish to see him suffer merely for suffering's sake. But in light of Harding's record it seemed highly likely that he had in fact committed the crime of which I had been convicted.

To my mind there was only one way to know for sure.

After my conversation with the trustee I gathered my closest friends and explained to them the situation and what I planned to do about it. All agreed to help me. Several days later we gathered in the back room of the prison auditorium. Ralph Petrozziello was there, along with two other members of my crew, Ozzy DePriest and Paul Minot. Billy Irish arrived last, with John Harding in tow.

Up to that point I had purposely kept away from Harding. Billy had invited him to the auditorium to meet "the real Myles Connor," knowing he would jump at the chance. When the two men entered the room, I was immediately taken aback by how much Harding looked like me. He was short, close to my height, with the same stripped-down build I'd had after my long hospital stay. His flame-red hair was a near-perfect match to mine.

Harding hesitated when he saw the four of us. "Hey, Myles," he said at last, trying to sound as if he wasn't afraid, and failing miserably.

"Any idea why you're here?" I asked.

Another shrug. "Not really. No."

"Think about it," I said. "When the reason comes to mind, be sure and let me know. In the meantime, I'm going to ask you some questions. Thing is, I already know the answers to most of them."

I nodded to my crew and the four men moved toward Harding,

surrounding him on all sides. Ralph, who had fashioned a shank for the occasion, pressed the instrument's sharpened tip against the small hollow at the base of Harding's neck. Of the five of us, Ralph definitely had the worst reputation. Don't get me wrong—Ralph was a stand-up guy and a friend of the highest caliber, but when provoked he had a violent temper. Every man in Walpole knew better than to fool with him.

Harding swallowed hard. His face was gray, his upper lip flecked with sweat. Suddenly, the tang of urine filled the room. I looked down at Harding's crotch and saw a dark stain spreading across his denim pants.

"He fucking pissed himself," Ralph said.

"It's simple," I told Harding. "Lie to me and I'll have you killed. The first question's an easy one: What are you in for?"

"Burglary." His voice was barely a whisper.

"You want to rethink that?" I asked.

Harding hung his head, as if resigned to his fate. "No."

Ralph hit him hard in the stomach then and he doubled over, struggling to get his breath back. But we didn't give him the chance.

I'm not proud of what happened after that. I still cringe remembering what we did to that man. Despite everything, he lied right up until the end. In fact he would have died lying if I hadn't stepped in.

"Could he be telling the truth?" I wondered out loud.

"No way," Billy said without hesitation.

"We pulled his fucking file," Ozzy reminded me.

"Let's kill him," Ralph suggested.

I shook my head. Harding's confession was my only shot at clearing my name. He would be no use to me dead. More important, killing him would be a pointless and hateful act. I wanted no part of it.

"John, please," I pleaded with the man. "I'm the only guy in here who wants you alive. Please, just tell me the truth."

He blinked up at me through swollen eyelids. "I hurt little girls."

"And the girl in Revere?"

Harding coughed, wincing at the pain in his ribs. "What do you want to know?"

"Did you do it or not?" I asked.

"Sure I did it. Little blond girl on a hill. I took some money from her, didn't I?"

I didn't answer. One of the charges against me was that I'd stolen four dollars from the girl. "Pull yourself together," I told him. "We're going to get you cleaned up and take you to the warden right now. We'll get this written up and you can sign an affidavit in front of him." I paused, staring down at him. "You say we laid a hand on you and we'll kill you right in front of the warden, understand?"

Harding nodded, then wiped his mouth, smearing blood across his cheek. "Do you think the police knew you were innocent?" he asked as Billy hauled him to his feet. " 'Cause I've got a real good friend in the MDC."

At the mention of the Metropolitan District Commission, I snapped to attention.

"Oh yeah," I said. "Who's your friend?"

"Detective Deschamps," Harding answered. "He's like an uncle to me. He protects me, even gives me money sometimes."

"You think he knew you did this?" I asked, trying to contain my rage.

Harding paused. It was almost as if he understood the importance of what he was about to tell me. "Sure," he said. "He knew."

A prison confession is one thing, but an acquittal on account of such an admission is something else entirely. In light of what happened with my original jury trial, I was wary of going through the same thing again. Fortunately, I wouldn't have to. Because such a short amount of time had passed since my conviction, my attorney was able to skip the lengthy appeals process and go directly to the judge who had originally heard the case to ask for a dismissal.

Despite this positive turn of events, a reversal of the charges against me was by no means a sure thing. The judge in the case, a man named Eugene Hudson, was known for being extremely tough on defendants. But he also had a reputation for fairness.

At our first meeting with Judge Hudson, in late November 1970, Harding, who had been transferred to the prison in Bridgewater, confessed once again to having raped the girl. But at our second hearing, a week later, he patently denied having committed the crime. His change of heart didn't come as a surprise to me. I had a strong suspicion that Hurley and Caselli had been down to Bridgewater to see him, along with Jack Zalkind, the Suffolk County assistant district attorney who had prosecuted the original case against me. If there's one thing cops and prosecutors hate more than losing the first time around, it's having their convictions overturned. Reversals generate huge amounts of bad publicity, something any district attorney needs to avoid at all cost if he or she is to win reelection.

Jack Zalkind had a reputation for being an extremely zealous prosecutor. Just a few years earlier he had been the lead prosecutor in a series of trials involving high-ranking members of the New England mob. Working closely with the FBI and a turncoat hit man named Joseph "the Animal" Barboza, the first person ever to take advantage of the newly created Federal Witness Protection Program, Zalkind was able to put four men on death row, two in prison for life, and send mob boss Raymond Patriarca to the Atlanta Federal Penitentiary.

It was quite a list of accomplishments, though even then the veracity of Barboza's testimony was questionable. In the years since, proof of widespread corruption in the Boston FBI office along with the contradictory testimony of additional witnesses further weakened Zalkind's mob convictions. It was eventually proven that Barboza fabricated his claims out of a desire to get revenge for perceived slights and to cut a deal for himself, and that the men he testified against were actually innocent of the crimes of which they were convicted.

Clearly, Zalkind was not the kind of man to step aside and allow a rape conviction to be overturned because of a prison confession. "I want Mr. Connor prosecuted to the full extent of the law for what he and his associates did to Mr. Harding," he told Judge Hudson when we returned for the third and final hearing.

"Mr. Zalkind," the Judge replied, glowering down at the prosecutor, "because of the unusual nature of Mr. Harding's confession, I took him into my chambers last week and asked him a series of questions only the guilty party would have known the answers to. He replied correctly to each and every one."

Zalkind tried to protest, but he was cut off.

"I have no doubt about Mr. Connor's conduct," Hudson said. "But had I been in his position, I would have done the same thing. You will not use my courtroom to railroad an innocent man."

After my attorney filed a motion for a new trial, Hudson went on to dismiss the case. Because of the circumstances surrounding his confession and the prosecutor's reluctance to drag the young victim back into court, Harding was never charged with the crime.

It's hard enough to serve a prison sentence when you know you're guilty. Doing time for a crime you know you didn't commit is excruciatingly painful. When I returned to Walpole after the dismissal I felt like a free man. And to the extent that I had reclaimed the larger portion of my dignity, I was.

But there is a price to be paid for everything.

To this day I still believe that what we did to John Harding was justified: he was guilty of the crime, and without his confession I would not have been able to clear my name. But I also believe that nothing good can come of that kind of violence. Ralph, Ozzy, Billy, and I would be forever linked by what we had done in that cramped room behind the auditorium. It was a bond that would extend far beyond Walpole's towering perimeter, a debt of friendship that I was bound to repay.

Nine

———

Not long after the rape conviction was overturned I was transferred from Walpole to the medium-security prison at Norfolk. It was early 1971 and I had served four years of my ten-to-twelve-year sentence for the charges from the shooting. Though I could not have foreseen it, I would be back in the art business much sooner than the police hoped. Meanwhile, I used my time at the more relaxed prison to study. That, and get into an adventure or two.

The transfer was meant as a reward for good behavior, but I viewed it as the worst kind of punishment. The nightmare I'd suffered at the hands of the medical staff there was still fresh in my mind, and the idea of going back made me queasy. On top of that, the prison population at Norfolk had a bad reputation, despite the laxity of the place.

It was ironic: the inmates at Walpole, by contrast, were stand-up guys. Old-school criminals who understood the meaning of loyalty, they lived, by and large, by an iron code of ethics. Whatever their disagreements were, men at Walpole did not rat on one another. Those who did were handled swiftly and discreetly. It was, at times, a brutal system, but it succeeded at keeping order.

Norfolk, on the other hand, could be an unpredictable place. The majority of the inmates there were junkies. Like all addicts, they would do anything for a score. Many had been sent to Norfolk as a reward for informing on fellow prisoners at other facilities. If the choice had been mine, I gladly would have stayed at Walpole.

Luckily, a number of my friends were also at Norfolk, including Ozzy DePriest, who was transferred from Walpole around the same time I was, and Bobby Donati, a kid I'd known from my days playing in clubs in Revere Beach. Though not a wise guy himself, Bobby had ties to the Italian community. He was always a very active thief, taking full advantage of any opportunity that came his way. Like me, he was an avid art collector, with a particular passion for oriental rugs.

Another upside to Norfolk was the number of college extension courses offered there. The educational opportunities at Walpole were unimpressive at best. There was a range of interesting classes to choose from at Norfolk. Having nothing better to do, I quickly took advantage of the offerings.

Growing up, I was never a particularly good student. It wasn't that I didn't have the ability to succeed at school; learning always came easily to me—perhaps too easily. As I said before, I have always had a surprising facility for recall of facts. There were just so many more interesting things than schoolwork—animals, music, art, girls—on which to focus my mental energy. But in prison the distractions were far fewer. I did well in my classes, earning straight A's.

When not in formal classes, I studied subjects that were of particular interest to me, making good use of the prison library and of books I requested from friends and family members. Aside from art and the current market for fine art and antiques, areas I always made a point of keeping abreast of, I was particularly interested in religion. I immersed myself in the study of Buddhism, Christianity, Islam, the American Indian religions, and even the occult.

Because of my good grades in the extension classes, near the end of my stay at Norfolk I was given an opportunity to take the SAT test. I surprised everyone—including myself—with near perfect scores on both sections of the exam. Somehow, the local press got wind of my achievement, and one of the Boston papers ran a story questioning the legitimacy of my scores. Essentially, the author accused me of having cheated. The article caused quite a stir at the time. Many people found it hard to believe that someone of above average intelligence could be doing time in the state pen. Others argued in my favor.

Eventually my story caught the interest of two professors from Cambridge, who endeavored to set the record straight once and for all by having me take the exam again, this time under close supervision. The warden at Norfolk agreed, and I was allowed to retake the test. I performed even better the second time around.

As a result of all the publicity surrounding my scores, I was offered admission and scholarships to two prestigious universities in the Boston area. The schools also offered to transport me to and from the prison for classes. Not surprisingly, Department of Correction officials shot down the proposal. Given my predilection for running, I could see why they were reluctant to let me leave the prison grounds.

I would have served out the remainder of my sentence at Norfolk in relative peace and quiet, diligently availing myself of the prison's educational opportunities, if it hadn't been for an incident involving Ozzy DePriest. Instead of academic pursuits, Ozzy had found a more lucrative way to pass the time at Norfolk. With the help of friends on the outside Ozzy was smuggling large quantities of pharmaceuticals into the prison, then selling them for considerable profit.

It was a thriving business for a while. But when Ozzy was busted with a substantial stash of drugs in his cell it seemed all but certain that he'd be facing additional time on the inside.

Never one to walk away from a friend in need, I quickly devised a plan.

Prison, I have come to learn, is a place of intense social stratification. In an environment where loyalty means everything, where the decision to trust someone has to be made at a glance, traditional identifying markers take on heightened significance. Italian, black, skinhead: these and other classifications can be matters of life and death. This is true for staff as well as inmates, and that includes those men of the cloth who ply their godly wares within the prison walls. At every prison I've had the pleasure to know, the clergy conform to surprisingly rigid stereotypes.

In New England prisons the Catholic priest always heads up the largest and most powerful congregation. Irish, Italians, Poles: everyone who's anyone is a Catholic. Like his flock, most of whom are career criminals, the priest is always a stand-up guy. It's his job to settle grievances between groups and stick up for men at parole hearings. If he knows what's good for him, he does his job well.

The rabbi, though far less powerful, is inevitably an inmate favorite. The rabbi is generally the one to resolve disputes between inmates and staff. He's always bringing in food and other treats, and lobbying for better treatment for all the prisoners.

The Protestant minister, on the other hand, is almost always the least likely to bend the rules to help an inmate. The minister at Norfolk, a man named George Dodson, was extreme in his contempt for the inmates. A spineless bottom-feeder with a pathological need for validation from the administration, he spent most of his time shooting down guys at their parole hearings. He was helped in his efforts by his inmate clerk who was a known informant. Not surprisingly, Dodson was universally despised. Inmates hated him for being the prick he was, while the staff disdained him for being a two-faced asshole. I figured pinning Ozzy's rap on him would be a piece of cake.

Ozzy had been put in isolation after being caught with the drugs, but I was able to get messages to him through a friendly guard. Screws, as we called the guards, could be invaluable allies. In every prison there were sympathetic screws who could be persuaded to do favors for inmates.

The next time I saw this particular guard I pulled him aside. "Tell Ozzy I'll take any extra merchandise he still has."

Not long after this exchange an associate of Ozzy's passed me a package with nearly a thousand dollars' worth of pills inside.

The next morning, taking the package with me, I paid a visit to the prison library, where I stashed the drugs in the stacks, behind a thick row of Bibles.

Snitches may be the lowest form of prison life, but that doesn't mean they don't have their uses. There are times when a smart con can use an informant to his advantage. This was one of those times.

Later that morning I approached a well-known rat on the yard. "I'll tell you a secret," I said. "But you can't tell anyone, okay?"

My words were music to the man's ears. He nodded eagerly.

"This rap Ozzy's facing was a setup. The real culprits are Dodson and his clerk."

"The minister?" the snitch asked, fairly drooling at the information.

I nodded. "Dodson's the one who brings the stuff in from the outside. He hides it in the library. Up in the top tier of the stacks where all the Bibles are." I paused, looking at the rat, watching his face as he processed the information, weighing its worth. "You won't say anything, will you?"

"Of course not," he assured me.

"I'm heading over to the weight room," I told him. "Wanna come?"

He shook his head. "Nah, I've got some stuff to take care of."

I bet you do, I thought as I walked away across the yard. Turning to look back over my shoulder, I saw the man making a beeline for the administration building.

Originally designed as a model of a progressive penal reform, the grounds at Norfolk looked and felt more like a college campus than a prison. Inmates were housed in a handful of dormitory-style brick buildings spread around a grassy quad. On pleasant afternoons we often gathered in small groups on the steps of these buildings. If not for our monochrome prison uniforms and the conspicuous lack of members of the opposite sex, we might have been any group of students lounging between classes, chatting about a lecture we'd just attended or which girl we were going to ask to an upcoming dance. Only we weren't, and the topic of conversation at Norfolk, though often centered on women, was usually of a much less wholesome nature.

Aside from providing a comfortable gathering place, the dormitory steps were the perfect vantage point from which to observe the comings and goings in the administration buildings. After allowing sufficient time for the snitch to do his work, I settled myself on the dormitory steps to observe the fallout of my actions.

I figured the warden would act quickly on the information I'd fed his snitch, and I wasn't wrong. I hadn't been watching for long when I saw a handful of guards run into the building that housed the minister's office. A few minutes later they reappeared with the minister and his clerk in tow.

Several days later the warden called me into his office.

"You son of a bitch," he said. "I know you had a hand in what happened to Dodson."

The setup had been a fine piece of handiwork on my part. I wanted more than anything to take credit for it. But I managed to bite my tongue. "I don't know what you're talking about," I told him.

"No?" the warden growled. "Well, I'm sending you back to Walpole anyway."

I tried my best to look crestfallen.

The fall of 1971 was a dark time in the nation's prisons. That September a bloody riot at New York's Attica prison ended in the deaths of ten hostages and twenty-nine inmates when state troopers dropped tear gas into the yard and stormed the facility. For those of us on the inside the riots highlighted not only the atrocious conditions in which we prisoners lived but also our powerlessness in the face of a brutal system. Attica brought simmering discontent to a full boil in prisons all over the country.

In the days immediately following the riots Walpole inmates were sharply divided over how to respond to what had happened at Attica. At the best of times the atmosphere in any prison teeters on the brink of all-out chaos. There were many at Walpole who believed violence was the only way to show our solidarity with the Attica inmates and air our grievances. Other, saner voices called for nonviolent demonstrations. Fortunately for everyone involved, those inmates advocating peaceful means eventually won out over those crying for a repeat of what had happened at Attica.

In late September the inmates at Walpole embarked on what would become a five-day work stoppage. The solidarity with which the strike was carried out was impressive, to say the least. All of the six hundred men at Walpole participated, bringing the prison to a virtual standstill.

Among our demands were furloughs for work and education, conjugal visits for married prisoners, better medical care, and permission for death row inmates—who at the time were kept locked down in horrific conditions in Block Ten—to mix freely with the general population. Our most controversial demand was a repeal of the so-called "two-thirds law," which mandated that all prisoners serve out two-thirds of their sentence before they could be eligible for parole.

On the third day of the strike savvy inmate council leaders issued an invitation to members of the press to come inside the prison walls and talk with the prisoners directly. It was a brilliant move. The next day the entire population of the prison, many of us wearing black armbands in memory of the Attica dead, gathered in the auditorium to meet with reporters from most of the major media outlets in New England. By the fifth day Governor Francis Sargent, under intense media scrutiny, pledged to act on our demands.

The strike was officially over. Yet hostility—and justified skepticism regarding the governor's ability to bring about the promised reforms—lingered. In early October prisoner leaders, frustrated by the lack of visible progress in fulfilling their demands, called for another work stoppage. This second strike, which lasted a week, was followed in mid-November by a two-week lockdown of the entire prison after rumors of a planned riot and inmate takeover reached the warden. Then in March 1972, the Massachusetts legislature defeated a bill to reform the two-thirds law, and full-scale violent riots broke out at Walpole.

The troubles started on St. Patrick's Day, when a white inmate knifed a black inmate in the maximum-security wing. What happened next is not entirely clear, but according to prisoners who were present during the incident, at least one guard then ran through the cellblock shouting, "Race riot!" This call was quickly answered by the inmates, who began setting fire to the piles of garbage that littered the floor of Block 10.

Most of the inmates from the minimum-security side, including myself, were in the auditorium watching a movie when the fight broke out. By the time the film ended the air was thick with the acrid smell of burning garbage. As the guards attempted to funnel us down the smoke-filled main corridor to our cellblocks, mayhem erupted. Guys started throwing things: ashtrays, a television set. Soon the minimum-security wing was burning as well. As the violence escalated, terrified guards deserted their posts, leaving control of the cellblocks to us. Within a matter of hours we had full control of the prison.

Tensions escalated further over the weekend after guards tried to force maximum-security inmates back to their cells. The confrontation quickly turned violent, and several guards and inmates were seriously injured. The move was a major misstep on the part of the new prison superintendent, Robert Donnelly. In the wake of the clash, inmates broke off all communication with Donnelly. He later apologized for his actions over the prison public address system, but by that time he had lost the trust of the inmates.

By Sunday inmates had succeeded in destroying almost all of the cell locks, along with the electrical system, plunging the blocks into smoky darkness. Later that night angry prisoners descended on the library, pulling down the stacks, setting piles of books on fire. The prison pharmacy was pillaged, the gym flooded. Someone managed to break the locks leading into the execution chamber and a crowd of angry prisoners thronged inside, smashing the electric chair, claiming pieces of this gruesome symbol of the system's power for themselves.

At one point I wandered into the auditorium to find that a group of inmates had smashed through the wooden floor with the intention of digging an escape tunnel. It was a wildly ill-conceived plan. As anyone who has ever set a fence post will tell you, the reality of digging a hole is always more arduous than one imagines it will be. But the group was so optimistic and determined that I didn't have the heart to tell them this.

There's a belief among many people who've never been on the inside that convicts naturally gravitate toward chaos and violence, that, like animals, we thrive in an atmosphere of utter lawlessness. While this may be the case for a few truly deranged inmates, the truth is that most are grateful for the security that locks and guards provide. For the weaker inmates, riots are a time of intense fear. Many of these men (Albert DeSalvo being one of them) spent the duration of the riots barricaded in the prison hospital, terrified for their lives. Even inmates like me, with nothing to fear, far prefer the day-to-day routine of prison life to the insanity of riots. None of us wanted to live in filth, squalor, and darkness forever, but neither were we willing to surrender until at least some of our demands were met.

Obviously, both sides would have to compromise. The question was how to find common ground before the situation devolved even further.

Soon after my return from Norfolk I had become active in the Walpole chapter of the Jaycees. Originally created to help young people develop business skills through community service, but perhaps more commonly known for its county fair booths and country club dances, the group was working to establish chapters in many of the nation's prisons. I jumped at the chance to join, mainly because it was something to do besides sit in my cell. To be honest, though, the knowledge that my membership in the organization could help me when I finally came up for parole also factored into my decision. Regardless of my motives in joining, however, I took my membership seriously and was soon elected president of the chapter.

On the Monday evening of the riots, in an attempt to maintain some semblance of normalcy, I convened our regular weekly Jaycees meeting in what was by now a ransacked classroom. I had no idea how many men, if any, would attend, but the room was packed. Clearly people needed a forum in which to air their grievances. The atmosphere was calm, as inmates offered suggestions for bringing about a peaceful end to the standoff. All agreed the first order of business was to restore a line of communication between ourselves and the administration. How this could be accomplished was a matter of debate.

Halfway through the meeting, to everyone's surprise, Superintendent Donnelly walked into the room. It was a gutsy move on his part. He had erred in his use of force on the inmates in maximum security, but his presence at the meeting signaled that he was willing to correct his mistake. After nearly two hours of intense questioning of Donnelly by the Jaycees board, we all returned to our cellblocks with the message that the superintendent was truly contrite about his earlier decision to use force on the prisoners in the maximum-security wing and was ready to negotiate.

Later that night the block leaders met to discuss a response to Donnelly's overture. After much debate someone finally suggested bringing in a mediation team from outside the prison. It seemed like a reasonable plan. But since none of the block leaders felt they could deliver the message to Donnelly without compromising their position, I was asked to do so.

Despite being active in the Jaycees and well liked by my fellow inmates, up to that point I had never participated in prison politics. It simply wasn't something I aspired to, and I was somewhat surprised to find myself in the position of intermediary. But I deemed it a true honor to be trusted in such a way by my fellow inmates.

I returned to Donnelly with the block leaders' proposal. He quickly rejected the idea, saying he believed it was the superintendent's duty to act as mediator. But he agreed to bring in a team of outsiders to arbitrate the dispute. It seemed like a question of semantics to me, but clearly it mattered to Donnelly. I delivered this counterproposal to the inmates, who quickly agreed to it. A five-man citizen team would be brought into the prison to hear our demands and relay them to Donnelly.

The creation of the arbitration team was a pivotal point in the standoff. Within a matter of days, the team was able to negotiate an end to the hostilities. All six hundred prisoners voluntarily returned to their cells. To further defuse tensions, Jaycees from outside the prison volunteered to come inside and walk the cellblocks. For several days, they roamed the prison, talking to inmates, listening to the men's grievances. Eventually Donnelly, too, proved good on his word. It took some time, but many of our demands were finally met.

Though I didn't know it at the time, my role in the negotiations would soon come to benefit me personally as well. But first, Walpole prison had one more surprise in store for me.

In the summer of 1972 I received an unexpected letter from a college student named Martha Ferrante. As part of her course work at the University of Massachusetts, the young woman explained, she was volunteering at a halfway house for newly released convicts. There she had met a friend of mine from the Walpole crafts room, a young man to whom I had taught scrimshaw. He was having trouble finding materials and had mentioned me as a possible resource. But the rules of his parole forbid any contact with convicted felons. Would it be possible, Martha wondered, for her to meet with me sometime on his behalf?

Would it be possible? A visit from a liberal-minded young coed with a soft spot for cons? Carefully I reread the letter, like a desert traveler checking his eyesight upon glimpsing an oasis. My reply went out in the prison mailbag the very next day, and soon we had made arrangements for Martha to visit.

Prison can do strange things to men. After long stretches with no physical contact with women, most cons will take whatever they can get, wherever they can get it. I've seen guys overlook all manner of shortcomings in their desperation to appease their overwrought libidos. At times the visiting room at Walpole resembled a cut-rate brothel, with inmates engaging in all manner of covert sex acts, often with women they wouldn't have been caught dead with on the outside.

But I'm proud to say this wasn't my style. Thanks to my music career, there had been no shortage of beautiful women in my life. Even after six long years in prison my standards were remarkably high. As my meeting with Martha approached, I focused on the real purpose of her visit, keeping well in mind the fact that college girls come in all shapes and sizes.

It's probably for the best that I didn't spend too much time fantasizing about Martha, for the truth is that my imagination couldn't have possibly done her justice. When I finally did meet her I was taken aback by how beautiful she was.

There was no denying the fact that she was physically attractive; she would have been considered so by anyone at any time. But she had a natural beauty that was particularly well suited to the prevailing style of the early seventies. Her brown eyes were striking even without makeup; her long dark hair fell effortlessly across her shoulders.

Visiting Walpole was in many ways a humiliating experience, especially for women, who were subjected to physically invasive searches before being allowed inside. But in spite of the indignities she'd had to endure, there was a warmth and openness to Martha's face that spoke volumes about her personality. That's not to say she was all sweetness and light. There was also a rebellious glimmer in her eye with which I immediately identified.

Despite the circumstances I found it remarkably easy to be with Martha. As our conversation turned from scrimshaw materials to more personal topics, we discovered that we shared a number of similar interests, including a mutual love of art and of animals. By the time she left I had fallen hard for her.

Martha must have felt something for me as well. She continued to visit me throughout the summer, initially under the pretense of needing additional information on scrimshaw materials. But the real reason for her visits quickly became clear to both of us.

Despite our feelings for each other, our meetings grew increasingly bittersweet. With three years left on my sentence before I could even be considered for parole it was difficult for me to justify any kind of relationship with Martha. Though she never said anything, I knew the trips to Walpole were taking their toll on her.

Then, late in the summer of 1972, we were granted an unexpected reprieve: based in part on my conduct during the riots, Superintendent Connelly had recommended me for early parole.

It was an incredible opportunity, but I knew the real work would be convincing the parole board to accept my petition. Fortunately, as president of the Walpole Jaycees, I'd had the opportunity to come into contact with many influential members of the community. A number of these men came forward to help me, along with officials who knew me from the March standoff, my teachers from Norfolk, and my father's friend John Regan, the state trooper who'd sat watch over me during my stay at Mass General. Regan had been promoted to state police detective by then and was part of a task force that investigated crimes committed within the state's prisons. It was a job that brought him to Walpole from time to time. Because of that, we had managed to stay in touch.

By the time I went before the parole board my file was brimming with letters of support, including one from the governor's office and another from the commissioner of correction.

With so much support behind me, the board had little choice but to grant my parole. In October 1972 I walked out of Walpole prison.

Ten

___

I faced a choice: still wild, or tame? I applied to the University of Massachusetts, Boston, and was accepted. But I could not make up my mind whether or not to register for classes. If I did, I knew I would have to apply myself fully to my studies. But with so many other opportunities vying for my attention, I wasn't sure I could do so. I was intent on following my music career, but first I had to decide whether to try the straight and narrow or not.

Soon after I got out of Walpole my friends and family hosted a welcome-home party for me. Everyone who meant anything to me was there—family members, childhood friends from Milton, band groupies, associates from my Revere Beach days, guys I'd run with in prison—many of whom I hadn't seen in nearly seven years.

It was an unlikely collection of people, one more suited to an episode of *This Is Your Life* than a social gathering. Al Dotoli was on the road at the time with a band he was managing and couldn't be there, but many of my former bandmates showed up. Also in attendance were Billy Irish, Ozzy DePriest, and Bobby Donati. Of my closest friends from Walpole, only Ralph Petrozziello, who was still serving out the remainder of his sentence, was absent.

Naturally, my older sister, Patsy, came. Much to Patsy's chagrin, an old classmate of hers from Milton High School named David Houghton was there as well. As a teenager, David had had a huge crush on my sister. When we lived on Oak Road he had developed a habit of lurking in front of the house late at night, half-hidden—or so he thought—by a telephone pole. He fashioned himself a young Marlon Brando, complete with leather jacket and motorcycle cap. But despite his flair for fashion, Patsy never reciprocated David's feelings.

I, on the other hand, adored him. Sensing this, and no doubt seeing an opportunity to get closer to my sister, David took me under his wing. During the time he and Patsy were in high school together he was like an older brother to me, taking me to the movies or out to the local burger joint for fries or a shake. In return I put in a good word for him with Patsy whenever I could. I lost track of David for a time after he and Patsy graduated, but in the years before my incarceration he had reappeared in my life, showing up regularly to hear me play.

I was thrilled to see David at the party and quickly introduced him around. To my surprise, he and Bobby Donati hit it off immediately. It was the beginning of a friendship that would last for years to come.

It was my party, but as far as I was concerned someone else was the guest of honor: Martha Ferrante had driven down from her parents' house in Northampton to be there. Nothing could have made me happier. Despite the fact that it was our first meeting outside the walls of Walpole prison, I felt as if we'd known each other our entire lives.

Al Dotoli came to my mother's house to see me as soon as he got back into town. Al had big plans for me, and he didn't want to waste any time getting my music career up and running once again.

"I could get you work tomorrow," he told me, stretching out his lanky frame on my mother's couch as if to illustrate the ease with which my career could be revived.

"I'm sure you could," I agreed, somewhat reluctantly. Even after six years in prison, I knew I still had a huge following. If anything, the Back Bay incident and my time in Walpole only added to the mystique of my rock-and-roller persona. The question now was whether I wanted my old life back at all.

"But?" Al asked, sensing the hesitation in my voice.

"There's a lot to think about," I said. "Like I might be going to college."

Al balked. "Who says you can't play music and go to school?"

"You know I hate doing things halfway."

Al leaned forward, setting his elbows onto the table. "I've been around this business for a while now," he said, "and I've learned a thing or two. I can tell talent when I see it, and you've got it in spades. You can be something, Myles, something big. I've always said that. But you've got to do it now, while you're still young."

I knew he was right. Playing rock and roll was a young man's profession. Prison had already eaten up what could have been the best years of my music career. If I wanted to salvage what was left of it, I couldn't afford to waste any more time.

"You're only young once," he said, as if reading my mind.

I smiled. Al's devotion to me was as persuasive as any argument he could have made. "I need some time," I told him. "To think things over, weigh my options."

Al sighed, slumping back in a posture of exasperation he often adopted in his dealings with me.

I wish I could say the choice was difficult, that I agonized over my decision, torn between the thrill of my old life and the heady hush of academia, that my conscience pulled me in one direction while my youthful heart dragged me in another. But let's be honest: college never stood a chance. I registered at UMass, and even attended a few classes. But in the end my college career lasted less than a week.

The high that comes from performing, from being onstage and connecting with an audience, is like nothing else in the world. It's as addictive as any drug, as powerful as any religion, as satisfying as even the best sex. Offered the chance to relive that feeling, I found it impossible to walk away.

Besides, having prided myself on my rebelliousness for so long, the thought of becoming part of the very system I scorned seemed like the worst kind of capitulation. Rock and roll was all about refusing to toe the line. That's what I was all about. That and the urge to get back to collecting, by whatever means necessary.

Acting as my personal manager, a role he would fill for the next three decades, Al Dotoli quickly put together a band for me. It was an impressive group of musicians. As usual, I sang and played guitar; a kid named Bean, who'd been in my band at Walpole, backed me up on bass; Harry French was our drummer; Chucky Norton, Paul Donsanto, and Danny McBride, later of the band Sha Na Na, took turns playing guitar. Good to his word, Al soon had steady work for us. That winter and into the spring we played in clubs around the Boston area and on the New England college circuit. By summer of 1973 we were regular headliners at a place called the Beachcomber, on Wollaston Beach in Quincy.

If I had one worry concerning my decision to put off school, it was that Martha would disapprove. But nothing could have been further from the truth. She was thrilled to see me doing something I so clearly loved, and came down from Northampton as often as she could to hear me play.

Like my Sunday afternoon concerts at Walpole, the Beachcomber gigs attracted a surprisingly diverse audience, from the highest of Boston's high society to the lowest Southie thugs. Brahmins and bookmakers, coeds and cons: they all rubbed elbows on the dance floor at the Beachcomber. And I did my best to keep them coming back.

Much of my appeal as an entertainer has always had to do with the fact that I know how to put on a good show. That's not to say I don't have real talent. Certainly, my musical ability drew people in. But they also came to forget themselves, to indulge in the fantasy of freedom, to laugh at themselves and the world around them. My popularity, whether in Walpole or Wollaston Beach, lay in my ability to fulfill that fantasy. Like any good musician, I took my work very seriously. At rehearsals my band members and I were meticulous in our preparations. But once we got in front of an audience we broke loose. We quickly became known for our onstage antics.

Al Dotoli's contribution to our success cannot be overstated. A born producer, Al had a gift for spectacle. Using my outlaw persona to our advantage, dubbing me the "President of Rock and Roll," Al created a thrilling signature show for the band. I worked out a terrific cover of Johnny Cash's "Folsom Prison Blues," referencing Walpole Prison instead. Another Johnny Cash hit, "Riot in Cell Block Nine," quickly became our signature song. Al rigged flashing lights and police sirens to simulate an actual riot. When we were done playing, the entire band would leap off the stage, brandishing our guitars as if they were guns, spraying the crowd while the sound of machine-gun fire blared from the speakers. This was long before the days of mosh pits and stage diving, and the move was a surefire crowd-pleaser. But it wasn't without physical risk. One night we were playing at a place down in Dennisport named Jason's. The club had particularly low ceilings, and when we went to do our stage jump, Bean, who was the tallest member of the band, hit his head and knocked himself out. Everyone, including me, thought it was part of the show. It wasn't until we climbed back on stage and saw blood pouring out of Bean's forehead that we realized he wasn't pretending. Fortunately, we managed to revive him, but he never performed the move with quite the same gusto after that.

It didn't take long for the audiences at the Beachcomber to begin resembling their prison counterparts in more than just their diversity. As my popularity grew so did the number of Walpole alumni at my concerts. My shows soon became an informal arena for guys looking to hook up with their buddies from the inside. If they could connect themselves to me, so much the better.

"You've got a hundred best friends out there," Martha said one night. "And every one of them has a story to tell with you in it. Bank robberies, cop shootings, museum heists. Who knew you had so much time on your hands?" Her tone was light, but I could tell that so many people wanting a piece of me bothered her.

She was right to be concerned. Al was worried as well, and moved quickly to make sure my shows didn't become gathering places for ex-cons, even going so far as to ban certain individuals from the clubs we played in. His actions did not make him popular with the Walpole crowd.

To the authorities my success was proof of the inherent injustice of the world. I was a cop shooter, after all, a punk kid who didn't know the meaning of respect. I should have been locked away somewhere, notching off the days in miserable solitude, instead of signing women's breasts in a Wollaston Beach nightclub.

Looking back, I can see that it wasn't just my success that goaded them, though surely that was part of it. What infuriated them—what has always infuriated those in authority—was my ability to take everything in stride. I had breezed through six years at Walpole as if it was a lark. Now, as if to add insult to injury, I'd reclaimed my music career with similar ease.

Once again, I was the thorn in their side, the collar everyone wanted. Once again, all eyes were on me, watching, waiting, hoping I would slip up.

By the end of the summer of 1973 I was riding high. I had a wonderful girlfriend and a growing following. For a few brief months it seemed as if I had succeeded in outrunning my past. But as anyone who has spent time on the inside will tell you, prison loyalties run stronger even than bonds of blood. Mine would soon be tested.

During my first year out of prison, I had managed to keep my nose clean. Music kept me busy and well above the fray. I didn't hit a single museum, or anything else. That's not to say I wasn't there with a hand up when guys needed me. Anyone who came to me looking for help got it. But for the first year of my parole my paychecks were all legit. In 1974 Al got me into the studio to record some preliminary songs for an album. The band members from Sha Na Na, who were enjoying national success at the time, graciously agreed to back me up in the studio. Danny McBride played guitar, Chico Ryan played bass, Lenny Baker played saxophone, and Jesse Henderson was our drummer. We recorded a sensational cover of the Elvis Presley hit "I Was the One," and were poised to make a terrific album, when my old friend Ralph Petrozziello showed up at the Beachcomber one Sunday with other plans for me.

Ralph was the last of my Walpole crew to be released. He came out of prison anything but reformed, itching to get back to what he did best. There's only so much one man can do on his own, and most of that falls into the category of petty crime: small-time holdups and burglaries, drugs, the occasional contract job. Real scores require at least two guys, if not more. It wasn't long before Ralph decided he needed a partner.

"How'd you like to make some money?" he asked me as we sat at the bar after my show.

"What do you think this is?" I responded, motioning to the empty stage. "Charity work?"

He shook his head and leaned closer to me. "I mean real money. Not this nickel-and-dime shit they're paying you here."

I would have been offended if he hadn't been right. My music provided me with a steady paycheck, but it was steadily meager. If I hadn't been living with my mother at the old house on Oak Road, I would have needed some other form of income to get by. Ralph, on the other hand, was clearly cashing in, dressed to the nines and driving a nice car, taking his girlfriends out for fancy dinners and champagne.

"I've got a tip from some of my friends," he said, lowering his voice a notch. "There's a boxcar full of electronics coming into the Dedham freight yard tomorrow night. I've got a guaranteed buyer for whatever I take. But I can't do it alone."

I shook my head, catching sight of Ralph's expensive Italian shoes as I did so, the leather buffed and gleaming. I've always been a sucker for the finer things.

"Say the word and the job is yours," he said, turning slightly on his stool, glancing around the bar. "But don't wait too long. There's at least a dozen guys in here who would kill for a piece of this gig."

In the end it was the money that got me, the money and what it could buy—and not just fine wine, expensive clothes, and extravagant weekends away with Martha, though these were things I could appreciate.

Like all collectors, I am a man driven by the desire for possession. Unlike most people, for whom the pleasure of looking is enough, I am not content with mere appreciation. I don't deny having stolen art for its value, monetary and other. But there is much more that I have taken out of love or lust, the possession of which is worth far more to me than the pieces themselves.

By 1974, my collection had grown to include, among other things, Chinese porcelains, Japanese bronzes, Asian watercolors, and antique weapons of every description. I had acquired a number of full suits of armor, both Japanese and Western. My sword collection alone boasted dozens and dozens of the finest examples of Japanese craftsmanship, including *katanas* and their slightly longer cousins *tachis* (traditional samurai swords), *naginatas* (large pole weapons), *tantos* (samurai knives), *kwaiken* (small, delicate knives used by samurai women), and *nodachis* (large two-handed swords). I displayed many of these pieces at my mother's house in Milton, having converted her dining room into a museum room. The rest I stored in her attic or in a shed in the backyard. But despite the impressive size of my collection, it wasn't enough.

If I accepted Ralph's proposal, I knew, I'd soon have enough money to buy whatever I wanted. My decision was an easy one.

"I'm in," I told Ralph as we left the club that night.

Eleven

If rock and roll was easy money, the Dedham job was embarrassingly so.

Ralph didn't offer any specifics about how he'd come by his information in the first place. It was clear to me that we were merely doing the grunt work for someone higher up the food chain, that our buyer was the one who'd tipped us to the haul in the first place. Conveniently, they'd even lent us a large commercial van for the job. Knowing Ralph's affiliation with a certain criminal organization, my money was on them, but I knew better than to say anything.

On the night of the heist Ralph picked me up at my mother's house in Milton and we drove together in the van to Dedham. As a rule, I've never been one to give the consequences of my actions much thought. Perhaps because of this I rarely get nervous about jobs. If things go smoothly, I always figure, it's all well and good. If not, I'll cross that bridge when I come to it.

It was the wee hours of the morning when we pulled into the Dedham freight yard. The sky was clear, the half-moon low on the horizon. The season had turned and there was a sharp chill in the air. We had dressed for the cold, in dark wool peacoats and knit caps.

"You ready?" Ralph asked, brazenly pulling the van up right beside the tracks, cutting the engine.

I nodded, feeling an electric rush of adrenaline. We weren't expecting any drama. In fact, neither of us was armed. Still, my heart was hammering the way it did before a gig. It was not an entirely unpleasant sensation. "Let's go." I said, popping the passenger door.

Hefting the bolt cutters he'd brought with him, Ralph opened his door and climbed out, his shadow looming in the slanted glare of the yard's floodlights. I stepped out after him, and we moved stealthily toward the freight cars, squinting to read the markings in the semi-darkness.

"This one," he said, finding what he was looking for at last, waving me closer, wrangling the heavy bolt cutters.

There was a loud crack as the metal lock broke. Ralph and I slid the car's heavy door open and clambered up inside. With the cold as encouragement, we worked quickly, transferring the freight by hand, moving silently from the boxcar to the van and back again. By dawn we had finished and were back in the front seat, heading for the Roslindale warehouse where we'd arranged to deliver our haul.

We were happy with our share of the Dedham score, and Ralph's friends in Roslindale were equally pleased. I don't remember the exact figure they paid us, but I do recall that it made the pittance I took home after a gig look like pocket change.

Ralph soon had another job for us, this one involving a semitruck-load of fur coats. We had found our niche. As the jobs continued to roll in we quickly realized that we needed at least one more pair of hands. Eventually Ralph's brother, Sal, joined our crew.

In the spring of 1974 Ralph's contacts approached us with a particularly lucrative proposal: they wanted us to clean out a Quincy warehouse that had just received a large shipment of leather coats. As usual, we agreed to take on the job.

On the night of the heist we met at Sal's place in Dorchester. Sal was a married man, one of the few of us not to be living with his parents, and his wife was particularly sympathetic to our line of work. As a result, we often gathered at their apartment.

Our past successes had made us perilously cocky, and we were in high spirits as we set out for Quincy. Ralph was driving the truck that had, as usual, been supplied to us by his contacts, while Sal and I rode along, windows open to let in the warm spring air. We arrived at the warehouse and parked around the back of the building, pulling the truck right up to the loading dock. Ralph jimmied one of the windows with a pry bar and the three of us crawled through it. I was the last one in.

"Sometimes I'm embarrassed at how easy this is," I commented as I joined Sal and Ralph on the floor of the darkened warehouse. They smiled back at me, two Cheshire cats, the white half-moons of their teeth catching what little light was shining through the windows.

Suddenly, as if answering my boast, a siren wailed in the distance. We all stopped to listen. The whine of a police siren wasn't exactly a rarity in Quincy, and we were all hoping the same thing: that this one had nothing to do with us. But it quickly became clear that this was not the case. The first siren was answered by a second and a third, all moving closer by the instant.

"We must have tripped a silent alarm," Ralph said.

I glanced out the back windows and saw the whirl of revolving lights on the brick wall of the warehouse directly behind us. "Head for the front of the building and scatter!" I told my partners.

Ralph and Sal disappeared into the sea of coats. I quickly followed suit, clambering out a window near the front of the warehouse. I hit the ground running, spurred on by the sound of yet another approaching cruiser, and ducked into an alleyway.

No sooner had the sirens begun to fade behind me than I heard the unexpected sound of Barbra Streisand singing "The Way We Were." Up ahead in the darkness I could just barely make out a parked car, lights out, engine purring quietly.

To tell you the truth, I've never been a big Streisand fan. Her songs are just too sappy for me. "The Way We Were" was a huge hit that winter, and I'd been forced to listen to it more times than I cared to. Normally I would have been supremely irritated at having to hear it one more time. But her voice that night was a welcome beacon in the darkness.

Cautiously, I approached the car, peering in through the open windows. Two figures were sprawled in the backseat, writhing against each other. I couldn't help laughing. Apparently I'd stumbled across some sort of lover's lane.

"Excuse me," I said, bending down toward the open window.

Startled out of their sexual reverie, the couple glanced up at me.

"I'm sorry," I repeated, producing my Smith and Wesson as proof of the seriousness of my request, "but I need to borrow your car."

The woman moved quickly, tucking her shirt in as she lunged for the door. But the man, still groggy from the wash of hormones, blinked up at me, stunned.

"Get out of the car," I told him urgently, waving the gun for emphasis.

"Jesus, John!" the woman yelled, reaching into the backseat and grabbing the man's arm. "Didn't you hear him? Get out of the fucking car."

Finally, John obeyed.

I slid into the front seat and peeled away, but not before turning the radio off, catching Babs in midphrase.

Ralph's friends' jobs were highly lucrative, and I was able to start adding to my collection once again. But as profitable as the contract work was, the three of us soon began to talk about branching out on our own. I've never liked working for other people, even when the work is of an untraditional nature. Helping someone else get rich just doesn't make good financial sense.

Early one morning, as Ralph and I were driving through Roslindale, I suddenly had an idea.

"Pull over!" I shouted.

"What?" Ralph asked, nervously glancing in the rearview mirror. "Is there someone following us?"

I shook my head, motioning to a parking lot on our right. "I want to show you something."

Ralph cut the wheel sharply and we skidded into the lot. "Christ," he swore, "you scared the crap out of me!"

"There," I said, pointing out a low-slung brick building on the opposite side of the street.

"You mean the bank?" Ralph asked.

"Yes, I mean the bank. And her." What had caught my eye was the lone figure of a woman strolling from her car to the front door of the bank. "Opening time," I observed as we watched her fish a ring of keys from her purse and unlock the front door.

Ralph smiled. "It's a shame she's all by herself."

"My thoughts exactly."

The Roslindale heist would be our first full-fledged bank robbery. Ralph, Sal, and I took our time preparing for the job, casing the place from our post across the street, as we had that first morning. We soon discovered that an armored truck made regular stops at the bank to pick up cash three mornings a week. It didn't take us long to conclude that our best opportunity for a big haul would be to hit the bank on one of these days, when the money was literally bagged and waiting for us.

With a few minor exceptions the bank's opening routine varied little from day to day. The woman—the manager, we assumed, for closer observation had confirmed that she was also the one to open the vault—always arrived fifteen to twenty minutes before the other employees. It was a brief window of opportunity, but if we moved quickly, we could make it work.

The only remaining question was how we would get into the building.

"How about the roof?" Ralph suggested as we sat in his car one morning waiting for the manager.

I laughed. "Sure. We'll just bust a hole and lower ourselves inside."

Ralph shrugged. "Why not? I'd say a couple of sledgehammers would do the trick."

I scanned the flat roofline. It wasn't the most subtle approach, but it might just work. There'd be no covering up for ourselves. But then, once we had the cash and were gone, what did that matter? In fact, I found the thought of the cops walking in to find a gaping hole in the ceiling of the bank quite amusing.

J ust after midnight on the morning of the heist Ralph, Sal, and I met in their parents' garage in Roslindale. Dressing the part is always important. If nothing else, in our black clothes and work boots, we looked like seasoned professionals. Each of us was armed with a pistol, in my case a Walther 9 mm that would accompany me on countless future jobs. I had brought ladies' stockings to serve as masks, and I handed one to each man as we made our final preparations.

Ralph had stolen a painter's ladder for the job, as well as a pickup truck in which to haul it and our other tools. *Borrowed* might have been a more accurate word, as we planned to abandon both the truck and the ladder at the bank. We finished loading our provisions and set off into the night, with Sal driving the truck while Ralph and I rode together in Ralph's Lincoln. It was after 2:00 A.M. when we finally arrived at the bank. We parked at the back of the building, which was well hidden from the street, unloaded our supplies, and scrambled up the ladder to the roof.

My biggest worry was that someone would hear us. The bank was located in a mainly industrial neighborhood, which meant there wouldn't be many people around at that time of night. But it was an extremely noisy undertaking and I was nervous nonetheless. I kept watch at the edge of the roof while Ralph and Sal did the physical work. Much to my relief, it didn't take them long to accomplish their task. Within a matter of minutes they had broken through the roof.

Ralph lowered himself into the building first while Sal and I passed down the remaining gear. Once the three of us were inside we quickly scouted the interior of the bank, finalizing our script before settling in with a deck of cards to wait for morning.

At eight-thirty, half an hour before the bank opened, we took our positions behind the front counter. Not long after, we heard the sound of a car pulling into the parking lot, followed by the staccato ticking of the manager's pumps on the sidewalk. Her key rattled in the lock and then she was inside, humming the tune to the ABBA hit "Honey, Honey" as she crossed the lobby.

I lowered my makeshift mask in preparation for confronting the woman, while Ralph and Sal did the same. In moments like this, I have found, it is better not to think, but to focus solely on the task at hand. In this case, what mattered most was keeping the woman calm so we could be in and out before the rest of the staff arrived.

> *How you thrill me, ah-hah*
> *Nearly kill me, ah-hah . . .*

The woman rounded the corner of the counter and stopped short, the next words catching in her throat, the sound high and tight.

"We're here to rob the bank," I told her matter-of-factly. "Do what we ask and you won't get hurt."

She glanced at the three of us, her brain working overtime to process what she saw. Involuntarily, her gaze shifted to the panic button at a nearby teller's station.

I shook my head. "The safe," I told her, motioning with the Walther.

She nodded, slowly, resolutely. Trying, I knew, to get a handle on her fear so she could do as we asked. Like any reasonable person, she was not about to defy three men with guns.

"Move it!" Ralph barked, conscious, as we all were, of the moments ticking steadily away.

The urgency of his tone spurred the woman to action. Silently, she made her way to the safe and dialed the combination with shaking hands. The door swung open, revealing several large bags of cash, bundled and ready for the armored truck.

Ralph and Sal grabbed the bags while I led the woman into a nearby office and tied her to a chair. It was an oddly intimate act, my hands on her wrists and stockinged calves. Up close I could see that she was older than I had first guessed, her skin beneath her makeup slightly flawed. There was a sour smell coming from her, the tang of fear in her sweat.

"No one's going to hurt you," I told her, glancing at my watch. It was nearly nine o'clock. At least she wouldn't be tied up for long.

Leaving her, I sprinted out the back door to find Sal and Ralph waiting for me in the Lincoln. As I slid into the backseat, Ralph gunned the engine and the car leaped forward, streaking the blacktop behind us with twin ribbons of hot rubber.

Our haul from the bank was well over $100,000: not a bad day's work for a day that began and ended before most people punched their time clocks.

Even as we counted out the money in Ralph's bedroom, with the smell of his mother's fried eggs and ham wafting from the kitchen, I knew the Roslindale heist would not be our last.

As gratifying as the money was—and believe me, it was—the attention the heist received was equally so. There was a story about the robbery in the Boston paper, along with a photograph of the ragged hole in the bank's roof: our handiwork in black and white, a slap in the face of every cop in the area.

It felt undeniably good, and I wanted more.

Ralph, Sal, and I split the proceeds from the Roslindale bank heist evenly. I used part of my share to buy a rare Muramasa samurai sword I'd had my eye on for some time. Sengo Muramasa was a Muromachi-period (sixteenth-century) swordsmith whose blades were famous for their sharpness. An extraordinarily skillful smith, Muramasa was known for his insanely violent temper. According to Japanese legend, Muramasa's blades took on their maker's brutal characteristics, urging anyone who wielded them to either kill or commit suicide. For this reason, in the early seventeenth century they were banned by the shogun Tokugawa Ieyasu. As a result, many Muramasa blades had their signatures altered or removed, making the ones that survived even more valuable to collectors. Acquiring the sword was a feather in my cap.

I also bought myself a sweet little TVR Griffith coupe, a custom British-made sports car. Mine was a beautiful specimen, green-light green, with a butter-soft leather interior, a V-8 engine, and a delicate racing frame, one of only several hundred in existence. Affectionately known as a coffin on wheels because of its tendency to pulverize any unlucky soul who happened to get into an accident in it, the Griffith was the fastest thing money could buy at the time, topping out at 160 miles per hour. Just sitting behind the wheel was a rush.

The best thing about the Griffith was the speed with which it allowed me to make the trip up to Northampton. Martha, who was still at UMass, where she was studying art history, spent most of the week at her parents' house. But I drove up nearly every weekend, either to stay with her there or bring her to Boston or wherever I happened to be playing. Thanks to Al Dotoli, who was a skilled manager, my band and I continued to enjoy regular gigs at clubs and colleges around New England.

Martha's interest in fine art easily rivaled mine, and we spent much of our free time together visiting museums. Over one of her vacations we drove down to New York City and spent several days wandering through the collections at the Metropolitan Museum of Art. The trip was nothing short of a religious experience for me. Muslims have Mecca, Christians have the Vatican, and serious collectors like me have the Met.

But even as I wandered in awe through the hallowed halls of the great museum, I was pondering the best way to rob it. I couldn't have imagined how soon I would return to do just that.

Twelve

Given the complex trajectory of my life, it's difficult to pinpoint any one event as utterly definitive. The Forbes Museum, the Ellsworth jailbreak, the Back Bay shooting: there's no doubt each of these incidents altered the course of my future. Yet even after six years in Walpole these changes were not irreversible. At any time, it seemed, I could re-chart my life toward legitimate success, through either music or school. Even after the Roslindale bank heist the way remained entirely open, the possibilities endless.

But all that changed the night Ralph brought Tommy Sperrazza and Johnny Stokes into the Beachcomber. Though I would not know the full extent of their influence on the course of my life for a number of years, the appearance of these two men marked a point of no return.

I had met the pair a few months earlier, when my band and I played a concert for the inmates at the state prison in Concord. Sperrazza and Stokes were both active in the Concord Jaycees. As former president of the Walpole chapter, I was allowed to speak briefly with all the Concord members after the show. Neither man made much of an impression on me at the time. In fact, it was only later, after Sperrazza reminded me of our first encounter, that I recalled meeting him at all, and then only vaguely. It was an inauspicious beginning to a relationship that would have dire consequences for all involved.

Though still in their early twenties, Sperrazza and Stokes were already hardened criminals. Both had spent the better portion of their lives in state-run institutions, as either juvenile wards or adult convicts. Now they were on the run, having escaped from Concord while on work furlough.

"What do you say we let them in on our next job?" Ralph asked, pulling me aside at the bar late that evening.

I hesitated. I loved Ralph like a brother, but his temper could make him unpredictable in stressful situations. Sperrazza and Stokes were clearly cut from the same cloth. The thought of having three loose cannons as partners did not sit well with me. But having been a fugitive myself on more than one occasion, I could not possibly turn my back on the pair.

Besides, in planning our next bank robbery, Ralph and I had both acknowledged that we would need at least one more set of hands, if not two.

"Okay," I agreed. "But they play by my rules. No one gets hurts."

In many ways our partnership with Sperrazza and Stokes was a perfect match. Since escaping from Concord the fugitives had robbed several banks. But their methods, which involved walking unmasked and with revolvers drawn into whatever bank they stumbled across, were crude at best, dangerous at worst. The fact that they had not yet shot someone or been wounded themselves was a miracle—though avoiding bloodshed seemed to be of little concern to the pair, who, as escapees, had next to nothing to lose.

If Sperrazza and Stokes were too brazen in their tactics, Ralph, Sal, and I were not brazen enough. We all knew we'd gotten lucky with the Roslindale bank in that the building hadn't been sufficiently alarmed. If it had been, our early morning arrival would have been detected right away. We'd have to hit our next bank during business hours.

If there was one aspect of our strategy that didn't need refining, it was the timing. Clearly, planning our robberies to coincide with a scheduled armored car pickup was the best way to maximize profits.

Not to mention the fact that such timing ensured that the tedious job of collecting and bagging the money was already done for us.

The bank we chose for our first job with Sperrazza and Stokes was in Danvers, a small town north of Boston, not far from Salem, Massachusetts. I was familiar with the area from previous trips to Maine. Danvers was just off Route 1, the road we always took when driving up to see my mother's family in Sullivan. The bank had everything we were looking for in a safe and profitable hit: it was large enough to be worth our while, small enough that security wouldn't be extreme, and most important, it was close to the highway, meaning we could slip away with relative ease.

As with the Roslindale heist, we did our homework, scouting the bank for several weeks before finalizing our plans. We were pleasantly surprised to learn that the employees not only bagged the money for the armored truck but brought it out from the vault in anticipation of the truck's arrival. If we could hit the place just before the truck got there, it would be a shamefully easy score.

It was my idea to add a switch car to the mix, meaning we would use one car—preferably a freshly stolen one—as our initial getaway vehicle, while leaving a second car parked somewhere close but out of sight. As the most experienced driver of the group, it was decided, I would man the getaway car, while Ralph, Sperrazza, and Stokes went in. Sal had opted out of this particular heist.

By the time the day of the robbery arrived Sperrazza and Stokes were champing at the bit. Not accustomed to having to wait, and lacking all appreciation for the benefits of planning, the pair had complained constantly about wasted time, pressuring us to speed the process up. In fact, our divergent views on the merits of planning would be a constant source of conflict on every heist I pulled with the two fugitives, as would our philosophies concerning the treatment of civilians. Sperrazza and Stokes had little regard for human life and were known to use violence at the slightest provocation. I, on the other hand, was adamantly opposed to harming anyone except as an act of self-defense.

With the money from our previous jobs Ralph had bought a car wash and garage in Brockton, which he used as a combination chop shop and storage facility for his ever-growing automobile theft enterprise. He had also worked out a system with a friend in the Walpole license plate shop who, for the price of a few well-placed bribes, was able to send him clean car tags. All of this meant we had nearly unlimited access to untraceable switch cars.

Early on the morning of the Danvers job Sperrazza, Stokes, and I met Ralph at his car wash, where he already had a clean switch car tagged and waiting.

"Either one of you so much as touches your gun," I told Stokes and Sperrazza as we went over the details of our plan one last time, "and this is the last job you pull with us. Understand?"

One consequence of the extended periods of time Sperrazza and Stokes had spent in institutions was that, when confronted by an authority figure, they could often be surprisingly pliant. But this was not always the case, and I had to be careful how I played this card. Fortunately, on this occasion my threat worked. After some initial hesitation, both men agreed.

With the matter of the use of firepower settled, we set out from the car wash. Ralph and I rode together in his Lincoln, while Sperrazza and Stokes followed behind in the stolen switch car. We arrived in Danvers just before opening time, parked the Lincoln in an alley close to the highway, and rode the last few remaining blocks to the bank together.

As planned, I waited outside in the switch car while Ralph, Sperrazza, and Stokes went inside. I'd been slightly reluctant to take on the position of driver, knowing the lack of self-control common to all three men. But the role was absolutely crucial to a successful getaway, and in the end, having secured Stokes and Sperrazza's promise that there would be no violence, I'd decided it was worth the risk to have me behind the wheel.

Still, I was nervous as I watched the trio pull their masks over their faces and disappear through the front doors of the bank. As I waited for them to come out again I strained to make out the activity in the lobby through the front windows, nervously listening for gunshots while at the same time keeping my ears open for the sound of police sirens.

Fortunately, everything seemed to be going smoothly inside, and I heard neither. The threesome were in and out of the building in a matter of minutes—far less time than it would have taken to make a conventional withdrawal—each carrying a heavy canvas deposit bag. Ralph slid into the front seat beside me, while Stokes and Sperrazza piled into the back. I hit the gas and we were out of the parking lot before the doors slammed shut.

"Everything okay?" I asked Ralph as we sped away.

Ralph nodded, peeling his mask off, but his expression was that of a father who'd been left in charge of two unruly children.

"Like taking candy from babies," Sperrazza gloated.

Stokes chuckled. "You see that asshole in the suit? I thought he was gonna piss himself for sure when I pulled out my forty-five."

"No guns," I yelled over my shoulder. "I said no fucking guns. Remember?" In the rearview mirror I saw Sperrazza shrug.

It was a gesture I normally would have felt compelled to answer, but at the time I had more pressing things to worry about. *At least no one got hurt,* I told myself, letting the subject go, turning into the alley where we'd left the second car.

Ralph opened his door and leaped out, followed by Stokes and Sperrazza. Moving quickly, the three men transferred the bank bags to the trunk of Ralph's car, then climbed into the car themselves.

"See you back in Roslindale," I called. Then I pulled out of the alley, heading for Route 1 and the city.

So successful was the Danvers heist that over the course of the next year and a half we used the same template to rob nearly a dozen banks, always hitting our targets just before the arrival of the armored truck, always using a switch car in our getaway.

In addition to Sperrazza and Stokes, who accompanied Ralph and me on many of these heists, we developed a regular crew, which included Bobby Donati, Billy Irish, two friends of Ralph's named Joey Santo and Bobby Fitzgerald, and Ralph's brother, Sal. David Houghton, who had become close friends with Bobby Donati after meeting him at my welcome-home party, occasionally joined us as a driver or lookout, though never as an active participant. David held a steady job and had never been in trouble with the law, and we all liked him enough to want to keep it that way.

My music career and these wild-one activities meshed nicely. My band was playing the college circuit by then, and these gigs, many of them in small, affluent towns like Danvers, provided me plenty of opportunities for scouting potential targets. Not all of them were banks.

My travels with the band had introduced me to a surprising number of small regional museums, most of which I had not even known existed. Many were associated with schools or historical societies. To my surprise, some actually housed pieces of real value. Few employed much in the way of security. I spent much of my downtime when we weren't playing casing alarm systems and memorizing floorplans for possible return visits.

Over the course of the next several years, using the information I gathered, I would successfully rob dozens of museums. Most of them were in New England, but I also hit several prestigious institutions in New York City, Washington D.C., and Toronto. My methods varied. Sometimes I only planned the heist and left the actual breaking and entering to my crew members. Other times I used deception to get what I wanted. But the result was always the same. The combined take from these thefts was enormous, eventually numbering in the millions of dollars.

One of the first of these targets was the Mead Art Museum in Amherst, Massachusetts. One day while I was on my way to case a small bank in nearby South Hadley, I stopped into the Mead, which was part of the Amherst College campus. Small yet pretentious, with an overblown sense of itself—not unlike many of the young women who made up the college's student body—the Mead possessed all the qualities I found particularly unattractive in a museum. But despite its unpleasant personality it nonetheless housed some interesting works of art, most notably the painter Robert Henri's dark and seductive "Salome" and a fair-sized collection of Dutch oil paintings.

As I was winding up my leisurely tour of the galleries I spotted a small but interesting Dutch Baroque painting through the open door of the curator's office and, wanting to get a better look, stepped inside. The act was entirely innocent on my part. But the curator, who returned to the office moments later, clearly did not see it that way.

"What are you doing in here?" he snapped, immediately identifying me as someone of a lower caste.

"I noticed the painting from the hall," I said truthfully, motioning to the canvas. "It's very pretty. Is it a Flinck?" By this point in my self-education, I could identify nearly every period in both Eastern and Western art, as well as most minor masters. Govert Flinck was well known for having been a pupil of Rembrandt's.

The curator glanced dismissively at the piece, as if someone of my social standing couldn't possibly appreciate its full aesthetic value. "This is a private office," he said icily, not bothering to answer my question. "And I will kindly ask you to leave."

I shrugged, my gaze passing discreetly over the window behind his desk, taking careful note of the lack of any visible alarm. The man couldn't have understood the potentially dire consequences of his words. For a moment I actually pitied his ignorance.

"Now!" he said.

When I met up with Stokes and Sperrazza outside the bank later that afternoon, payback was the only thing on my mind.

"Either of you have pressing plans for tonight?" I asked.

Both men shook their heads.

"Good," I told them. "I've got just the job for us."

As museum jobs go, the Mead wasn't especially memorable. Getting inside required nothing more than breaking a small pane in the curator's window, undoing the lock, and climbing inside. But the personal satisfaction it brought me was on par with the most daring heists of my career.

The pieces we took were chosen more for their symbolic value than their monetary worth. From the Native American gallery I selected several beaded deerskin bags and a number of Navajo pots, the kind of artifacts a curator would be especially proud to have in his museum. We also took two Dutch oil paintings. One, which we selected from the main collection, was an exquisite Pieter Lastman rendering of St. John the Baptist. The other was a lovely church interior we took from the curator's office; on closer inspection, it turned out to have been painted not by Govert Flinck but by his contemporary Hendrick Cornelisz van Vliet. Together the two paintings were worth nearly half a million dollars.

Thirteen

As my profits from the bank robberies grew, collecting came to serve a practical purpose, solving the problem of what to do with my growing fortune. For obvious reasons, conventional investments were out of the question. By putting my money into art and antiques, I turned my dirty cash into legitimate goods. And not only that: my knowledge of the market enabled me to make a killing in the process. It was a near-perfect system. I loved fine art; I made a lot of money buying and selling it; and I loved the thrill of bank robbery, which helped fund my investments.

Martha accompanied me to many of these auctions and soon became an expert in her own right. Eventually I was able to send her to auctions in my place when a show or some other commitment kept me from going myself. By this time we had been together for well over a year and were completely committed to each other. But despite this fact, and despite her involvement in the auctions, I was careful not to tell Martha too much. It wasn't that I didn't trust her; to the contrary, I didn't think for one second that she would betray any of my secrets. But I was realistic about the position I could put her in by telling her the truth. I didn't want to see her called to the stand someday, forced to decide between obeying the law and perjuring herself for me.

As far as Martha knew, my financial successes were due entirely to the wise decisions I made as a collector, not a totally implausible assumption given my considerable expertise. Still, Martha was a very bright woman, and she likely had her suspicions. If she did, she didn't say so.

As I scouted more museums, I soon recognized that my growing collection could serve another, possibly even more lucrative purpose than merely being a de facto bank account. Recalling my experience at the Boston Children's Museum several years earlier, I quickly realized that my best course of action would be to get to know the museums and their staff as a knowledgeable collector.

Whereas in the past no one had given the name Myles Connor a second thought, I knew my notoriety would now make it difficult for me to pass myself off as a benevolent and merely curious art enthusiast. If I was to gain the trust of museum staff, it would have to be as someone other than myself.

Realizing this, I set about creating an alternate identity for myself. Combining my middle name, Joseph, with a variant on the first initial of my first name, I settled on the alias of Michael Joseph. But for what I had in mind, a mere pseudonym would not be enough of a cover. My background would have to be sufficiently convincing as well.

Most people are suckers for titles. Barring *count* or *duke,* both of which are far too flashy for the persona I had in mind, the one title that I knew would inspire universal awe and respect was *doctor.* But a doctor of what? Posing as an M.D. was out of the question, as I would never be able to survive intense questioning on the subject. History and art were equally risky, given the fact that so many people who worked in museums had Ph.D.'s in one or even both of these subjects.

After evaluating all my options, I finally settled on psychology as the best choice for my field of expertise. Several of the classes I'd taken at Norfolk had been in psychology, so I had a fair grasp on the basics. Beyond this, it seemed, the subject lent itself quite easily to the work of a good bullshitter. For my alma mater I chose Harvard. As long as I was reaching high, I figured, I might as well aim for the stars.

As impressive as my academic pedigree and my connections were, I knew my collection would be the real door opener. To understand why this was the case, it helps to know a little something about museum culture in general. Most museums, especially small ones, live and die by the generosity of individual collectors. No only do the Dr. Josephs of the world contribute large sums of money to institutions whose work they deem worthy of supporting, but they also can be counted on to bequeath their collections to these same institutions.

By now, my personal collection of Japanese weapons alone rivaled that of almost any museum in the country. Any museum, of any size, would have been foolish not to cultivate a relationship with someone like me. But for small museums especially, a bequest of the sort Dr. Joseph was in the position to give could have a huge impact on the status of the institution.

Over the course of the next few weeks I made the rounds of a number of small museums in New England, bringing along my best pieces for show-and-tell, introducing myself as Dr. Michael Joseph, respected collector of Asian art and antiquities. Soon, like farmers escorting a fox into their henhouse, one curator after another walked me through his collection, proudly pointing out the most valuable items.

One of the first museums I hit using information I'd gained as Dr. Joseph was in western Massachusetts. For a number of reasons, I am still not at liberty to identify the institution, except to say that it was a highly specialized regional museum of respectable size. There was nothing in its collection that appealed to me personally. By then my own collection was far more impressive. But one of my many connections in the underground art world had an outlet in Europe for exactly the kind of pieces the museum specialized in.

Recognizing an opportunity to make a tidy profit, I set about devising a plan to rob the place. Built specifically as a museum, the building presented an imposing façade. It also boasted impressive perimeter security. But even the best security system has its Achilles' heel. During a visit as Dr. Joseph, I'd observed that one of the third-floor windows on the back of the building appeared not to be alarmed. It was here, I decided, that we would make our entry.

Because the heist was shaping up to be a straightforward case of breaking and entering, I decided to send several of my crew members to do the job for me. Paying them generously with the proceeds from my latest bank robbery, carefully describing the layout of the museum and exactly which pieces I wanted, I dispatched three of my associates.

Fortunately, my suspicions about the third floor proved to be correct. Using a painter's ladder, my friends climbed up the side of the building, popped the window, and let themselves inside. Working off the shopping list I'd given them, the crew filled three duffel bags before exiting through the same window. As at the Children's Museum, logistics meant they could take only relatively small pieces. But despite this constraint, the men made off with tens of thousands of dollars' worth of valuables. Since I had already paid them for their work, the take was pure profit for me.

For the most part, my meticulous planning paid off when it came time to carry out our heists. But not every job went smoothly. One of the few museums in New England whose collection of Japanese arms and armor came close to rivaling my own was the George Walter Vincent Smith Museum in Springfield, Massachusetts. Opened at the very end of the nineteenth century by Smith and his wife, both avid art and antiquities collectors, the museum was designed to resemble an Italian villa.

The museum housed a number of impressive collections, including works of the classical and Renaissance periods, a stunning collection of Middle Eastern rugs, and a number of early American oil paintings. But the Smith Museum's Asian art collection—which included many fine examples of Japanese art and armor from the time of the samurai; Japanese ivory carvings, lacquers, and ceramics; the largest collection of Chinese cloisonné in the Western world; and an elaborately carved Shinto shrine—was of particular interest to me.

Disguised as Dr. Joseph, bringing several of the most valuable swords in my collection along for show-and-tell, I visited the museum and introduced myself to the staff. As was inevitably the case, they were thrilled to make my acquaintance. One of the curators offered to show me around.

As we toured the building I noted with chagrin that the museum had a good perimeter security system. Determined to find a way around it, I spent the next several days and nights observing the comings and goings of the staff. I soon discovered that the museum employed only one nighttime security guard. If two or three of us could hide inside the museum until after closing time, I decided, we could easily overpower the guard and have the run of the place.

I quickly set my plan in motion. My first step was to come up with a suitable cover for myself. For obvious reasons, this was one museum visit I could not make as Dr. Joseph. Nor could I risk being recognized as Myles Connor. Finally, I settled on disguising myself as an old man. If it had worked with Al Dotoli, my closest friend, I figured it would work with the museum staff. Next, I enlisted the help of a friend from Walpole named Billy Oikle, who readily agreed to participate in the robbery.

On the afternoon of the heist the two of us arrived at the museum well before closing time. We purchased tickets without incident and went inside, strolling the galleries as if we were ordinary visitors, making our way toward the Asian art galleries.

Two of the more impressive items in the museum's collection were a pair of massive bronze Japanese temple guardians. I had taken special note of the statues on a previous visit, not only because of their beauty but because they were easily large enough to conceal two grown men. As closing time neared and the galleries emptied of visitors, Billy and I slipped behind the bronzes to wait.

As we crouched behind the two enormous statues, I felt a frisson of excitement, that Aladdin-in-the-cave feeling all over again. It was all I could do to keep myself from being distracted by the overwhelming amount of art and antiques so close by. But I managed to focus on the task at hand until, about an hour later, we heard the sound of the guard's hard-soled shoes on the marble floor.

He paused for an instant at the entrance to the gallery, the beam of his flashlight raking the dark room. Then he started walking again, passing just in front of our hiding spot. I nodded at Billy, and the two of us rushed forward, tackling the guard, sending his flashlight skittering across the floor.

As a rule, museum guards are not heroes. Who can blame them? They certainly don't get paid enough to risk even minor injury doing their jobs. This man was no exception. After a brief, instinctive struggle, he quickly surrendered. Not that he had much choice in the matter. Using rope we'd brought along specifically for that purpose, Billy and I quickly had the guard's hands and feet tied.

"Good evening," I said, showing him my Walther, but keeping my voice as even as possible. I've always found that calm—and, inversely, panic—is contagious. It's a lot easier to get someone to do what you want when they're not terrified. "You're not going to do anything stupid, are you?"

He shook his head.

"Good," I told him. "And we're not going to hurt you."

With the guard immobilized, Billy and I headed off to gather our booty. We hadn't gotten far when I heard a faint knocking sound.

"What the fuck is that?" I wondered out loud, stopping to listen more closely, motioning for Billy to do the same.

We both froze. For a moment everything was quiet; then the knocking came again, louder this time, more insistent. It was someone pounding on the front door.

I rushed back to where we'd left the guard.

"You expecting someone?" I asked, waving the 9 mm in front of his face. I hadn't observed anyone coming and going when I'd watched the place.

He flinched. "I-I've got a buddy who comes by to visit me sometimes," he stammered, genuinely scared. He hesitated a moment, than added, "Guy's a cop."

I turned to look at Billy, who had turned white as a ghost.

"Fuck the score!" he said. "Let's get out of here."

I couldn't have agreed with him more. In an instant we were off and running, sprinting for the back door. Needless to say, we left the George Walter Vincent Smith Museum empty-handed.

• • •

Not all of my museum thefts were as dramatic as the Springfield heist or as profitable as that first contract job. In fact, many of the pieces I took during this period were small items I stumbled across in museum archives, pieces I felt a special affinity for. Don't get me wrong, many of the items I took were valuable—a quality sword guard could, at the time, fetch upward of $25,000 at auction. But for the most part I took only things I really loved.

The thefts themselves were uncomplicated. Left alone in the archives to "study" a certain piece or collection of pieces, I would secrete the items I wanted in a briefcase or coat pocket. My actions hardly seemed wrong. Stealing from a museum archive is a lot like robbing your grandmother's attic. The pieces I took would, I reasoned, not even be missed by overburdened museum staff. I, on the other hand, loved and appreciated them. I wasn't the first collector to have succumbed to this temptation, and I certainly wasn't the last.

Though my motives for visiting museums as Dr. Joseph were far from pure, I truly enjoyed meeting people who shared my passion for collecting. The time I spent talking to curators and other museum staff, many of whom I came to regard as friends, was always stimulating and often highly educational. There was one institution in particular, a relatively large and highly respected regional museum that I will refer to here only as the "Bartlett Museum," where this was especially true.

The more I got to know the staff at the Bartlett Museum, the more I liked them. They were, without exception, a truly dedicated group of people, deeply attached to their collection. Where greed, or at least self-advancement, was clearly the motive of so many of the curators I came in contact with, the Bartlett staff appeared genuinely to relish the opportunity to meet and talk with anyone who shared their interest in art.

There was one man in particular, a young, up-and-coming curator named James Letsky, with whom I developed a particularly close friendship. Letsky's specialty was Asian art, and I learned a lot from our lengthy discussions on the subject.

Partly out of loyalty to Letsky, and partly out of respect for the museum's staff, I made the decision not to take anything from the Bartlett's archives. But I continued to visit the museum on a regular basis.

Though Letsky had swallowed my Dr. Joseph act hook, line, and sinker, there was one staff member at the Bartlett who clearly had not. An old battleship of a woman whose glasses hung from a chain around her neck to rest on her cashmere-clad bosom, Philippa Lear was one of the museum's senior curators, specializing in Chinese ceramics. Lear made no pretense about her feelings for me, which swung between extreme suspicion and outright loathing.

"She doesn't like me very much, does she?" I asked Letsky one day after we'd run into her in the hallway outside Letsky's office and she'd greeted me with one of her signature dismissive sneers.

"What, Philippa?" Letsky replied, brushing the question off. "She hates everyone."

But the very next day, when I was alone in the archives studying a beautiful example of a Kamakura-period *tanto* blade, I looked up to see Lear watching me. She caught my gaze and held it for a moment. Then, slowly, she smiled at me. It was not a friendly expression, not in the least. It was, without doubt, a warning. Then her lips closed over her gray teeth and she turned her back on me, her glasses swinging across her chest.

As I spent more time in the archives, it soon became clear to me that someone was stealing from the museum. Letsky had a list of various items that were missing from the inventory. Ironically, the pieces were the kind of things I would have chosen: sword guards and small porcelains. Philippa Lear no doubt must have thought I was the culprit, but I was not. Over the course of several months of observation I determined that the thieves were most likely two janitors who had unfettered access to the archives.

It's a testament to my respect for the Bartlett that I made the decision to tell Letsky about my suspicions. It was the only time in my life when I have turned on a fellow criminal. But in this instance my loyalty to the museum and the art it housed outweighed my loyalty to the thieves. Still,

I was relieved when, for lack of any hard evidence, the men were merely reassigned to a different area of the museum.

Incredibly, not long after the incident with the janitors I was offered a position as an assistant curator of Asian arts at the Bartlett. It was a huge honor. Had the situation been different I would have jumped at the opportunity. But under the circumstances I clearly could not accept. Dr. Joseph could not have withstood the scrutiny of the hiring process. Someone, no doubt Philippa Lear, eventually would have proven me a fraud, a discovery that I'm sure would have brought her substantial satisfaction.

Several years later, when I was very publicly indicted for a number of crimes, I immediately thought of Philippa Lear and the pleasure she must have gotten seeing my picture on the TV news and having her suspicions confirmed. At the same time, I felt a twinge of guilt for Letsky, who must have been horrified to discover that he had been harboring a notorious art thief—though I'm happy to report that his association with me didn't harm his career in any way. He went on to become the director of the Bartlett and, during his tenure, oversaw the museum's significant expansion. Today, the Bartlett is regarded as one of the finest institutions in the country.

Years after my involvement with the Bartlett, I would learn that I was not the only art thief with a soft spot for the museum. In the early 1990s a Pennsylvania history professor and lover of antique porcelains was convicted of pilfering the archives of a number of museums into which he had been welcomed as a scholar. Unable to bear seeing beautiful works of art languishing in dusty basements, the professor stole items he considered especially precious. He then donated them to the Bartlett, where he knew they would be cared for and exhibited.

As my collection of Japanese swords continued to grow, I became interested in having my swords officially documented. Because false signatures have been a major problem during certain eras of sword production, documentation is very important to any serious collector.

A sword that has been judged to be authentic by one of the two major Japanese sword study associations, the Nihon Bijutsu Token Hozon Kyokai (NBTHK) or the Nihon Token Hozon Kai (NTHK), can easily be worth ten times as much as an unauthenticated sword.

The judging process, or *shinsa,* is extremely rigorous and tightly controlled. Experts closely examine every aspect of the weapon, including the distinctive *hamon,* and rate the sword according to its aesthetic appeal, workmanship, and historical significance. They then issue papers, or *origami,* attesting to the sword's various attributes.

Though I had no doubts about the authenticity of my swords, I knew that having a *shinsa* performed on my entire collection would have a huge impact on its value. Accomplishing this, however, would be no small feat. *Shinsa* are very rarely performed outside of Japan, and then normally only in conjunction with special events.

Knowing my best chance lay with the NTHK—without exception, the NBTHK conducts its *shinsa* only at the Japanese Sword Museum in Tokyo—I contacted the organization directly to request a judging. Along with a written description and photographs of my extensive collection, which I knew would impress the potential judges, I made a generous cash offer for their services.

As we all know, money talks. In this case, it must have made a persuasive argument. I soon received word from the NTHK that they would be sending over a *katana* expert, Joshi Nakamura, and his team to evaluate my swords. I was elated, and quickly began making plans for Nakamura's arrival.

Nakamura's visit was a huge coup for me, not only because of the effect his *shinsa* would have on the value of my collection but also because my association with him added greatly to my credibility with museums. Having promised James Letsky that I would introduce him to the esteemed judge, I dutifully brought Nakamura to the Bartlett.

Letsky eventually returned the favor by introducing me to a number of curators and directors from museums outside of New England. These connections allowed me—or more precisely, Dr. Joseph—access to the archives of some of the most highly respected museums in the United States and Canada.

Over the course of the next several months, disguised as Dr. Joseph, I visited a number of these institutions, including the Smithsonian Institution in Washington, D.C., the Royal Ontario Museum in Toronto, and the Metropolitan Museum of Art in New York City. Like any good visitor, I never left without a souvenir. Only my mementos didn't come from the museum gift shops.

I chose my keepsakes carefully. They were, by necessity, small and discreet, compact enough to slip under a coat or into a small bag. From the Smithsonian I took an important *tanto* blade; from the Royal Ontario Museum an intricately decorated sword guard, or *tsuba;* from the Met a beautiful Persian *jambiya,* or dagger, with an intricate carving of Marco Polo on the hilt.

Fourteen

Like all good businessmen, I knew the importance of diversifying my assets. After several years of robbing banks, hitting museums, and putting the profits into my collection, I was ready to invest my money in a different venture. I didn't have to look far for the ideal opportunity.

The mid-1970s were a boom time for heroin consumption and distribution in the United States. The recent expansion of opium production in the Golden Triangle region of Southeast Asia had resulted in a steady flow of the drug into the country, while the return of soldiers from Vietnam—many of them already addicts—ensured a solid customer base on which to expand. In short, the heroin business was the Starbucks of its day. Everyone wanted his own franchise.

As with any retail enterprise, the success of our fledgling business relied in no small part on finding a dependable and inexpensive supplier. Fortunately, Ralph had just such a person in mind. While on vacation in Miami he had met and struck up a partnership with a purveyor from Tijuana, Mexico, named Héctor Sánchez.

It was an ideal arrangement. We didn't even have to cross the border. Every couple of weeks Sánchez would send one of his mules up to San Diego with a package. Ralph would fly down with the money and an exchange would be made.

For the first few months our transactions went smoothly. Then one day Sánchez contacted Ralph with a special request. Saying he needed some extra cash, Sánchez asked for three payments up front at the next delivery. He'd make it worth our while, he promised. The demand wasn't entirely unusual. Drug dealing is an unpredictable business. Opportunities requiring large amounts of money can arise out of the blue. Ralph and I figured this was what had happened. We agreed, and at his next meeting with the mule, Ralph handed over the extra payments.

But when Ralph flew down to San Diego two weeks later for his next scheduled delivery the mule was a no-show. A phone call to Sánchez confirmed what Ralph and I already suspected: that the Mexican had no intention of giving us our money or the merchandise we were owed.

If he had known us better, he might have understood what a huge mistake he was making.

One of the first rules of business—any business, but the drug business in particular—is that you can't let anyone take advantage of you. The first person to screw you and get away with it sends a clear message about your vulnerability to all future associates. Ralph and I could not let Sánchez's defiance go unchallenged. I knew what Ralph wanted to do to the man. But I had an idea of my own, one that, if carried out correctly, would broadcast our message to all of Tijuana.

As luck would have it, just a few weeks earlier one of Ralph's friends had knocked over a train carrying military surplus. The guy had gotten away with an impressive haul, including a substantial stash of the explosive C-4 and various detonation devices. Knowing how much I loved unusual weapons, he'd offered me first dibs on the lot.

I didn't have much use for any of the stuff at the time, but I figured I might at some point in the future—if not, I told myself, I could still have a hell of a lot of fun blowing things up. If I had known an opportunity to use the explosives would present itself so soon, I might have purchased even more of the C-4 than I did.

As much as it would have pleased Ralph to take Sánchez out,

killing the man seemed far too extreme to me. Besides, my real hope was that we might intimidate him into giving us our money back. To accomplish this we needed to demonstrate not only that we meant business but also that the consequences of not paying us back would be even more severe the next time around. Sánchez's house, I concluded, might be a perfect target. Ralph had visited Sánchez's home once before and was confident he could find it again. The only remaining question was how we would get to Tijuana.

Flying across the country with a suitcase full of C-4 and a remote detonator was out of the question. Driving seemed equally risky, knowing Ralph's and my propensity for speeding and the number of highway patrolmen between Boston and the Mexican border. In the end we decided to take the train.

I was especially enthusiastic about the idea of making the trip to San Diego by rail. I've always found the forced idleness of train travel to be highly relaxing. And the route we'd be taking, the Southwest Chief, traveled through a part of the country I'd never seen before. All in all, I figured, the three-day ride would provide plenty of welcome distractions from the task that awaited us.

It's safe to say I've never packed so carefully for a trip. The night before we were to leave, Ralph and I divided the C-4 between two large suitcases, padding the plasticized bricks with socks and undershirts. These bags, we had decided, would be checked for the trip. One of the advantages of C-4 is that it's incredibly stable. Still, neither of us was especially comfortable with the idea of riding all the way from Boston to San Diego with the explosives under our seats.

"Careful with those," I cautioned the porter at South Station as he loaded the suitcases, both marked FRAGILE, onto his dolly.

"Whadda you have in here," the man joked, "your grandmother's china?"

"Something like that." I smiled, then reached into my billfold and pulled out a twenty. "Just take good care of them, okay?"

"Will do," the elderly porter said, discreetly accepting the tip and slipping it into his pocket.

. . .

We left Boston on a Tuesday morning and arrived in San Diego around noon the following Friday. After three and a half days on the train we were both ready to get to work. Ralph, who always had trouble sitting still for more than five minutes at a time, was especially antsy.

After having lunch at a restaurant near the station, we took a taxi to a rental car agency, where we'd reserved a car for the next leg of our trip. Despite the obvious risks involved with carrying military-grade explosives into a foreign country, I wasn't overly concerned about the border crossing. Then as now, security measures at the border were focused almost exclusively on cars entering the United States. If we were searched, it would most likely be on our way out of Mexico. Still, Ralph and I took the precaution of unpacking the bricks of C-4 and taping them to the bottom of the rental car for our trip across the border.

Needless to say, we were careful to avoid potholes on the trip down.

We arrived in Tijuana in the afternoon and drove up to Sánchez's place to get a look at the property while there was still some daylight left. The house, a rambling, single-story ranch perched on the dry hills directly overlooking the Tijuana bullring, was just as Ralph had described it. At the back of the structure, jutting out over the precipitous hillside, was a large, hacienda-style covered porch. This, I concluded, would be our initial target. The stiltlike construction of the porch meant it would be easy to take down, and if we timed things right, the spectators at the corrida would even get a free fireworks display.

If Sánchez still refused to pay, we'd take down the whole house.

Having scouted out the property, Ralph and I found a room at a nearby motel and made our final preparations, packing everything we would need—several hundred feet of ignition wire, the remote detonator, and the C-4 itself—into two large duffel bags. Knowing we had a long night ahead of us, we tried to get some sleep. But after the long train trip and the days of anticipation we were both restless. We tossed and turned in the dark for several hours, finally setting out for Sánchez's house at around three in the morning.

We parked just up the hill from the property and, after watching from the car for some time to make sure everyone was asleep, made our way down to the house. Working in the dark, Ralph and I carefully placed the explosives around the foundation of the porch, wiring each brick of C-4 to the ignition device. With our prep work finished, we returned to the car and settled in to wait for daybreak. Once we were certain everyone was out of the house we would set off the charges with the remote detonator.

Sánchez's wife and two children were the first to leave in the morning. Watching them pull out of the driveway, I breathed a sigh of relief. The maid left next, heading down the hill into town with her shopping basket. Finally, just before noon, Sánchez appeared in the front courtyard.

"Let's do it now," Ralph suggested. "It'd scare the crap out of him."

It was tempting, but I shook my head. I wanted him far enough away that we wouldn't run into him, or any of his cronies, on our way out of town. Eventually Sánchez would know it was our handiwork, but I was hoping to be across the border before he figured out that we were responsible.

We watched as Sánchez climbed into his Mercedes and pulled out of the driveway.

"Ten minutes," I said, checking my watch. I turned on the radio, catching an AM station from San Diego, Carl Douglas's static-scarred voice singing, "Everybody was kung fu fighting . . ."

"Now!" I told Ralph at last.

For a split second after he punched the remote, nothing happened. "Shit," I started to say, thinking we'd screwed up the wiring, but the word never left my mouth.

The explosion rattled the windows of the rental car, spewing rock and pulverized concrete across the hillside, obliterating the porch.

"Motherfucker!" Ralph gasped appreciatively, awestruck by our handiwork.

There was no denying it was a beautiful sight. I smiled. "Now let's get the hell out of here."

A week later I called Sánchez from Boston.

"I heard you've been doing some unexpected remodeling," I said.

"Fuck you, Connor," Sánchez replied. "I know it was you and Petrozziello. You're lucky I didn't catch you. I would have cut your fucking balls off and fed them to you."

"No," I corrected him, "you're the lucky one. You get us our money by the end of the month or I'm coming back down there to blow up your whole fucking house. With you in it."

"Go fuck yourself!" Sánchez snarled, slamming down the phone.

Despite his defiant attitude, I could tell from the tone of his voice that he believed me and that he was scared. Two weeks later Ralph received a plain brown envelope in the mail with a San Diego postmark and no return address. Inside was a full refund.

Fifteen

In the spring of 1974 Bobby Donati came to me with a proposal: he wanted me to help him rob the Woolworth family estate in Monmouth, Maine.

Because oriental rugs were Bobby's area of expertise and because most rugs are housed in people's homes rather than museums, much of Bobby's attention was focused on private art collections. The New England elite were Bobby's bread and butter, and he was careful to keep abreast of their comings and goings, familiarizing himself with their seasonal routines and their various vacation properties. In the same way an experienced bird watcher knows the migration habits of the cardinal or the chickadee, Bobby knew exactly which weekend the Boston Brahmins departed en masse for their vacation homes in Hyannis Port or Martha's Vineyard, leaving their Beacon Hill mansions—and everything in them—untended.

Bobby had had his sights set on the Woolworth estate for some time. He wasn't the only one. Just two years earlier, in the spring of 1972, thieves had robbed the place of nearly fifty paintings. Newspaper reports pegged the total value of the items taken at well over $250,000.

But as staggering as the theft was, the stolen pieces represented only a fraction of the art the family owned. Using their considerable fortune, the dry-goods heirs had amassed one of the best known collections of fine art in the country. Much of it was housed at the Monmouth estate.

"I don't know," I said when Bobby first approached me with his plan. "The place has got to be wired like Fort Knox by now."

Bobby shook his head. "I've been up there. I've checked it out. There's nothing."

I was incredulous. "You're telling me that after getting taken for a quarter of a million dollars they haven't even installed an alarm?"

"Yup." He smiled. Then, sensing I still didn't believe him, he added, "I'll take you up there and you can see for yourself."

A few days later we drove to Maine together.

The estate, known at the time as Clearview Farm, was located some five miles outside of Monmouth, on a hillside overlooking Cobbosseecontee Lake. It was a sizeable property, a thousand acres of woods and pastures—and even a small orchard and cemetery—straddling the sparsely trafficked two-lane road that followed the lake's western shore. A self-proclaimed "gentleman's horse farm," it was originally conceived as a retreat for the Woolworth brothers, Norman and Frederick, whose shared passion was horse racing. Norman had passed away a few years earlier and his widow, an avid art collector herself, now owned the estate, but Frederick still kept a home there. His house was to be our target.

Bobby, who had obviously done his homework, gave me a brief but thorough tutorial on the property as we drove the last few, winding miles to the estate, explaining that the only permanent resident was a caretaker who lived in a small cottage just down the hill from the main house. I could see why Bobby was so tempted by the prospect of robbing the place. In theory, at least, it seemed like the perfect setup.

"Here it is," Bobby announced proudly as we came over a small rise and emerged from the woods.

The property, though grand, was less ostentatious than I had imagined. On one side of the road the land sloped gently toward the lake. On the other side a long gravel drive curved upward past a large, fenced pasture to the main house and massive horse barn.

Bobby slowed the car and pointed to a small cottage on the downhill side of the road. "That's the caretaker's place."

"He's got an awfully good view of the house," I commented. In fact, the caretaker's front windows looked directly across the horse pasture toward the main residence. It seemed highly unlikely to me that we could get in and out of the property undetected.

Bobby smiled and shook his head. "*That's* Frederick's place," he said, pointing toward the thick woods on the far side of the pasture.

It was early enough in the season that the trees were not yet in leaf. Through the tangle of bare branches I caught sight of a large white structure.

"There's a better view from the road up ahead," Bobby explained as we continued along the road, leaving the pastures and the main house behind us, entering the woods once again. "There!" He pulled the car to the side of the road.

On the hillside above us, nestled among the trees, was a handsome cottage with a large, columned porch and distinctive double gambrel roofline.

"The mother lode!" Bobby declared.

That night we returned to the estate and, under the cover of darkness, hiked up to the cottage. Using flashlights, we were able to look in through the ground-floor windows at some of the artwork inside. What I was able to glimpse was impressive, to say the least. The walls were covered with paintings and prints. Even the furniture was museum-quality. I recognized, among other things, a Frederick Waugh seascape and a beautiful example of an eighteenth-century banjo clock. More impressive than the objects themselves was the fact that the Woolworths lived casually with such masterpieces. For a collector like me, the realization was staggering.

Our nighttime visit also confirmed what Bobby had told me earlier: that the house was not alarmed. In fact, there weren't even adequate locks on the windows and doors. It would be ridiculously easy to jimmy our way inside. And the isolated location of the house meant we could literally drive a truck right up to the front door.

Bobby hadn't been exaggerating: we had hit the mother lode.

· · ·

With summer fast approaching, time was of the essence. Once June arrived, we both knew, the cottage would be host to a steady stream of visitors. If we didn't pull off the job soon, we'd have to wait until fall.

Back in Boston, we set to work assembling an experienced crew. First on our list was Billy Irish. After much discussion, Bobby and I also agreed to include David Houghton. David had been begging for a bigger role in one of Bobby's heists for some time, and we both figured the Woolworth estate would be a relatively safe way for him to indulge his craving for adventure.

Bobby had somehow gotten hold of a catalogue detailing the entire Woolworth collection. It was like a Sears catalogue of American art. Over the next few weeks we familiarized ourselves with the contents, taking note of the most valuable pieces in the lot, educating ourselves on what we should take and what we could afford to leave behind.

By the end of May we had made several more reconnaissance trips up to the estate and were ready to go. On the afternoon of May 25, driving Bobby's car and a panel truck I had borrowed from Ralph Petrozziello, we headed for Maine.

On the night of the burglary the weather was perfect, warm and clear. The trees were in full leaf, hiding the house almost entirely from the road below, providing us with thick cover under which to perform our task. A bright crescent moon hung overhead, casting just enough light in which to see.

We arrived after midnight to find the estate reassuringly quiet. The windows in the caretaker's house, as well as the main house, were dark. The cottage, at least what we could see of it from the road, appeared dark as well. We parked both vehicles at the bottom of the driveway, and Bobby climbed up alone to make sure the place was empty. About ten minutes later he reappeared, flashing us two thumbs up before climbing into his car.

I started the truck's engine and followed him up to the cottage, parking just behind him on the gravel apron outside the front door. Moving quickly, the four of us assembled on the front porch, flashlights in hand. Using a pry bar he had brought along, Bobby tried to jimmy the front door, but cracking the lock was tougher than we had anticipated. Finally, he gave up, smashed a small glass panel near the handle, and reached inside. Within a matter of seconds the four of us were standing in the dark foyer.

It was time to get to work.

As planned, we fanned out through the house. With the exception of David Houghton, we were all old hands at breaking and entering. We worked quickly and quietly, methodically combing through the Woolworths' staggering collection, looking for the pieces we'd already identified using Bobby's catalogue. At the top of our list were three N. C. Wyeth paintings: the original oil painting for a cover illustration of Robert Louis Stevenson's *Treasure Island;* a portrait of a farmer holding a pig, titled "Pennsylvania Farmer"; and "Dark Harbor Fisherman," a stunning oil painting of fishermen hauling in their glittering catch. Bobby was also particularly interested in two Andrew Wyeth watercolors. These five pieces alone, we knew, were worth upward of $200,000. The previous thieves had reportedly cut the paintings they took from their frames. I was well aware of the risk of damage involved in doing so, and made it clear to everyone how important it was to keep canvases and frames intact.

While we were trying to locate the Wyeths, I stumbled across not just one but two Simon Willard grandfather clocks that I had not known were part of the Woolworths' collection. Willard, who produced timepieces in Massachusetts during the eighteenth and early nineteenth centuries, was one of the finest craftsmen of his time. His clocks, examples of which still hang in the White House and the Supreme Court, are universally considered masterpieces.

I immediately went to tell Bobby. "You've got to see these clocks," I said after finding him in a nearby sitting room.

Ignoring my request, Bobby gestured to the far wall, illuminating one of the Wyeth oils, "Dark Harbor Fisherman," with the beam of his flashlight. "First, help me with this," he said.

Together, we lifted the painting, which was a good four feet by five feet, from the wall and carried it through the dark house and out to the truck.

"Now what about these clocks?" Bobby asked as we walked back to the house.

"Not just clocks," I said, peering into the woods below us, noting with relief that the main house and the caretaker's house were both still dark. "Simon Willards. I'll show you."

Bobby followed me inside and down the main hallway to where one of the clocks was. "It's awfully big," he commented, shining his flashlight on the cabinet.

"These things are priceless," I told him. "It'll be well worth the effort. C'mon, give me a hand."

Bobby shrugged. "If you say so."

As we were loading the first clock into the truck, Billy and David appeared with several framed pieces, including the Andrew Wyeth watercolors. "I spotted a nice little pair of dueling pistols in the library," Billy told me. "Something you might like."

Thanking him for the information, I rushed back inside and made my way to the library. Billy was right: the pistols, made of silver and ornately carved bone, were just the kind of thing I liked. I took them as an addition to my collection.

Because of the isolated location and the relatively small risk of our being discovered, the Monmouth job was, without a doubt, the most leisurely heist I ever pulled. We were in the house for well over an hour. In that time we took nearly three dozen pieces, including both Simon Willard clocks, all three N. C. Wyeth paintings, and the two Andrew Wyeth watercolors. The total haul was worth nearly a quarter of a million dollars.

With everything finally loaded in the panel truck, Bobby and David set out for home, while Billy and I, driving the truck, cut through Vermont and New Hampshire, heading for Martha Ferrante's house in western Massachusetts, where we planned to store our haul for the time being.

Now, I know what you're thinking: there's no way Martha couldn't have known, or at least suspected, that the artwork was stolen; as smart as she was, it's just not possible. But the honest-to-goodness truth is that, during this period of time, there was absolutely nothing remarkable about me showing up at her house with a truckload of art and antiques. As far as she knew, the things we carried up to her attic that day had been purchased legitimately at auction. This was what we told her, and she had no reason not to believe us.

As you might imagine, the biggest problem with a heist like the one we'd just pulled off was liquidating the merchandise. Putting the pieces on the block at Sotheby's was not an option. In time we might be able to sell the lesser-known pieces at auction, but the real moneymakers—the Wyeth paintings—would immediately be recognized as stolen, even decades down the road.

Fortunately for us, there was—and still is—a thriving black market for fine art.

Contrary to what most people would like to believe, art and crime have always shared uncomfortably close quarters. A good deal of the art on display in many of the world's finest museums has been acquired through unconventional means. Throughout much of the nineteenth and early twentieth centuries, classical antiquities were often illegally excavated and taken clandestinely from their countries of origin. Countless pieces of stolen Greek, Roman, and Egyptian art found their way into museums in the United States, Britain, and Europe with the full knowledge of museum staff. During World War II, artwork was routinely confiscated from Jewish owners by the Nazis. Many of these pieces later showed up in the collections of major European museums. As recently as 2008, dozens of museums in the United States, including the Metropolitan Museum of Art in New York and the Museum of Fine Arts, Boston, were found to have purchased looted Thai artifacts.

Often these thefts are justified by the museums themselves, who insist they are better equipped to care for the artifacts than more "primitive" facilities located in the countries from which the pieces have been taken. That, or they deny knowing the artifacts were stolen in the first place. Whether any of these things are true or not is a subject of intense debate. What is certain is that curators continually turn a blind eye to the questionable provenances of many of the pieces they purchase or are given.

In this case, even blind museums were out of the question. To find a buyer for the Wyeth paintings we would have to explore the unquestionably black corner of the trade, a domain inhabited mainly by private collectors.

For many people, mention of the black market in art brings to mind the infamous James Bond villain Dr. No, whose underwater lair was decorated with stolen masterpieces. While there are a small number of real-world collectors who fit this mold—extremely wealthy status seekers for whom exclusive possession of a great work of art is a high in itself—the motivations of the overwhelming majority of illicit collectors are less spiritual in nature. In the underground world of organized crime, stolen art acts as a kind of universal monetary unit. Easy to transport and readily converted into any currency, art is most often traded for weapons or drugs. The majority of these pieces never even leave their shipping crates, but are shuffled from one storage facility to another, like so many sacks of pirates' gold.

Though not a member of any criminal organization himself, Bobby, like Ralph, had grown up on the fringes of that world and had many friends in the community. So when he told me he'd found a buyer for the Wyeths, I made certain assumptions.

"We can trust this guy, right?" I asked.

Bobby nodded. "Absolutely."

On the morning of June 18 I rented a small U-Haul and drove up to Martha's house in Northampton to retrieve the three N. C. Wyeth paintings and the two Andrew Wyeth watercolors. Things were moving quickly. Just the day before Bobby had called to say that the deal was a go. I was to meet the buyer that afternoon in Mashpee, a small tourist town on the western edge of Cape Cod.

Our rendezvous spot was the parking lot of a shopping center that housed On the Rocks, a local nightspot where my band and I were regular headliners. In fact, we had a gig there later that night. I figured I'd have just enough time to broker the deal for the paintings before the rest of my band arrived for the show.

Inland, the day was hot and humid, uncomfortable even. But by the time I reached the Mid-Cape Highway a pleasant breeze was blowing in off the bay. I cut southward across the Cape's broad upper arm, skirting Otis Air Force Base, heading the last few miles into Mashpee. I was right on time.

I turned into the shopping center a few minutes ahead of schedule and pulled the U-Haul into a space at the far end of the parking lot. It was a Thursday, the weekend's onslaught of tourists just beginning to arrive. The lot was nearly full, every other car a station wagon crammed with coolers and beach blankets. The shopping center's little supermarket was doing a brisk early-season business in beer and charcoal.

No sooner had I cut the engine than two men emerged from a nearby van and started toward me.

"You're Bobby's friend, right?" one of them asked, approaching the U-Haul's open driver's side window.

Nodding, I popped the door and climbed out. "Myles," I said, offering him my free hand.

His grip was limp, his palm clammy. "Johnny," he told me, not bothering to introduce his associate.

I nodded, surveying the parking lot over his shoulder. It was impossible to tell whether or not we were really alone. But nothing seemed out of the ordinary.

"This way," I said, heading toward the back of the truck, motioning for Johnny and his shadow to follow. I undid the lock and slid the door open, revealing the five carefully wrapped Wyeths inside. Then the three of us climbed up into the U-Haul together.

"You've got the cash?" I asked.

"Sure," Johnny replied. "It's in the van."

I glanced over at him, catching the unmistakable timbre of a lie in his voice, the way he threw the words out there with all the assurance of someone bluffing an ace. I'd been set up.

Turning toward the open door, I saw a virtual army racing across the blacktop, pistols drawn.

"FBI!" the frontmost figure bellowed. "Get out of the van! Now!"

Every interaction I've had with the FBI has led me to believe that most federal agents rarely get the opportunity to leave their desks. As a consequence, when something big happens—the imminent arrest of one of New England's more notorious criminals, for instance—every G-man within a hundred miles wants to be there for it. The Bureau is renowned among cons of all stripes for its overzealous use of manpower.

The Mashpee arrest was a perfect example of FBI overkill.

Despite the fact that my two "buyers" were clearly informants, leaving only one "real" criminal—me—for the feds to wrangle, there were at least two dozen agents on the scene. They swarmed on the truck, appearing seemingly from nowhere. As flattered as I was by all the attention, I found it unsettling to know I'd had twenty-odd sets of eyes watching my every move. They made a big show of cuffing all three of us, hustling Johnny and his shadow into the back of one unmarked car and me into another.

My companion for the ride to the nearby Barnstable County Jail was the lead agent on the case, a handsome, dark-haired Irishman named Bernie Murphy, with whom I would become extremely well acquainted over the course of the next eighteen months. Murphy was unabashedly elated to have collared me. I was his ticket to bigger and better things, just as I'd been for Deschamps and the other MDC cops back in Revere.

We didn't say much to each other; I knew better than to answer any of Murphy's questions. But as we neared our destination he leaned across the seat, bringing his face just a few inches from mine.

"I've got you now, Connor," he said with a gloating smile. "Let's see you get out of this one."

For an instant I was back in that basement cell in Ellsworth, the deputy sheriff's words still ringing in my ears. *Oh no you don't:* the challenge that had sent me over the wall and into the Union River. Only this time there was nowhere to run.

The door opened and a pair of hands reached inside, pulling me to my feet. I wrestled myself free and ducked my head, meeting Murphy's gaze once again. Now I was the one smiling.

"Just watch me," I told him.

Sixteen

My first phone call from the jail was to Ralph Petrozziello. I was in serious trouble and I knew it. I needed a good lawyer, and Ralph's attorney, a man named Martin Leppo, had helped him out of a number of jams. Until then I hadn't needed Marty's services, but he represented more than a few of the guys on my crew and we were casual acquaintances. He was a regular at my gigs; in fact, he owned a beach house not far from Mashpee.

"Call Marty and let him know the FBI's got me in Barnstable," I told Ralph.

As luck would have it, Marty was at his beach house at the time and was able to come right away.

"The first thing we have to do is get you out of here," he said when he finally got in to see me. "I assume you can post bail?"

"Bail's not a problem," I told him. "But you know I'm still on parole. The board's going to send me right back to Walpole."

Marty shook his head. "Not if I can convince them otherwise."

As soon as I was out on bail I drove up to Northampton to see Martha. My arrest had made headlines in the Boston papers, and I knew I had some explaining to do. The question in my mind was what, exactly, I would tell her.

Martha wasn't stupid; she knew full well the kind of person I was and who my associates were. She had met me in prison, after all, and I have no doubt that my roguishness was part of what made me attractive to her. But the Woolworth robbery and the bank heists were, I knew, much more than Martha had bargained for. She'd already had her suspicions. I worried that the Mashpee arrest would serve to confirm them once and for all.

As I'd feared, Martha was not thrilled by this latest development. But she was also very much in love with me, and love can make us overlook all sorts of transgressions.

"I swear," I told her, "I was selling the paintings for Bobby. I had no idea they were stolen."

Once again I felt uncomfortable lying to Martha. Once again I told myself the lie was for her own good, that she was better off not knowing the truth. But even I could see the justification was a hollow one.

"You really expect me to believe that?" Martha asked.

"Yes," I said, thinking: *It's what you have to believe.*

She grew uncharacteristically quiet. "Yes," she said at last. It was not a statement of faith so much as it was one of surrender. "Yes, I believe you."

As much as I wanted to believe that Marty Leppo could keep me from getting sent back to Walpole, I was skeptical. I knew better than to put my faith in the generosity of the parole board. I had already decided I would not be going back to prison, no matter what the board's decision. I began working on a contingency plan to ensure I wouldn't have to.

My idea was simple. If the board voted to revoke my parole, my crew would spring me from the hearing, by force if necessary.

I had no trouble convincing my friends to help me. The parole board was universally detested by everyone on my crew, all of whom had been forced to make at least one appearance before it. With few exceptions, the individuals who volunteered to sit on the parole board were contemptible human beings, small men who relished wielding their modicum of power. It was their holier-than-thou attitude that bothered us most, the pleasure they clearly took in sending ex-cons back to prison. The thought of turning the tables on them was extremely appealing. In fact, as the date of the hearing neared I found myself half hoping for an unfavorable decision.

The board met at the parole office down in Brockton, a rough-and-tumble suburb south of Boston. It was a place we all knew well. Inside the main entryway was a large lobby. Leading off the lobby was a long, wide corridor with rows of desks for the secretarial staff on either side. At the end of the corridor, glass double doors opened onto the hearing room, affording everyone in the lobby a clear view inside.

It was a perfect setup for what we had planned: Ralph, Billy, Sal, and Joe Santo would wait in the lobby while I went in for my hearing; when the board announced their decision, I'd give a signal—a hand across my forehead—if the news was bad. At that point the foursome would come rushing in, weapons drawn, and put the board and the parole officer, who was nothing more than a postman with a gun, down on the floor.

To my mind the biggest challenge would be keeping Marty in the dark. He knew and had represented everybody involved, and easily could have blown the whole setup if he'd recognized any of them. Fortunately, on the day of the hearing he was far too preoccupied with the details of the meeting to suspect a thing.

When Marty and I arrived at the parole office on the afternoon of my hearing my crew was already there, waiting in a van in the parking lot. I could see Ralph behind the wheel, his face hidden behind over-sized sunglasses. Everyone else was in the back, well out of sight.

"Slow it down a minute, Myles," Marty said as we went inside. "We have some good arguing points. The feds haven't proven anything yet."

I smiled. "Who said I'm worried?"

Normally, going before the parole board is akin to having a root canal without anesthetic. The process is an exercise in humiliation. As an ex-convict, you're expected to offer up repentance for any past misdeeds, to swear off all your friends and the life of crime into which they led you once and might lead you again. And the best all this bowing and scrape can get you is another year or two under the thumb of the system.

At my last meeting with the board I'd put on a good show, promising to walk the straight and narrow. And for the most part I'd meant it. But this time I was so sure they were going to screw me once again that I couldn't muster my usual charm.

From my seat before the board I could see straight down the corridor toward the lobby. Each time another one of my friends appeared, my attitude worsened.

Marty, on the other hand, was valiant in his efforts to convince the board to spare me. He reminded them of my exemplary conduct during the riots at Walpole and the near universal support I'd garnered in favor of my original parole.

"What's wrong with you?" Marty asked testily as we waited in the corridor while the board deliberated.

"Not a thing," I told him.

"Well, you didn't exactly charm them, did you?"

I shrugged, imagining the smug looks on the faces of the board members melting at the sight of Ralph's machine gun. Then the glass doors opened and we were called back inside.

Marty shook his head. *You're screwed,* the gesture said.

Looking at the board, their features set in grim parodies of disappointment, I was certain he was right. I took a seat as directed and waited for the verdict.

"Mr. Connor," the head of the board began, clearing his throat self-importantly, "after careful consideration, and despite grave misgivings, we have decided to take no action at this time. The terms of your parole remain unchanged, awaiting court action in the federal case."

A reprieve, I thought, stunned by the unexpected decision. Instinctively, I reached up and wiped my brow, not realizing what I'd done until it was too late.

Out of the corner of my eye I saw Ralph start down the corridor, followed closely by Billy, who was already opening his coat and reaching for his gun. Joe and Sal were just a few steps behind them. Frantically, I waved them off, trying to keep my gestures inconspicuous, but they were all too focused on making it to the end of the corridor to notice.

One of the secretaries rose from her desk and stepped directly in Joe's path. For an instant I was worried he might do something we'd all regret, but Joe politely moved aside, allowing her to pass.

"You will be expected to keep your nose clean this time, Mr. Connor," the head of the board droned on. It was the same paternalistic speech I'd heard numerous times before. "Mr. Connor? Are you listening to me?" He stopped talking and glanced out the glass doors, looking directly at Ralph, who by now was mere feet away.

My heart stopped. Out of the corner of my eye I saw Billy's gun slide back under his coat.

"Who is that man?"

I waved at Ralph, trying desperately to pantomime my intentions. He looked at me quizzically. Keeping my hands beneath the chair and out of the board's sight, I waved him off again. Finally, he understood and turned back. "Old friend from Walpole," I said. "Must be here meeting with his parole officer."

The man nodded, watching Ralph retreat down the corridor. "As I was saying, Mr. Connor, you're expected to steer clear of these types from now on."

"Yes, sir," I agreed, glancing at Marty, who was completely oblivious to what had just happened. "You won't be sorry," I said, putting on my best poker face.

"I hope not, Mr. Connor," he said gravely.

With that, I was dismissed.

Seventeen

I've always wondered what those old fogies on the parole board really think, whether they truly believe their cautionary speeches have an impact on the behavior of the cons they're preaching to. If they do, they're hopelessly naive. A man will promise anything if he thinks it'll get him paroled. I've known guys who've apologized for crimes they didn't even commit, knowing remorse was their only ticket out of the joint.

I had absolutely no intention of following through with my promise to the parole board. In fact, keeping my nose clean was just about the last thing on my agenda.

In the late fall of 1974 my crew and I began planning what would be our last big bank job together. Our target was the Norfolk County Trust Company in Milton, Massachusetts. We were all familiar with the establishment. Al Dotoli had his business account there, and the band's paychecks were drawn on the bank. Whenever my bandmates or I needed to cash a check we went to Norfolk Trust. As a consequence, we had become friendly with several of the tellers, who in those days were almost all young women. There was one teller in particular, an attractive brunette named Barbara Drew, with whom I was on especially good terms.

Despite Barbara's conservative exterior, she had a mean wild streak. Barbara and her boyfriend, a former classmate of mine and now a Milton cop, were regulars at the Beachcomber. On nights when he was working, Barbara often stayed on to party with us after the shows. The more I got to know her the more I grew to believe she could be convinced to help us with the bank heist.

Our initial plan had been to kidnap the bank manager at his home, drive him to the bank, and force him to open the safe for us. But as we hashed out the details it became clear to me that a kidnapping was far too dangerous. There was simply too much that could go wrong, too many opportunities for someone to get badly hurt. On the other hand, if Barbara gave us even limited assistance, we could forgo the kidnapping and pull off the job with relative ease.

Approaching Barbara with my proposal was perhaps the riskiest part of the plan. It was one thing to use her friendship for small favors at the bank—cashing unendorsed checks for friends, for example—but quite another to involve her in a full-scale robbery. I would have to be extremely careful in feeling her out. If she balked and told someone—especially her boyfriend—we'd be screwed. Still, I had a good feeling she would agree to help us.

The following Sunday at the Beachcomber I pulled Barbara aside after the show.

"So," I asked, "you like working at the bank?"

"It's a job." She shrugged, then took a drag off her cigarette and exhaled wearily.

"It must pay pretty well," I commented, "working with all that money."

"You'd think it would, wouldn't you?" She seemed mildly buzzed, groggy and giddy at the same time.

"You ever think about taking a little extra for yourself? You know, just to even things out."

She sucked at the cigarette again, smiled slyly. "All the time."

"Then why don't you?" I prodded, lowering my voice, letting my shoulder touch hers. I liked this part of the game.

She turned her head slowly and looked over at me, her blue-shaded eyelids fluttering open. Suddenly she was wide awake. "What do you have in mind?" she asked.

It was a question with many possible answers.

• • •

As it turned out, Barbara was an even bigger asset than I had anticipated. She was well acquainted with the procedure for preparing the weekly Brinks pickup, a task that required the head teller to be at the bank first thing every Wednesday morning to unlock the vault in which the money shipment was kept overnight. There were two locks on the vault: a standard dial, to which the head teller knew the combination, and a timed lock, which the teller was in charge of setting the night before. If we could overpower the teller, we'd have easy access to the cash.

Barbara was extremely smart, with an uncanny ability to see all the angles. Under slightly different circumstances we would have made quite a team. Clearly, she'd given the idea of a possible robbery a fair amount of thought before we'd come along. She volunteered to trip the bank's alarms several times during the days leading up to the robbery. That way, if we did set off the security system during the break-in, the police would think it was yet another false alarm.

While we were making our final preparations for the Norfolk County Trust Company robbery, Tommy Sperrazza and Johnny Stokes, who were still on the run, came to me with a side proposal. They'd been scouting a small bank up in Northampton and wanted me to partner with them on the heist. It was a straightforward job, the kind of robbery that was almost second nature to me by then, and I readily agreed to participate.

As usual, we planned the heist to coincide with the Brinks pickup. On the afternoon of the robbery we met in the parking lot of the Northampton VA Hospital, on Route 9 just north of town. I had driven up in my Griffith the night before to see Martha. Stokes and Sperrazza, along with Ozzy DePriest, who'd come on board at the last minute, had made the trip up from Boston that morning in separate cars: Tommy and Johnny in Tommy's Chevelle, and Ozzy in a Ford he'd stolen off the street that morning. Our plan was to use the stolen Ford in the robbery, then dump it in the woods behind the hospital, hike back to the parking lot, and drive our own cars back to Boston.

The robbery itself was unremarkable. Stokes and Sperrazza went inside while Ozzy and I waited in the getaway car. As soon as they were out with the cash we hightailed it up Route 9 and down the dirt track that ran back into the woods behind the hospital.

It was early evening by the time we walked the mile or so to the VA parking lot. We climbed into our respective cars—Ozzy and me in the Griffith, and Stokes and Sperrazza in the Chevelle—and headed south with the Chevelle in the lead. We'd been driving for close to half an hour went I saw the Chevy's brake lights flash. Stokes, who was driving, pulled the car to the shoulder of the road. Thinking something was wrong, I did the same. Only then did I see the real reason for the unexpected stop: a young woman was standing by the side of the road. She walked to the Chevelle, leaned in the passenger window, and said something to Sperrazza. Then the door opened and she climbed into the backseat.

As we pulled away I could see the three heads silhouetted in the Chevelle's rear window: Stokes in the driver's seat, Sperrazza on the passenger side, and the girl leaning over the seat to talk to them. I wasn't thrilled about the idea of taking on a hitchhiker. I became even less so when I saw Sperrazza climb into the backseat with her. But there was little I could do about the situation. As long as the girl was a willing participant in whatever was going on in the car, I figured I might as well let it slide. Unfortunately, it quickly became clear that this was not the case.

"What the fuck is he doing?" Ozzy asked as we watched Sperrazza climb on top of the girl and push her down. She tried to fight him off, her arms flailing wildly, but she wasn't strong enough. I had to do something.

Telling Ozzy to roll his window down, I pulled the Griffith up alongside the Chevy at the next straightaway.

"Pull over!" I called across the seat.

Stokes leered at us from the driver's seat, then shook his head.

"Pull the fuck over!" Ozzy yelled.

Suddenly, headlights appeared coming toward us. Quickly I slammed on the brakes and fell back behind the Chevelle again as the oncoming car passed.

"My Walther," I told Ozzy, nodding toward the glove box.

Ozzy opened the latch, grabbed the gun, and handed it to me.

I pulled even with Stokes's window again. "Pull the fuck over!" I yelled, pointing the gun at him. "Now!"

This time he complied, slowing the car, then pulling it to a stop on the shoulder of the road.

I parked behind it and leaped out of the Griffith, followed by Ozzy. "Get out of the car!" I yelled, banging on the rear window, motioning with the Walther.

Glaring at me like a petulant child, Sperrazza climbed out of the backseat. "What's the matter?" he asked defiantly.

"What's the matter?" I was stunned. "You're trying to rape that girl, and you're asking me what's the matter?"

He shrugged. "It's not like it's a big deal. We do this all the time."

I wanted to punch him, or worse. Enraged, I flexed my palm on the Walther, sickened by Sperrazza's admission—*we do this all the time*—contemplating for a brief instant the idea of shooting him.

"Get back in the car," I told him, then, turning to the Chevelle's passenger window, I spoke to the girl. "Where are you going?"

"Spencer," she said, naming a town just a few miles down the road.

"You're riding with us," I told her, offering her my hand, helping her out of the car.

She squeezed into the Griffith's tiny front seat with Ozzy, and we headed off down the road. Ten minutes later, we dropped her off. The incident was over, but neither Ozzy nor I could get over what we'd witnessed.

"You should have killed him," Ozzy said as we pulled away from the girl's house and headed back toward the highway. I could tell he was dead serious.

It would have been remarkably easy to do so. I could have shot Sperrazza dead without any repercussions. Neither Stokes nor the girl would have said anything, of that I'm certain. Clearly, Ozzy wouldn't have, either.

If I had known what was to come, if I had understood the consequences of my inaction, I would have killed him then, without so much as a second thought. But I didn't. If I made a list of all my regrets, of every decision I wish I could retract or revise, my choice to spare Sperrazza far outranks all the others. It was a decision that would haunt me for the rest of my life.

By January 1975 we were ready to act on our plan to rob the Norfolk Trust Company. The thought of working with Stokes and Sperrazza again made my stomach turn, but by then there was no cutting them out of the job. Vowing that the Milton robbery would be my last interaction with the two fugitives, I gathered my crew for one final meeting.

It was decided that Tommy Sperrazza and Joe Santo would overpower the teller as she unlocked the bank. Johnny Stokes would wait in the switch car. As usual, I would act as lookout and getaway driver.

One of the newer members of my crew at the time was a kid named Steven Gregory. Gregory wasn't the sharpest criminal mind, but he had a good heart and a willingness to do whatever was asked of him. He also owned a marine uniform, though he had never been in the service.

"You still have your uniform?" I asked him.

"Yup."

"What about your duffel bag?"

"That too."

"Good," I told him. "Sperrazza can wear the uniform into the bank. They can put the cash in the bag. No one will suspect a marine strolling down the street with his duffel over his shoulder. I'll park around the corner and Tommy can walk back to meet me." I nodded to Santo. "You'll head off in the opposite direction. Any problems with that?"

Both men shook their heads.

I turned back to Gregory. "In the meantime I want you to go to Kustom TV in Quincy and buy a couple of police scanners. And wear the uniform. It'll look better that way."

Gregory nodded. "Whatever you say, boss."

That Sunday at the Beachcomber I sought out Barbara between sets. "We're on for this Wednesday," I told her. "Can you work your magic with the alarms?"

I was prepared for her to back out or at least stumble on the answer, but she didn't miss a beat.

"You got it," she said.

On the morning of Wednesday, January 29, Santo, Sperrazza, Stokes, and I met at Giuliani's Garage in Quincy, just a mile or so from the bank. Though not an active member of my crew, Ricky Giuliani was an old friend of mine, and my associates and I often used his service station as a rendezvous point. It was bitterly cold out, damp and foggy, the low gray clouds spitting an unpleasant mixture of snow and icy rain.

I was the first to arrive, driving a rented Ford Torino. (Though we still made use of Ralph's inventory of stolen cars from time to time, we had found that renting vehicles was often far more expedient.) Sperrazza, Stokes, and Santo got to the station next, having driven down from Dorchester together in Sperrazza's Chevelle. The car stopped next to mine. Santo and Sperrazza, who was wearing Gregory's fatigues, got out of the Chevy and climbed into the Torino for the ride to the bank. Then we took off for Milton together, with Stokes following behind.

It was about twenty minutes before eight when we reached the bank. I pulled off the street and into the parking lot while Stokes, in the Chevelle, headed for our designated rendezvous point, down a nearby side street. About five minutes later the teller's car pulled into the bank's parking lot, her pale face visible behind her car's rain-streaked front windshield.

I handed Santo one of the two police scanners I'd sent Gregory to buy, keeping one for myself. "Keep it on," I told him. "Just in case."

Santo nodded.

"And remember to go easy on the girl," I reminded him and Sperrazza.

We all watched the teller get out of her car and start toward the bank. Her stride was just slightly hurried, her manner businesslike. As she neared the front door, she slid a ring of keys from her pocket.

"Now!" I told Santo and Sperrazza. "Go now!"

Pulling their masks on, the two men jumped out of the Torino and sprinted for the front door of the bank, their guns drawn. The teller's key was already in the lock when Sperrazza grabbed her from behind, jabbing the barrel of his pistol into the small of her back. Santo spoke briefly to the woman, who appeared too stunned to offer any resistance. Within a matter of seconds the door was opened and the three of them disappeared inside.

Seconds later the police scanner crackled, shattering the early morning silence, a call from Milton dispatch. Tensing, I glanced up and down the empty street. Barbara had sworn the front door was unalarmed. Could she have been wrong? I wondered. Or, worse yet, setting us up? I fine-tuned the scanner, catching a snippet of friendly banter, two stiffs trying to keep each other awake. Nothing to be concerned about. At least not yet.

Inside, Santo and Sperrazza got to work. The first order of business was to persuade the teller to open the vault. With this accomplished, Santo began transferring the money, which was already bundled and bagged for the Brinks pickup, into Gregory's marine duffel.

While Santo dealt with the cash, Sperrazza took the teller to a small office in the back of the building. This was the part of our plan that most worried me. As I waited in the car I wondered if I'd made a terrible mistake in assigning the task of dealing with the teller to Sperrazza. I had repeatedly instructed him not to use physical violence with the woman, but with Sperrazza there were no guarantees that things wouldn't get out of hand.

Just before eight o'clock, as I waited anxiously for Santo and Sperrazza to finish the job, the dispatcher's voice came over the scanner again, this time with the news that something had tripped the alarm on the back door of the Norfolk Trust. They'd done it, I thought: Santo and Sperrazza were out of the building, but they still weren't out of danger.

The scanner blared a response, an impatient voice answering the dispatcher's call. "That's the fifth alarm we've answered there this week," the cop complained before reluctantly agreeing to head to the bank and check it out. "I'm on my way," he sighed.

The plan now was for Sperrazza and Santo to split up. Sperrazza would walk north up the back alley to meet up with Stokes, while Santo, carrying the duffel, would head in my direction. Knowing Barbara's false alarms would buy us only so much time, I glanced toward the mouth of the alley, hoping to see Santo emerge. One minute passed, then another. In the distance, a lone police siren wailed.

I turned the key in the ignition and the Torino's engine purred to life. Three minutes. Four. Where the fuck was he?

Finally, Santo ambled out of the alley with the duffel slung over his shoulder. I pulled away from the curb, meeting him as he crossed the street. He popped the passenger door and threw the bag into the backseat, then climbed inside.

"Everything go okay?" I asked as we drove away.

Santo nodded.

"And the girl?"

"She'll be fine," he said, pausing to catch his breath. "Sperrazza had to clock her with his forty-five."

"Why the fuck did he do that?" I asked, angry at myself as much as at Sperrazza. I should never have allowed him to have anything to do with the teller, I thought.

Santo shrugged. "I think we got a good haul. At least it sure felt like that on my shoulder." He grinned, then turned suddenly and glanced into the backseat. "Shit!" he swore. "I knew I forgot something."

I felt my stomach hit the back of my throat. "Forgot what?" I asked.

"The scanner," he said. "I left the fucking scanner in the vault."

I paused for a moment with my hand on the wheel, contemplating what to do. Leaving the scanner behind was a major fuckup. The cops would be able to trace it back to Kustom TV in a matter of hours. But there was no going back for it. Now there was more than one siren, and they were getting closer by the second.

"We'll just have to hope it doesn't matter," I told Santo. Punching the accelerator, I felt the Torino's wheels spin briefly, then catch the street.

Eighteen

Even with Santo's sloppy mistake, it appeared as if the Milton bank robbery had been a success. As was always the case when a crime of this sort was committed in the Milton area, police immediately suspected that I'd been involved. In the days following the robbery I had a number of unfriendly visits from detectives. But as usual, no one was able to come up with any concrete evidence linking me to the crime.

With the bank robbery behind us, I hoped to cut all ties with Sperrazza and Stokes. After the incident with the hitchhiker and Sperrazza's treatment of the bank teller, I could barely stand to be around the pair. But extricating myself from my relationship with the two fugitives wasn't easy.

On the afternoon of Saturday, February 22, 1975, Sperrazza called me at my mother's house in Milton. He was highly agitated, saying he and Stokes were skipping town and that they needed my help.

"Is this about that thing over in Roslindale?" I asked. The night before, at the Beachcomber, I'd heard several people talking about the fact that Stokes and Sperrazza had been involved in a fight outside a Roslindale bar. "What the hell happened?" I asked Sperrazza.

"I don't know, Myles. I think I shot a guy."

"What guy?"

"Some local kid," Sperrazza answered. "He and his buddy thought we were horning in on their territory."

"Is he okay?" I asked.

"I guess so."

"Fuck, Tommy!" I said. "You can't just go around shooting people."

"We need your help, Myles," Sperrazza pleaded, ignoring my rebuke. "We need to disappear for a while. Just till everything dies down."

"Sorry," I told him. "You're on your own." Aside from the fact that I didn't want to involve myself in whatever dirty business Sperrazza and Stokes had gotten tangled up in, I already had plans for that evening.

My mother had been complaining for weeks that I never spent any time with her. I'd made reservations to take her out to dinner that night at Maison Robert, a snooty French restaurant in Boston's Old City Hall building. After that she and I were driving up to Northampton for the weekend. I'd already reserved a motel room. I told Sperrazza this.

"Could you get a room for us at Shaw's?" he asked, naming the motel where he, Stokes, and I had stayed on a number of occasions while scouting the Northampton bank job.

I hesitated, wondering just how much trouble the two of them were in.

"We just need you to register for us," he said.

Hearing the desperation in his voice reminded me of all the times I'd been on the run, looking for a place to stay. "Okay," I finally agreed, regretting my words even as I spoke them. "I'll meet you up there."

By the time I got up to Northampton I was regretting my decision even more. After my conversation with Sperrazza I'd found out that the shooting was much more serious than he'd made it out to be. At the time, the details of what exactly had happened that Friday night were still emerging. But the basic outline of the events was clear.

By all accounts, the evening started innocently enough. Sperrazza and Stokes were on a casual double date with two young women, Karen Spinney and Susan Webster. As the foursome were driving through Roslindale, they passed a local pub that Webster frequented, and Webster asked if she could go inside to look for a friend. They parked across the street from the pub and Sperrazza accompanied Webster inside. Stokes and Spinney waited in the car.

While Sperrazza went to the men's room, Susan Webster stopped at the bar to talk to Anthony DiVingo, a friend and sometimes boyfriend. She was still talking to him when Sperrazza returned from the bathroom. Not pleased to see his date getting friendly with another man, Sperrazza approached the bar and grabbed Webster's arm, snapping, "Let's go!"

"Hey," DiVingo responded, "take it easy."

The comment did not sit well with Sperrazza. "You want to take it outside?" he snarled, challenging DiVingo. Then, pulling Webster by the arm, he headed out the door.

By all accounts, DiVingo let the incident go, but Sperrazza wasn't willing to. Ten minutes later someone came into the bar and informed DiVingo that Sperrazza was still waiting outside for him. Accompanied by his friend Ralph Cirvinale, DiVingo headed outside to confront Sperrazza.

No sooner had DiVingo stepped through the door of the pub than Sperrazza pulled his forty-five from the waist of his pants and fired. The bullet passed through DiVingo's shoulder and, in a horrible twist of fate, continued on its path, striking Ralph Cirvinale, who was standing behind his friend, his mouth wide open in shock. Cirvinale was shot fatally in the mouth.

While horrified witnesses watched from inside the pub, Stokes, who was still in the car with Karen Spinney, opened fire on the wounded men. Sperrazza hightailed it across the street, forcing Susan Webster into the car with him. Then the foursome sped off into the night. It was a gruesome scenario, made all the more troubling by the fact that neither Spinney nor Webster had been seen since.

"You know you're in a shitload of trouble," I told Sperrazza when we met in the parking lot of Shaw's Motel late that night. I had already dropped my mother off at the Howard Johnson's in nearby Hadley.

"I haven't seen those girls since late last night. We gave them some money and put them on the train. I swear, Myles," he pleaded, no doubt sensing my skepticism. "They got spooked. They were worried the cops would think they had something to do with the shooting. I'm sure they'll come back once things cool down."

"They'd better," I told him. I glanced into the front seat of his car, where Stokes sat waiting, then across the parking lot toward the motel's office. "Come on," I said, wishing I hadn't agreed to help them. "Let's get this over with. I'll get you two a room, but after this you're on your own."

I was true to my word. The next afternoon I left Northampton and drove back home to get ready for my gig at the Beachcomber that night. Once again I thought I had washed my hands of Tommy Sperrazza. Once again I was wrong.

In the days and weeks to follow, Karen Spinney and Susan Webster failed to materialize. As the winter wore on, people grew more and more concerned. Though there was no direct evidence confirming that the women had been killed, everyone feared the worst. Knowing Sperrazza and Stokes as I did, I couldn't help drawing the same grim conclusion.

More than once I found myself thinking of the bank robbery we'd pulled together up in Northampton and the hitchhiker Sperrazza and Stokes had picked up on the ride home. The Roslindale shooting and the subsequent disappearance of Karen Spinney and Susan Webster further confirmed what I had felt in my gut that night: that the world would be a better place without Tommy Sperrazza in it.

But I didn't have much time to dwell on this fact. Unfortunately, I had problems of my own to worry about.

That December Judge Caffrey, the judge in the Wyeth case, had denied an important motion brought by my attorney. Despite this legal setback, my attorney, Marty, remained optimistic. I wasn't nearly so confident. Having been found guilty in the past of a crime I didn't commit, I had no expectation of being acquitted of a crime I was actually guilty of.

My father was understandably beside himself. I was looking at a good ten years in prison for the Wyeth paintings, plus the three years I had left to serve once my parole was revoked, as it most certainly would be if I was found guilty in the federal case. On top of all of this, rumors about my involvement in the Norfolk Trust robbery were starting to gain some traction.

"You didn't have anything to do with that bank robbery in Milton, did you?" my father asked me one night not long after the heist.

"Of course not," I assured him.

At the time I was cocky enough to think he believed me. But looking back, I'm not so sure. He was a cop, after all. He was also a good man. There's no way around the fact that I broke his heart.

"I want you to talk to John Regan," he said. "See if he can help you work out some kind of deal."

I shook my head. I had my doubts that my old friend and former bedside companion, who by then was working for the Department of Corrections' Office of Investigative Services, could do anything for my cause. Even if he could, I had no intention of making a deal. I'd serve out the full thirteen years I had coming before I'd rat on my friends.

"Just talk to him, Myles," my father pleaded. "For me."

Reluctantly, I agreed.

In the days leading up to my meeting with Regan, it occurred to me that I held a number of bargaining chips that were worth far more than any testimony I could offer, and that I might be able to make a deal with the federal prosecutor without compromising my loyalty.

The bargaining of fine art for freedom from prosecution is one of the dirty little secrets of the art world. Since there is not much that is stolen that cannot be replaced, in most cases of theft, recovery of the goods is of secondary importance to the capture and prosecution of the thief. In the case of fine art, however, its theft deprives the world of something no amount of insurance money can replace. Add to this the overwhelming pressure on museums to keep these thefts from being disclosed to the public, and the pressure the museums in turn put on law enforcement, and you end up with a system in which prosecutors will agree to almost anything.

There are many critics of these underground deals, those who argue that bargaining with art thieves contributes to future thefts. They're right, of course. But how many of us, faced with the choice between recovering a priceless masterwork and losing the man who took it, on one hand, or punishing the man who took it and losing the art forever, on the other, would choose the latter?

Surely, I thought, there was at least one piece out of the many I'd stolen that would be worth my freedom.

But when I broached the subject with Regan—speaking theoretically, of course—he was less than encouraging.

"I know Twomey," he said, referring to Assistant U.S. Attorney David Twomey, the chief prosecutor in the case. "He's not in the mood to negotiate. And even if he was, his hands are tied. Face it, Myles, nothing short of a Rembrandt could get you out of this mess."

I swear, these are the words he uttered. I'm sure he was using Rembrandt's name as an example, not an actual presumption. Yet his comment got me thinking. I knew I would need something big—really big—if I was going to bargain my way out of the Wyeth charges. And since I did not yet possess such a piece, I knew I would have to steal it. An actual Rembrandt wasn't part of the plan until several weeks later, when fate intervened in my favor as it had so often before, this time in the form of a cherubic young Dutch woman named Elizabeth.

Early in the spring of 1975 I was having dinner at my maternal grandparents' house when my grandfather brought up the topic of a well-known Rembrandt portrait that was on loan to the Museum of Fine Arts in Boston. The painting was of the artist's sister, Elizabeth van Rijn. Art was a favorite topic at my grandparents' dinner table. My grandfather, whose tattered *Mayflower* bona fides still provided the slimmest entree into Boston society, knew several members of the MFA's board, and it was not unusual for us to discuss current exhibits. After my conversation with Regan, I found the subject particularly interesting.

"Who's the benefactor?" I asked.

"The Paine family," my grandfather answered between bites of Sunday roast.

Descendants of Robert Treat Paine, a signer of the Declaration of Independence, the Paines were Boston royalty. The MFA was one of many local causes they generously supported. If anyone could persuade Twomey to contemplate making a deal, it would be the Paines.

"Do you know if it's insured?" I asked.

There was little point in stealing a painting like the Rembrandt if it wasn't insured. Unless you have a buyer lined up—like some crazy Arab sheikh who wants to keep the thing in his basement rec room—it's impossible to fence a famous piece of art like that. But an insurer will do anything to keep from making a full payout.

My grandfather looked at me suspiciously. "I happen to know that it is," he said. "But then, they'd be crazy not to insure it. It's got to be worth close to a million dollars."

"Really?" I commented, trying to sound nonplussed. "That much?"

In hindsight, I suppose I should have felt at least a twinge of guilt at the thought of robbing the Museum of Fine Arts. It was a place I knew and loved, having spent many afternoons there as a child, most of them accompanied by my grandfather. Much of what I knew about art in general, and Asian art in particular, had started with these boyhood visits.

But as much as the MFA had done to enrich my appreciation of fine art, the space it occupied in my mind at the time had more to do with denial than opportunity. Like the Forbes Museum—that symbol of the unwavering superiority of Milton's upper class—the Museum of Fine Arts embodied Boston's rigid caste system. It was, primarily, an institution run by and for the elite. Families like the Paines not only sat on the board and hung their art on its walls but socialized within the confines of the museum as well.

The idea of forcing Twomey's hand, while at the same time thumbing my nose at the bluebloods, was too good to pass up. The day after my conversation with my grandfather I paid my first visit to Miss van Rijn.

I have to admit, my first meeting with the famous Elizabeth left me slightly underwhelmed. That's not to say she wasn't beautiful. Like any Rembrandt subject, she was exquisitely rendered, her skin luminous against her rich surroundings, her dark cloak trimmed in radiant gold. Her blond hair was dotted with tiny shimmering pearls, her ears adorned with pearl drop earrings. As stunning as the portrait was, however, it was not something I would have paid a million dollars for. But then, the business of art is based not on individual taste but on the collective will of the market. At the time Rembrandts were fetching astronomical prices at auction.

Besides, the real question at hand was not one of aesthetics but whether or not I would be able to get my hands on the painting in the first place. Despite the fact that I had already robbed several museums on par with the MFA, I had never conducted a heist like the one stealing the Rembrandt would entail. This painting was not stored in some dusty basement but was on display and no doubt well secured. There'd be no sneaking out of the archives with the portrait hidden under my coat.

There's a notion among most laymen I've encountered that stealing a painting such as a Rembrandt requires outwitting state-of-the-art museum security. We've all seen the movies in which the thieves must dodge infrared beams or dangle from the ceiling, where the slightest misstep triggers steel security doors and silent alarms. Yet only once in my long career—at the Boston Children's Museum— had I encountered anything even remotely resembling these measures, and it had stopped me dead in my tracks. I knew better than to believe Hollywood's version of reality, yet neither was I foolish enough to compare the MFA to the Children's Museum. Steel doors or not, I knew the building would be nearly impossible to get into once it was closed to the public.

This left only one option: a broad daylight heist.

· · ·

The brazen nature of my plan meant nothing could be left to chance. As with any job I undertook, my first step was to familiarize myself with the museum's physical surroundings. A sprawling neoclassical masterpiece, the MFA sits right in the heart of Boston, between busy Huntington Avenue and the rambling wetland park known as the Back Bay Fens. The building itself, which takes the approximate shape of a sideways H, is made up of two distinct wings connected by a long central corridor and large rotunda. The southernmost wing faces Huntington Avenue, while the northernmost wing—or Evans Wing—looks out over the Fens. It was here, in a small gallery on the second floor of the Evans Wing, that the Rembrandt portrait hung.

At the time each wing had its own entrance, but most visitors passed through the Huntington Avenue doors. Several days of casual observation taught me that the Huntington entrance was also a popular hangout for Boston cops, who liked to sit in their cruisers in the semicircular driveway, eating donuts and drinking coffee.

The Fenway entrance, on the other hand, received little use. At one time, when the park had been an elegant place for Boston's elite to stroll, the Fenway portico, flanked by twenty-two soaring ionic columns, was the museum's main entrance. But by the mid-seventies the Fens was a muddy, overgrown, garbage-filled swamp that most Bostonians did their best to avoid. In other words, it was perfect.

Add to this the fact that, for the most part at least, museum security consisted of a handful of unarmed old men in blue blazers, and the job began to look frighteningly easy. If I played things right, I concluded, I could simply buy a ticket, walk into the Dutch room, and lift the Rembrandt from the wall.

If the actual theft was shaping up to be relatively straightforward, the getaway, I knew, would be much more complicated. I would need help—and lots of it. For this I turned to my old friends Billy Irish and Ralph Petrozziello.

Ralph, who was always game for anything, immediately volunteered his services as well as a getaway van.

Billy, who was more of a realist, was slightly less enthusiastic.

"Are you out of your fucking mind?" he asked when I told him what I was planning to do.

"It's a sure thing," I said. "As sure as they come."

He shook his head in disbelief. "As I suspected, you're out of your fucking mind."

"Just hear me out," I told him. "We'll go in the Fenway entrance. There's never anyone back there. Hell, we could park a tank back there and no one would give a shit."

"You're right about the Fens," Billy conceded, his forehead creased in thought. "It's a fucking cesspool."

"And the guards," I reminded him. "They don't even have guns." Seeing that he was coming around, I pressed on. "We act like we know what we're doing, and no one's going to stop us. I guarantee. The last thing anyone expects to see is a couple of guys walking off with a Rembrandt in broad daylight."

"And how do we get away?" he asked.

Luckily, I had an answer for him. "If we can make it across Huntington, it's a straight shot down Parker Street to Bromley-Heath. We can switch cars there."

A garbage-strewn, crime-ridden warren of a slum, the Bromley-Heath housing project was a virtual no-go zone for cops, the perfect place in which to disappear after the heist.

Billy's brow relaxed. "It might just work. *If* we can get across Huntington, and that's a big if."

"That's where you come in," I told him. "You think a couple of your buddies from the Shamrocks would be willing to drive crash cars?"

As their name suggested, crash cars were backup vehicles whose purpose was to run interference with the police, including going so far

as to crash into pursuing police cruisers if necessary. The Black Shamrocks, in which Billy was an active member, was one of the most notorious motorcycle clubs in New England. I couldn't think of anywhere
better to find drivers with the skills and the balls necessary for the job.

Billy smiled. "I might find a couple of takers."

As April approached, so did my first scheduled court appearance
for my role in the theft of the Wyeth paintings. Knowing that we
would have to act soon to secure the Rembrandt, I contacted Billy and
Ralph with a date: barring any unforeseen problems, the job would go
down the following Monday.

Nineteen

That two unidentified men walked into the Museum of Fine Arts on April 14, 1975, and walked out with a priceless Rembrandt is a matter of record. Such was the brazen nature of the heist that newspapers all over the world carried reports of it. But how exactly the thieves managed to slip away with the painting without getting caught has been a mystery for over three decades. Until now.

Here's exactly how we did it.

Around midmorning on Monday, April 14, my crew gathered at Ralph's car wash in Brockton. The forecast the night before had mentioned a possibility of rain. But fortunately, the weather had chosen to cooperate. It was a breezy spring morning, the sky a cloudless robin's-egg blue. The temperature had dropped close to freezing during the night and there was a lingering chill in the air, coupled with the promise of a slightly warmer afternoon.

Billy Irish and Ralph were there, along with Ozzy DePriest, who would be meeting us at Bromley-Heath with a switch car. Also in attendance were three drivers Billy had recruited: an ex-boxer named Billy Hogan, an Irish kid from Dorchester named Mickey Finn, and one of Billy's fellow Black Shamrocks named Bobby Fromm. All of us were armed, Billy with a .45, Ralph with an M-16 assault rifle. As usual, I was carrying my Walther. Already on his way to the museum was an eighth member of our party, another of Billy's friends who had been recruited to stand lookout on Huntington Avenue.

Since Billy and I would be the ones going inside, we were both wearing disguises. Billy had on a knee-length tan car coat and a long blond wig. I was wearing a short jacket, a leather chauffeur's cap, and a brown wig that covered my red hair.

"That's a nice look for you," I told Billy as we gathered to run through the details of the plan one last time. "You ever spend time at the Spahn Ranch?" I joked, referring to the Manson Family's notorious California home.

"Yeah," Billy replied, flashing me a roguish smile. "And I'm gonna go helter-skelter on you if you don't lay off."

Any heist is a performance. Robbing the MFA is the equivalent of playing to a packed house at Carnegie Hall. Not surprisingly, we were all suffering from preshow jitters. I tried my best to put everyone at ease. Tension can make people trigger-happy, and the last thing I wanted was for someone to get killed.

"These guards are just a bunch of old micks doing their jobs," I reminded everyone. "No one fires a shot unless it's absolutely necessary. And in that case, it's just a warning." I looked at Ralph to emphasize my point. "Got it?"

"Got it," he answered, but I wasn't entirely convinced.

As much as I loved Ralph, I knew he could be a loose cannon. I would have to keep an eye on him.

As usual, Ralph had provided the transportation for the job: a van for making our getaway with the painting and the two crash cars, a black and gold Torino and a black Monte Carlo. All three vehicles were stolen. All bore Ralph's Walpole plates, making them absolutely un-traceable.

We left the car wash just before noon. Mickey drove the van, while Billy, Ralph, and I rode in the back. Hogan was in front of us in the Torino. Fromm followed behind in the Monte Carlo.

From Brockton it was a straight shot north to Huntington Avenue, then a few short blocks east to the museum. As we turned off Huntington and onto Museum Road, which ran along the southwest side of the MFA grounds, I glanced out and saw the lookout in place. His job was simple: he was to stand at the corner of Forsyth and Huntington, on the far side of the museum. We'd be coming that way after the robbery; if there were cops on Huntington, all he had to do was wave a red handkerchief and we would know to continue east on the Fenway instead of crossing the avenue as planned.

After turning off Huntington, we continued along Museum Road, then turned right onto the Fenway.

I glanced at Billy. "You ready to do this?"

He grinned. "Let's rock and roll."

Hogan pulled the Torino into the semicircular drive that led to the Fenway entrance. We followed behind, trailed by the Monte Carlo. All three cars pulled to a stop, with the van directly in front of the wide granite staircase. Billy, Ralph, and I jumped out and made our way into the outer foyer, where Ralph was to wait while Billy and I went inside.

I don't remember exactly how much it cost us to get into the museum. My best recollection is that the two tickets together came to something in the neighborhood of five dollars. Whatever the price, it was a bargain. Smiling politely to the elderly volunteer who handed us our tickets, Billy and I pushed through the turnstile and started up the grand staircase that led to the second floor galleries.

We reached the upper landing and immediately turned right, passing through the long seventeenth- and eighteenth-century European gallery on our way to the Dutch and Flemish room. Weekdays were typically quiet at the museum, and that Monday was no exception. There were no more than a handful of patrons in the Evans wing, perhaps two or three of them in the Dutch room, a space large enough to accommodate a decent-sized crowd. A white-haired security guard stood in the doorway between the two galleries, fighting to keep his eyes open. Wasting no time, Billy and I crossed the Dutch room, bypassing a number of masterpieces, including Rembrandt's "Artist in His Studio" and Jacob Van Ruisdael's dramatic "Rough Sea," and stopped in front of the Rembrandt portrait.

By this point in my life, having stolen and handled numerous masterworks, I was not easily awed. But in those last few seconds before Billy and I took the canvas off the wall, my heart was stuttering like a jackhammer. I could tell Billy's was too. As he moved to flank the painting on the left, I glanced down and saw that his hands were shaking.

"Easy does it," I whispered to myself as well as to him.

Together we grabbed the frame and lifted the painting off the hooks that held it to the wall. Adrenaline surged through my body, cold and immediate, like the shock of injected Novocain.

I hadn't expected the Rembrandt to be especially heavy. The canvas was relatively small, around 24 by 16 inches. And old frames are never as heavy as you expect them to be—the wood, desiccated by age, becomes as light as kindling. Even knowing this, I was surprised by how insubstantial the portrait felt in my hands.

But there was no time to process any of these sensations. The guard was awake now. As we headed for the doorway he stepped forward to block our way.

"What are you trying to do with the painting?" he asked with a thick Italian accent.

Leaving the Rembrandt to me, Billy pulled out his .45 and aimed it at the guard. "Shut up or I'll kill you," he said.

The man froze, his face ashen with terror. Then, moving quickly, he took a step backward, ducking behind the gallery wall.

As I ran out of the Dutch room with the painting under my arm, I heard the sound of the guard's whistle.

Billy sprinted after me through the adjoining gallery, and together we plunged down the winding marble stairs and across the first floor foyer, toward the Fenway entrance. As I slipped through the turnstile, I felt the mechanism catch, trapping me between the metal bars. Had we triggered some kind of automatic security lock? I wondered.

I turned back and looked to Billy for help, but he already had his hands full. The guard from the Dutch room and a second guard were coming down the stairs, right on his heels.

"Go!" Billy yelled, clearly bewildered by the fact that I wasn't out the door yet.

Suddenly, three shots rang out, the bullets passing over my head and catching the stairs at the guard's feet. I turned to see Ralph firing from the outer foyer. The guard from the Dutch room stopped where he was, but his colleague, a trim man in his midsixties, kept right on coming.

In desperation, I threw all my weight against the turnstile and, hearing the sickening sound of wood splintering as I did so, realized the frame was wedged between the bars. I was stuck.

Realizing what the problem was, Billy rushed forward and added his weight to mine, pushing as hard as he could against the jammed stile. There was a loud crack as the corner of the frame broke away. The turnstile spun free, spitting me and the painting out the other side. Billy was right behind me.

We careened through the doors at the Fenway behind Ralph, who was already sprinting for the van. Undeterred by the sight of so many guns, the second guard, who I would later learn was a retired cop, raced down the steps, right behind us. Billy jumped into the van and I handed him the Rembrandt. But as I did so, the guard, who had caught up with us, grabbed a corner of the Rembrandt's frame.

"It's not worth it, pal!" a voice of reason—most likely the first guard—yelled out from the top of the stairs, but the guy wasn't listening. He had a good grip on the frame and he wasn't letting go. As hard as Billy pulled, he couldn't get the painting away from the guard.

Out of the corner of my eye I saw Mickey, who was still in the driver's seat, turn and point his gun at the guard. *Shit,* I thought, *this idiot is going to get himself killed.*

"Don't shoot," I yelled to Mickey as Billy and I struggled to get the painting away from the guard.

No doubt sensing a catastrophe in the making, Billy loosed his grip on the painting and smacked the guard in the head with his pistol. The blow caught the man hard and he buckled immediately, releasing his grip on the Rembrandt. Quickly Billy hauled the painting into the van. I jumped in after it and we pulled the door closed.

Seeing that we were all safely in the van, Hogan floored the Torino and pulled out onto the Fenway. As our van followed it, I turned back to see the Monte Carlo do the same. Seeing no red flag from our lookout, we turned down Forsyth. As we crossed Huntington Avenue I glanced out the van's back window and saw the lookout ambling away toward the Northeastern University campus, just as we had planned. For the moment, at least, there wasn't a cop in sight.

Almost home free, I thought as we angled southward onto Parker Street, still safely sandwiched between the Torino and the Monte Carlo. From the corner of Parker and Huntington it was a straight shot south to Bromley-Heath. I hated to disappoint Hogan and Fromm, but the way things were going it looked like we wouldn't need to use the crash cars after all.

But as we careened down Parker, past the Wentworth Institute of Technology, a Coca-Cola delivery truck loomed ahead of us. It was parked crossways on Parker, blocking the narrow street.

"Fuck!" Mickey swore, slamming on the brakes, screeching to a stop behind the Torino.

Ralph, who was in the passenger seat of the van, climbed out, brandishing his M-16. "Move!" he screamed at the driver of the delivery truck.

The man froze.

"There's no time!" I yelled at Ralph. I could hear sirens behind us, what sounded like a good number of cruisers on Huntington Avenue.

But Ralph wasn't listening. "Move your goddamn truck!" he bellowed.

"The sidewalk!" Billy yelled out the window, loud enough for Hogan to hear him up ahead in the Torino. "I think you can get around him on the sidewalk."

Taking Billy's advice, Hogan gunned the engine and the Torino leaped forward, lurching onto the curb, squeezing through the narrow opening between the truck's bumper and the brick wall of the Wentworth Institute. Ralph leaped back into the van.

"Go!" I yelled to Mickey. "Go!"

Following the Torino's lead, Mickey eased the van up onto the curb and around the truck, scraping the wall as we went. We were through.

With Fromm following in the Monte Carlo, we shot forward down Parker, the sirens fading behind us, then across Tremont, around Parker Hill and into the safety of the projects.

As promised, Ozzy was waiting for us at Bromley-Heath with a switch car, a stolen LTD from Ralph's stables. Working quickly, we ditched the van, stripping the plates off, and transferred the painting to the trunk of the LTD. With the van disposed of, it was time to go our separate ways. Taking the Torino, Ralph and Billy drove to nearby Dudley station, where they abandoned the getaway car and hopped on a train back to Dorchester. Where the others went, I neither knew nor wanted to know.

Elizabeth came with me.

The question of where to take the Rembrandt was one to which I had given plenty of thought. All the usual places—my mother's house on Oak Road, Martha's parents' home in Northampton, Al Dotoli's house in Quincy—were out of the question. Even if the cops couldn't pin the robbery on me, my reputation would make me the prime suspect, which meant that until the painting was recovered all my friends and associates would be under intense scrutiny. Leaving the portrait in some random storage locker didn't seem like a particularly good idea, either.

I needed to find a home for Elizabeth with someone I could trust absolutely, someone whom the police would never suspect of helping me. Fortunately, I knew just such an individual.

For obvious reasons, I am not at liberty to identify this person, even decades after the fact. Suffice it to say that Charlie, as I will call him, was an old friend of mine, a legitimate guy who had absolutely nothing to do with the criminal side of my life. When I left Bromley-Heath that Monday I drove straight to his house in Boston's southern suburbs.

I can only imagine what must have gone through Charlie's mind when I showed up on his doorstep unannounced, with a freshly stolen Rembrandt on my hands. He knew I was in trouble and facing considerable jail time because of the stolen Wyeths. And he must have suspected I was planning something. But he certainly could not have expected to be called upon to play a vital role in one of the most notorious art thefts in history.

As shocked as he must have been, he agreed to help me without hesitation.

At the time, Charlie's mother-in-law was living with him. Though she didn't know it, she was about to get a new roommate, and a famous one at that. For the next eight and a half months the portrait of Elizabeth van Rijn, one of the most sought-after pieces of art in the world, remained hidden beneath the old woman's bed. It was truly the last place anyone would have thought to look.

In terms of publicity, we couldn't have timed things better. The heist went down early enough that it made the front page of the evening edition of that day's *Boston Globe*. "$1m Rembrandt Taken from Boston Museum," the headline, flanked by a picture of the stolen painting, screamed. By the next morning every reporter in the city was wondering what the Boston Police Department was doing to get the Rembrandt back.

For their part, the police were playing it extremely cool. Two days after the theft they told the *Globe* that they expected a break in the case to come "at any moment."

"It's just a waiting game right now," Deputy Superintendent Leroy Chase told a *Globe* reporter. Describing us as "rank amateurs," Chase went on to say that the police "have had some tips." But despite Chase's display of confidence, it was obvious to me that the eleven Boston PD detectives and twelve FBI agents who'd been assigned to the case had next to nothing to go on. In fact, the authorities didn't even have enough evidence to bring me in for questioning.

They'd found the Torino outside Roxbury Station. But thanks to Ralph, there was no way they could link the car to us. The official descriptions of me, Ralph, and Billy were so vague as to be laughable, identifying us only as "white males, about twenty years of age." The only other clue investigators had to go on was a rubber glove I'd dropped on my way out of the museum, and I knew it wasn't talking.

All in all, I thought, we'd done pretty well for rank amateurs. It was going to be a long wait for Chase and his detectives.

Twenty

Now that the Rembrandt was in my possession, I had absolutely no intention of standing trial for my role in the theft of the Wyeth paintings. But I was not yet ready to make a deal.

Knowing the seriousness of the charges against me, I was realistic about the fact that whatever bargain I struck with the U.S. attorney's office would probably involve some prison time. At the very least there were weeks of negotiating to be done. Summer was coming and the thought of spending it at Walpole or on the sweltering top tier of the Charles Street Jail while Marty Leppo and David Twomey hammered out the details of a deal did not appeal to me. Unfortunately, with my trial date quickly approaching, the only way to avoid this fate was by skipping bail and going on the lam.

In preparation for this inevitability, I had asked a friend to rent an apartment for me down in the wealthy South Shore beach community of Cohasset. This was where I went after dropping the painting off at Charlie's house.

On April 23, the day the trial for my role in the Wyeth thefts was scheduled to begin, my attorney arrived at Judge Cafferty's courtroom on the twelfth floor of the old U.S. courthouse at Post Office Square. I had purposely not told Marty about the Rembrandt or my plans for it, or the fact that I had no intention of standing trial for the Wyeth thefts, and he fully expected to find me waiting for him. Needless to say, neither he nor the judge was amused by my absence.

Marty pled my case, begging for extra time, making frantic phone calls from the pay phone outside the courtroom, trying without success to track me down. I felt bad about leaving Marty hanging like that, but it had to be done. Despite Marty's efforts, Judge Cafferty quickly ran out of patience and declared me in default. I was officially on the run. It wasn't the first time in my life, and it wouldn't be the last.

Technically speaking, the Rembrandt theft had made me an instant millionaire. I spent the summer of 1975 playing the part.

The town of Cohasset proved an ideal place in which to lie low. It was just close enough to the city that I could keep abreast of developments in my case, but far enough away in both distance and income bracket that it wouldn't be crawling with Boston cops. The apartment I'd rented was on tony Jerusalem Road, in a large castlelike structure that had once been the home of a Boston business tycoon.

Once her classes ended, Martha came to stay with me. By then she was well aware of the fact that I had jumped bail on the Wyeth charges and was a fugitive, but I did not tell her about the Rembrandt. I can't speak for Martha, but I suspected that she knew we would not be together much longer. As a result, our time in Cohasset had a bittersweet quality to it. We spent nearly every waking moment together, often at the beach.

Billy Irish drove down daily from Boston with news and provisions.

"I ran into Al Dotoli," he told me one afternoon. "He says the FBI's got a fucking camera on the telephone pole outside his house. And that Bernie Murphy's been to visit him a time or two."

I wasn't at all surprised to hear this. Because Al was my personal manager and my closest friend, everyone assumed he knew where I was. It was the same when I'd been on the run nearly ten years earlier. Then, the cops had practically camped out at Al's house. Besides, I knew Murphy and two other agents had shown up at Martha's house the day after Judge Cafferty had declared me in default, and tried to intimidate her. She'd told them to get lost. I had every confidence Al would do the same.

Boston cops may not have been able to afford beach homes in Cohasset, but there was another, potentially more dangerous segment of the population that could. One morning while Martha and I were walking on the beach, she stopped to coo over twins who were out for a ride in their stroller. As she leaned down to admire the babies, I exchanged small talk with the father.

It wasn't until we were walking away that I realized the man I'd just been talking to was one of the Channel 7 news anchors. I passed several sleepless nights after that, but luckily the reporter must not have recognized me. Nothing ever came of our meeting.

With the exception of this one unsettling incident, life on the South Shore was uneventful—perhaps too much so. By August my Griffith was begging to be driven and I was itching to get away from Cohasset. As the summer drew to a close I grew more and more reckless, driving up to Boston to go to clubs or visit friends. I'm sure there was a part of me that wanted to get caught. I've never been able to withstand boredom, even—or especially—when the alternative is danger.

During one of my trips to the city I went to see Bobby Donati. I hadn't seen Bobby since I'd jumped bail, and I certainly hadn't told him I'd been involved with the MFA heist. But he knew me well enough to be sure I'd had a hand in the theft. I could tell as soon as I got there that he was dying to ask me about the painting. Of all my friends and associates, Bobby had the most knowledge of and greatest appreciation for fine art. The fact that I had actually touched a Rembrandt meant something to him.

"So how did it feel?" Bobby asked finally, with a devilish glint in his eyes.

"How did what feel?" I asked, feigning ignorance.

"You know. The Rembrandt." He was whispering, though there was no need to: we were entirely alone. "How did it feel to hold it in your hands?"

I winked at him. "I don't have the faintest idea what you're talking about."

He smiled. "Sure you don't." He suddenly changed the subject. "You ever think about knocking off the Gardner?"

"The Gardner Museum?" I asked, taken slightly aback by the abruptness of the question.

He smiled again.

Founded at the turn of the twentieth century by the unconventional socialite for whom it was named, the Isabella Stewart Gardner Museum was one of the gems of the Boston art world. Its small yet incredibly well-regarded collection of European and Asian art had all been hand-picked by Mrs. Gardner, who was one of the early twentieth century's foremost art patrons. For such a small institution, the museum boasted a surprising number of outright masterpieces, including Titian's stunning "Rape of Europa" and Rembrandt's darkly beautiful "Storm on the Sea of Galilee," the only seascape the Dutchman ever painted.

Unless one was interested in using them as leverage or stashing them in an underground lair, these renowned works were far too recognizable to steal. But there were plenty of smaller, less flashy pieces to choose from as well.

"Sure," I told Bobby. At that point in time, there weren't many museums in New England I hadn't contemplated robbing.

"What do you say we pay it a visit one of these days?"

I shrugged. "Why not?"

Less than a week later Bobby and I found ourselves strolling through the lush courtyard garden at the center of the faux Venetian Renaissance palazzo that housed the Gardner Museum.

"You know, she designed this place herself," I told Bobby. "She thought art should be an intimate experience." In fact, Isabella Gardner had been one of the first major art patrons to espouse this point of view. To this end, she had purposely designed the museum to feel like a private residence.

"I heard she could throw one hell of a party," Bobby mused, looking around at the building's ornate inner façade, a series of windowed galleries towering three floors above us.

I smiled, thinking about Isabella's legendary gatherings. Her contempt for convention—and the trappings of class—had been scandalous at the time. Rumor had it she'd even posed naked on more than one occasion. I'd always thought she and I would have been fast friends.

"Let's go see the Titian," I suggested.

After walking back through the garden, we climbed up to the third floor and made our way to the Titian gallery. True to Isabella's style, the rooms were crammed with all manner of precious antiques: Chinese mat weights and porcelain vases shared floor space with early American furniture; the walls were covered with canvases and prints; even the wallpapers were works of art, rich velvets and silks stamped into exotic patterns. At first glance the placement of these items appeared utterly chaotic. But there was a meticulous method to Isabella's madness, and it worked, like the bordello-red wallpaper in the Titian gallery, which perfectly evoked the lurid sexuality in "The Rape of Europa."

"This one's for me," I said, standing before the painting.

Bobby laughed. "It's kind of on the big side, isn't it?"

At nearly eighty inches square, the canvas was totally unmanageable. But I wasn't thinking in practical terms at the moment. We were window shopping, fulfilling some fantasy wish list that had nothing to do with practicality.

Next we went down to the second floor to check out the Dutch room. A rich, stately space with wood-beamed ceilings, a large, formal fireplace, and triple arched windows that looked out over the villa's interior courtyard, the gallery could not have been more perfectly conceived to showcase the pieces it housed. The dark interiors and rich colors used by the Dutch painters contrasted splendidly with the gold silk wallpaper against which they were hung, just as Isabella Gardner had intended them to.

"How much do you think these are worth?" Bobby asked as we made a slow circuit of the room. "Just the Rembrandts."

The Gardner's Rembrandts, which included a self-portrait of the artist and the spectacular seascape "Storm on the Sea of Galilee," were undeniably priceless. I hesitated to put an exact figure on them. "Millions," I said.

Like most people, Bobby was drawn to the big, flashy stuff. But he was no amateur. He knew as well as I did how difficult a Rembrandt would be to sell on the open market.

"That Vermeer," I said, pointing to a smaller oil painting of a girl playing the piano. "Now that's a real gem. There are only a handful of Vermeers out there."

As we strolled out of the Dutch room and into the adjoining tapestry room, Bobby suddenly stopped. "See that finial?" he said, pointing to a small bronze eagle atop a Napoleonic flagpole. "You've got your Titian; I've got that eagle." He smiled to himself. "That'll be my calling card: 'The eagle has landed.'"

"I'll remember that," I told him.

Picking out Rembrandts and Titians may have been the stuff of fantasy, but Bobby had lit a fire in me concerning the Gardner Museum, and we began to talk about a heist in more concrete terms. Over the course of the next few weeks we made several trips to the museum to scout out the alarm system and identify the building's vulnerabilities.

But on Friday, September 12, any plans Bobby Donati and I had for robbing the Gardner were put on indefinite hold.

That afternoon I drove up to Northampton to pick up Martha, who was back in school. We were on our way to have dinner at one of our favorite restaurants, in nearby South Hadley, when a team of FBI agents descended on us in the parking lot. As in Mashpee, they had taken no chances. There were at least a dozen officers, each with his pistol drawn.

"Myles Connor?" one of them asked.

"The one and only," I answered.

Twenty-One

Much to my dismay, I soon found myself back at the Charles Street Jail. Not long after my arrival I learned that Tommy Sperrazza was also there. He and Johnny Stokes had been arrested while I was in Cohasset. Stokes was already back at Walpole, but Sperrazza, who was also a client of Marty Leppo's, was awaiting trial for the murder of Ralph Cirvinale, the man he'd shot to death coming out of the Roslindale bar. Karen Spinney and Susan Webster, the two young women who had witnessed the crime, still had not been found, but there was no shortage of other witnesses, and it looked like Sperrazza's conviction was a foregone conclusion.

My first visitor at Charles Street was Marty Leppo. Though I'd had no direct contact with him since jumping bail, I had managed, through various mutual friends, to let him know that I was alive and well. Despite the circumstances, I have to think he was relieved to see me back in custody, where he could at least keep an eye on me.

"You know, that was a stupid stunt you pulled, skipping out on me like that," he said when we sat down together in one of the private attorney-client meeting rooms at Charles Street.

I shrugged. "I had some unfinished business to take care of."

He tried and failed to look disappointed in me. The truth was, he liked me too much to be angry with me for disappearing. "I'll bet you did."

Leaning back in his chair, he unbuttoned his suit jacket and smoothed his tie. Like me, he was a man who could appreciate a nice set of clothes. I had never seen him anything other than impeccably dressed. "You wouldn't happen to know anything about that missing Rembrandt?"

"Absolutely not," I said. I smiled at him, and the look he gave me in return said he knew I was involved. We didn't speak about the subject again.

The second person to visit me at the Charles Street Jail was my father. He would have come to see me no matter what, but I could tell as soon as we sat down together that he had an agenda of his own. After the usual pleasantries and a few requisite questions regarding my general well-being, my father got down to business.

"You don't know anything about that painting, do you?" he asked. Then, knowing better than to expect a straight answer out of me, he added, "Because if you do, John Regan would really like to be involved in its return."

It had been my intention all along to use Regan, partly because I liked him and knew what a feather in his cap helping to get the painting back would be, and partly because I relished the thought of screwing over Bernie Murphy. After his gloating remarks to me following the Mashpee arrest, I had no intention of letting him take even one iota of the credit for the Rembrandt's return. But I didn't tell my father any of this.

"Tell him to come see me," I said, trying to sound nonchalant about the idea, as if involving Regan as an intermediary was just one of many possibilities I had to consider.

Days later, Regan did come.

"Your father says you might be able to help get that Rembrandt back," Regan said.

"Possibly," I told him. "For the right price."

"Meaning?"

"Meaning I don't want to spend the next ten years in federal prison."

Regan nodded. "Fair enough."

"Look," I said, "I didn't take the painting, but I've got a good idea where it is. If I can make a deal with Twomey, I'll do what I can to see it gets back into the hands of its rightful owners. But I'm going to need someone to take custody of the painting." I stopped and looked Regan in the eye. "Someone I can trust."

Regan nodded, slowly and deliberately, as if he'd already given his response no small amount of thought. "You know, you're going to piss a lot of people off if you do this, Myles. The MFA's Boston PD turf. They're going to look like real assholes if they're not in on bringing that painting home."

I shrugged. Regan had known me for long enough to realize I wasn't afraid of the Boston police, or anyone else for that matter.

I knew I'd never see the outside of Charles Street Jail until the Rembrandt was safely returned, which meant I needed someone to deliver the painting to Regan. There was no question in my mind that the only person I trusted enough to fill this role was Al Dotoli.

Aside from being my manager and best friend, Al was as clean as they come, and a businessman to boot. I knew he had the authority needed to successfully carry off the exchange. Having seen him in action with nightclub owners and radio producers, I knew what a tough negotiator he could be. Al also knew John Regan from the old days in Milton. But most important, I had absolutely no doubts concerning Al's loyalty to me.

Soon after my meeting with Regan, Al came to visit me. Conveniently, the state police had arranged for us to have our own private meeting room at Charles Street.

"I heard you've been getting chummy with Bernie Murphy," I joked when we sat down together.

Al smiled. "We've said a few words to each other. He's a real personable guy."

"He know you're here?"

"I'd say it's likely. Most days I've either got him or his partner on my tail." He leaned closer. "Murphy told me the feds are willing to drop all charges if you can help them get the Rembrandt back."

"Fuck Murphy," I said. Then, softening slightly, I told him, "Look, I know where the painting is and I can get my hands on it, but I won't deal with the FBI." I paused, searching Al's face for any sign that he was wavering. "And I'm going to need your help."

"You know I'll do what I can," Al assured me.

I nodded my appreciation. "It might take me awhile to work out a suitable deal."

"Don't take too long," Al warned me. "The feds aren't the only ones interested in the painting. I've got every wise guy in New England breathing down my neck. Not to mention cops of every stripe. I came home last night to find a couple of insurance guys hiding in the bushes behind my house. I feel like fucking Elvis."

"I'll try my best," I promised him.

With all the important players on board, I met with Marty Leppo to discuss the details of a plea agreement. With the Wyeth theft, the bail-jumping charges, and the parole violation all hanging over my head, I knew I'd have to do some time, but I'd already made up my mind not to settle for anything less than a four-year concurrent sentence for all three. The Rembrandt was a major trump card, and I wasn't about to play it for pennies.

Telling Marty only that I was in a position to help negotiate the return of the Rembrandt, I laid out my sentencing demands.

Marty was cautiously optimistic. "I think I can convince Twomey to agree to that," he told me. "The MFA's leaning hard on him to get the painting back. I'm sure that FBI agent, Murphy, would act as a middleman."

Al Dotoli wasn't the only one Murphy had been following around. He'd also taken to shadowing Marty.

I shook my head. "I've already made arrangements to use the state police."

"You screw the feds and the Suffolk County DA on this deal and they'll make it their sole mission in life to put you away," Marty warned me. "Are you ready for that?"

"Bring it on," I told him.

Marty shook his head. "Twomey and Gabriel are going to need proof you can get your hands on the painting," he said, referring to Jim Gabriel, the U.S. attorney and Twomey's boss.

"No problem," I assured Marty.

Negotiating the return of a million-dollar work of art is no small feat; doing so from behind bars was challenging, to say the least. My first order of business was to furnish Marty with the proof he needed. To this end, I had Charlie snap a photo of the portrait alongside that day's *Boston Herald American* and send it to Marty's office.

"You'll never guess what I got in the mail the other day," Marty told me on his subsequent visit.

I smiled. "Have you shown it to Twomey?"

Marty nodded. "I had a nice long chat with him and Gabriel."

"And?"

"They're definitely interested."

Over the course of the next two months, Marty met with Twomey, Gabriel, and Regan on numerous occasions. Negotiating for stolen art is a highly controversial subject. There are plenty of people out there who believe that this kind of deal only encourages art theft. In the case of the Rembrandt, my celebrity and the nature of the crimes for which I had been convicted in the past meant all parties involved had to be especially careful about attracting unwanted media scrutiny. Certainly none of them wanted to be seen making a deal with a convicted cop shooter and known art thief.

By late December 1975 the U.S. attorney's office finally agreed to all of my demands. In exchange for the safe return of the Rembrandt they would drop the bail-jumping charges and pursue a four-year sentence in the Wyeth case, to run concurrently with the time remaining on my state sentence. Just as important, I could serve out that sentence in a state facility. I would be going back to Walpole.

But there was one remaining hurdle. If my federal and state sentences were to run concurrently, I first had to be sentenced in state court for my parole violation. Only then could the federal court impose a concurrent sentence. But the state court couldn't sentence me while I was in federal custody.

Marty Leppo offered a clever solution to this logistical quandary: Twomey and Gabriel would make a recommendation to the U.S. magistrate to reduce my bail to a personal bond. Once out on bail I would be taken into state custody for violating my original parole. With the transfer accomplished, I would plead guilty to the federal charges.

It seemed like a perfect resolution, but Twomey and Gabriel were still not satisfied. Given my proclivity for going on the run, the two men were rightly worried that I would use the brief window of opportunity between my release from federal custody and my handover to the state to slip away. To further complicate matters, they wanted the painting in their hands before they would make their recommendation to the magistrate. This last demand was something I could not agree to. The Rembrandt was my only bargaining chip, and I wasn't about to give it up before I got what I wanted.

Just after Christmas, Al Dotoli came to see me at Charles Street. He was visibly upset.

"Myles," he said, "you know I love you like a brother and I'd do anything for you, but this has gone far enough."

"What happened?" I asked.

"Eleven o'clock last night a big black limo pulls up outside my house and fucking Rudy climbs out with a briefcase full of cash."

Rudy was a well-known organized crime figure with influence over a massive crew. A visit from him was not to be taken lightly, even by someone like Al, who'd bumped into his fair share of wise guys in his time. "What did he say?" I asked.

"What the fuck do you think he said?" Al lowered his voice, doing his best impersonation of the gangster. "'I just came from a meeting at Raymond's office on the hill. The boys would like Myles to consider turning the painting over to us.'"

Suddenly I understood why Al was so shaken. "Raymond" was none other than Raymond Patriarca, who at the time ran the entire New England mob from the Federal Hill neighborhood in Providence, Rhode Island.

"What did you tell him?"

"I said I'd pass on the request."

I couldn't help smiling at the image of the old wise guy standing on Al's doorstep in Quincy with a case full of money.

"The situation has gotten out of hand, Myles," Al said forcefully. "The feds have been tailing me everywhere. I had a guy follow me to Paris, for chrissake." Al had spent much of December on tour with Dionne Warwick, both in the United States and abroad.

"They must be killing each other for that gig," I remarked.

Al wasn't amused. "I want this resolved. Preferably in time for it to make the front page of the Sunday *Globe* this weekend."

"It'll be sooner than you think," I told him.

At this point, the only thing standing in the way of a deal and the return of the painting were Twomey and Gabriel's fears that I would try to make a run for it. Fortunately, John Regan stepped in at the last minute to offer a compromise: he would personally vouch for the safe return of the Rembrandt and for my transfer from federal to state custody.

Regan's guarantee worked. After several long months of intense negotiating, we finally had a deal everyone could agree on. It was Wednesday, December 31, New Year's Eve. Because of the intervening holiday, my transfer and court dates were scheduled for Friday the second, two days later. The timing couldn't have been better. That afternoon I called Al and told him to come see me right away.

. . .

On the evening of December 31, Al and I met at Charles Street Jail for what would be the last time.

"It looks like you're going to get your Sunday headline," I told him. "I'm going to court on Friday morning. I'll call you as soon as my sentencing is official. You'll need to be ready to move."

Al nodded soberly.

I passed him a piece of paper with two phone numbers written on it. "This is Charlie's number," I said, indicating the first set of digits. "Tell him your name is Kevin. He'll be expecting your call."

"Do I know him?" Al asked.

"You won't be surprised when you see him," I admitted.

Al nodded. I could tell he was already working up a plan for the exchange.

"Call Regan next," I instructed him, pointing to the second phone number. "I'll leave it to you to arrange the handover."

I reached into my pocket, pulled out a Polaroid, and slid it across the table to Al. It was a photograph of the back of the Rembrandt, showing a distinctive sequence of numbers that were imprinted on the canvas. "Take this with you to the handover," I told him. "Make sure the numbers match."

Al glanced down at the Polaroid.

"I've given one to Regan as well. When you meet him for the transfer, say, 'It's a beautiful night out.' You'll be looking for him to answer, 'Yes, there are plenty of stars out.'"

Al may not have been a hardened criminal, but neither was he a rookie. If he had been, I wouldn't have trusted him with such a perilous undertaking. He and I had been in some hairy situations together, and I knew he could take care of himself. My confidence wasn't misplaced.

Rightly fearing for his safety, Al had already recruited one of his most trusted friends, who will be known here simply as B., to act as backup for him. With B. on call, Al set out to come up with a fail-safe plan for the return of the painting. His first order of business was selecting where the exchange would take place. It didn't take him long to do so. By the time he left the Charles Street Jail on the night of December 31, he had an exact location in mind: the Holiday Inn in North Randolph. The choice was dictated by geography more than anything. The motel was an easy drive from both Al's house in Quincy and John Regan's house in Milton. More important, it was located just off Interstate 93, making for a convenient getaway for Al.

Wasting no time, Al drove straight from his meeting with me at the Charles Street Jail to John Regan's house in Milton. Carefully timing the route as he went, he headed south from Regan's in the direction of the Holiday Inn, stopping at the Copeland Farms, a popular dairy bar and farm stand on Randolph Avenue, where he jotted down the number of the pay phone. He then called B. and asked the man to call him back at the number, to confirm that the phone and the number worked. Satisfied that they did, Al continued the last mile down Randolph Avenue to the Holiday Inn, still timing himself.

Making a circuit of the motel's large parking lot, which it shared with several other businesses, including Lantana and the Chateau De Ville, two large function halls, and Peter's, a popular disco, Al contemplated his options. If his plan was to work, he needed to locate yet another pay phone. Figuring he could use a drink, he parked his car and headed into Peter's. Despite the fact that it was New Year's Eve, it was still early enough that the nightclub had not yet filled with revelers. Al easily found a seat at the bar and ordered a drink. While he was waiting for the bartender to fill his order, he noticed a house phone at the far end of the bar. It was exactly what he'd been looking for. Not only was the phone easily accessible, but it was equipped with a number of lines, meaning the chances of it being busy at any one time were extremely slim.

Slipping off his stool, Al sidled down the bar until he was close enough to read the number on the phone. Repeating the precaution he'd taken at Copeland Farms, he then made his way upstairs and used the pay phone outside the men's room to dial the bar phone for verification. With the phone number at Peter's confirmed, Al headed back to his car.

The pay phones took care of his plan for dealing with Regan, but Al still needed to find a location where he could rendezvous with Charlie, preferably somewhere nearby but not part of the motel complex. It would be catastrophic if someone got to Charlie and the painting before he did. Scanning the boundaries of the parking lot, Al headed east toward a sparsely lit drive that led out of the lot to High Street. Once on High Street, he cruised south, with the wooded landscape of the Blue Hills nature preserve on his right and a residential neighborhood of quiet through streets on his left. Passing a ball field, he slowed slightly, noting a small dirt car park and some trash barrels. Then he turned east on one of the through streets and looped back toward North Main Street, still looking for a rendezvous point. At the intersection of North Main Street and Edwin Street, just a few blocks south of the Holiday Inn, he found exactly what he was looking for: a Dunkin' Donuts shop with ample parking and direct access to the northbound lane of North Main Street. With the logistics of his plan firmly laid out in his mind, and in no mood for celebrating, Al headed home to Quincy to try to get some sleep.

While Al was scouting the location for the handover, I drafted two letters—one to Al and one to Charlie—with last-minute instructions and assurances that the men could trust each other. I won't lie; I was nervous as hell that something would go wrong.

This operation is vital, I wrote to Al, *and must be carried out successfully; no mob, no insurance men, no FBI or police, and no failure.* In a final postscript I added one last piece of advice: *Whatever you do, don't remove the painting from the frame.*

The next day a friendly screw hand-delivered the letters to Al and Charlie. There was nothing more that I could do. The return of the Rembrandt was now out of my hands.

Twenty-Two

Friday, January 2, 1976, dawned bright and early at the Charles Street Jail. After the usual morning roll call—and the customary prebreakfast scramble to nab one of the few seats in the mess not covered in pigeon shit—deputy marshals arrived to escort me to the Federal Building, where I was to appear before U.S. Magistrate Willie Davis.

My court appearance was a mere formality. The details of my sentencing and transfer from federal to state custody had been worked out well in advance and thoroughly vetted by both Twomey and Gabriel. In keeping with the recommendation given him by the U.S. attorney's office, Magistrate Davis reduced my bail from $1 million to a personal bond. No longer a federal prisoner, I was handed over to John Regan.

While I was standing before Judge Davis, Al Dotoli had some business of his own to take care of. Having laid the groundwork for his plan on the evening of the thirty-first, he had only a few last-minute tasks to accomplish. The first of these was to call his backup man.

"I need you to go the Holiday Inn in North Randolph," Al told B. "Get me two adjoining rooms on the second floor. Tell them you want to be as close to the side entrance as possible. And whatever you do, don't give them my name. When you're done with that I want you to swing by here. I need a ride to the car rental agency."

Early that afternoon, making good on his word to Twomey and Gabriel, John Regan personally accompanied me from the Federal Building back to the Charles Street Jail. But before delivering me to the jail staff, he allowed me to stop and make one important phone call. The number I dialed was Al Dotoli's. Our conversation was brief and to the point. "It's a go," I told my friend. The rest, I knew, was up to him.

Having received the go-ahead from me, Al called Charlie. "It's Kevin," he said, using the code name I'd assigned him. "Be in the parking lot of the Dunkin' Donuts in North Randolph at seven fifteen. I'll be coming from Edwin Street. When I turn onto North Main Street, I'll flash my lights three times. Follow me into the Holiday Inn parking lot."

After getting a description of Charlie's car, along with his license plate number, Al hung up and called John Regan, who had gone home to wait for the call. "It's on," Al told the state police detective, identifying himself once again only as Kevin. "Stand by."

"I won't be alone," Regan warned him, making good on the agreement he and the U.S. attorney had come to over their months of negotiations. "David Twomey will be there as well."

"That's fine," Al agreed. "Wait for my next call."

Regan hung up and called Twomey, who immediately set out for Milton.

With Regan on alert, Al waited for darkness to fall to put his plan into action. He wasn't taking any chances. Al's Quincy property was bounded in the back by a steep ravine and thickly wooded marshland. On the far side of the ravine was a parking lot. Al had left his rented Plymouth Fury in the lot earlier that afternoon. His backup man, B., was also waiting in the lot, along with his two brothers. The men were armed to the teeth and ready to spring into action should the need arise; B. had parked his van so he could monitor Al's house, which was dark except for a single light in the upstairs bathroom.

As the sun set, Al had one last detail to see to. Taking a large mirror off the dining room wall, he carefully wrapped the piece in a sleeping bag and set it by the back door. With this final task accomplished, he headed upstairs. At exactly seven o'clock, Al turned off the bathroom light to signal to his backup man that he was on the move. Then he made his way downstairs out the back door, taking the mirror with him. Once the lights were out, Al knew, he had only a few minutes to get across the backyard and through the woods to the parking lot. Any longer than that and B. would come looking for him.

Picking his way along the narrow path that crossed the marsh, Al reached the parking lot without incident. Glancing around to make sure he hadn't been followed, he stowed the mirror in the trunk of the rented Plymouth. Then he climbed into the driver's seat, started the engine, and, with the van following at a discreet distance, pulled out of the lot, heading south.

Sticking closely to the script he'd written for himself on the night of the thirty-first, Al stopped at Copeland Farms and used the pay phone to call Regan. "Who owns the '69 Buick?" Al asked, referring to a car—not Regan's—that he'd seen parked in the lawman's driveway.

"My wife," Regan answered.

"Good," Al told him. "Wait three minutes, then get in the Buick and drive at a normal speed to the Copeland Farms on Randolph Avenue. Wait at the pay phone there for my next call."

"Hold on," Regan said, balking. "What's wrong with my car?"

"Bring the Buick or it's off," Al said forcefully, "and two sets of keys."

"Okay, okay," Regan quickly relented.

"And one more thing," Al told him. "If I so much as see a gun, the deal's off."

Noting the exact time, Al hung up and climbed back into the Plymouth for the final leg of his trip. Still shadowed by B., he cruised down Randolph Avenue and under the highway, then pulled into the Holiday Inn parking lot. Passing Pete's and the Chateau De Ville, he headed toward the east side the parking lot. Turning down High Street, he pulled up next to the ball field, took the sleeping-bag-wrapped mirror from the trunk, and, moving slowly so that anyone watching could see exactly what he was doing, placed the mirror next to a large trash barrel.

If he was being followed, Al figured now was the time his pursuers would show themselves. Knowing this, he'd given B. specific instructions concerning the decoy drop: B. was to pass Al on High Street, turn around, and make sure he got back into the Plymouth unharmed, then head back to the Holiday Inn parking lot and turn around once again; if the decoy was still by the trash barrel, B. was to pick it up and head home; if the decoy was gone, he would drive directly to the Holiday Inn to warn Al that someone was on to him.

As Al walked back to the Plymouth, he saw the van carrying B. and his brothers go past him on High Street, then slow and make a U-turn. Satisfied that B. had his back, Al climbed into the rental car and continued down High Street, looping west on Edwin Street. As he emerged onto Randolph Avenue, he was relieved to see Charlie waiting for him in the parking lot of the donut shop. Having confirmed that the painting was in place, Al continued back to the Holiday Inn.

Parking his rental car next to the motel's side entrance, Al climbed up to his rooms on the second floor and went inside. After checking his watch and satisfying himself that B. had in fact recovered the decoy, Al used the phone in his room to dial the number of the pay phone at Copeland Farms. Regan answered on the first ring.

"Drive down Randolph Avenue to the Holiday Inn parking lot," Al instructed him. "Behind the motel you'll see a big sign for Peter's. Park in the sign's shadow and wait."

Checking his watch once again, Al left his room, exited the motel through the side entrance, and crossed the parking lot toward Lantana and Chateau De Ville. Concealed in the narrow common alley between the two buildings, Al watched and waited for Regan to arrive. Almost immediately he saw the '69 Buick pull into the parking lot and roll to a stop behind the massive sign. His adrenaline spiking, Al pulled a black ski mask down over his face, crossed the lot, and approached the car. Seeing him coming, Regan rolled the driver's-side window down.

"It's a beautiful night out," Al said, repeating the exact words I'd told him to use.

Regan nodded. "Yes, there are plenty of stars out."

Hearing the response he was waiting for, Al opened the back door of the Buick and slid inside. "Show me your IDs," he told the two lawmen.

Hastily, Regan and Twomey pulled their wallets out and passed their IDs to Al, who examined the documents with his flashlight. "Okay," he said, finally satisfied. "I want you to get out of the car and walk over to Peter's. Go into the disco downstairs. Take a seat at the end of the bar and wait. If the phone rings and the barman asks for Paul Greeter, you take it."

Regan pulled the keys from the ignition and started to get out, but Al stopped him. "Leave the keys."

Regan protested. "You can't take my wife's car!"

"You brought a second set, right?"

Regan nodded.

"Leave the keys or it's off," Al warned, opening his own door.

Regan quickly acquiesced. "Okay," he agreed.

"Now get going," Al said. He watched Regan and Twomey disappear into Peter's, then slid into the Buick's driver's seat and started the engine. Following the same route he'd driven earlier, he looped east, down High Street and past the ball field, where, he noted with relief, the decoy was nowhere to be seen.

Turning onto Edwin Street, Al again headed for the Dunkin' Donuts. But this time, when he stopped across from the donut shop, he flashed his lights three times, giving Charlie the signal to follow him. As Al turned onto Randolph Avenue, he glanced in his rearview mirror and saw Charlie's car pulling out behind him. Slowing, he pulled into the Holiday Inn parking lot for what he hoped would be the last time and parked facing Randolph Avenue, with his trunk to the motel.

Charlie pulled in next to him, and the two men climbed out of their cars. They recognized each other immediately, but neither man said a word. Moving quickly, Al opened the Buick's trunk. Charlie followed suit, lifting the painting out of his trunk, pulling away a corner of the sleeping bag in which the Rembrandt was wrapped to reveal the series of numbers on the back of the canvas. Al produced the Polaroid I'd given him.

After both men had confirmed that the numbers matched, Al took possession of the painting, giving Charlie the Polaroid in return. While Charlie got back into his car and sped away, Al hastily loaded the Rembrandt into the trunk of the Buick, then tossed Regan's keys on top of it, closed the trunk, and headed for the side door of the motel.

For an agonizing two minutes, while Al sprinted up the stairs to his room, the painting sat in the Buick's trunk, unattended and entirely vulnerable. Despite the fact that he'd taken every precaution to make sure no one had followed him, Al's heart was racing as he opened the door to his room and ran to the window. Seeing the Buick still in its spot, he breathed a huge sigh of relief. Al's ordeal was almost over, but before he could wash his hands of the painting entirely, he had one last phone call to make: to the bar at Peter's.

Al dialed the number with shaking hands, half expecting Regan himself to answer, but it was the bartender who picked up.

"I'd like to speak to Paul Greeter," he told the man. "I believe he's right there."

On the other end of the line, Al heard the barman calling for Greeter, followed almost instantly by Regan's voice: "That's me!"

"Hello?" Regan spoke into the receiver.

"Go outside," Al instructed him. "Run, do not walk. Your wife's car is parked at the Holiday Inn, facing the street. Open the trunk. If what you want is in there, turn and face the building, put your hands in your pockets, and count to five. Then get the hell out of here."

Al hung up the phone and looked out the window of his room toward the nightclub. Within seconds, the front door burst open and the two lawmen came running out, their trench coats flapping in the stiff January wind. They reached the Buick and stopped while Regan unlocked the trunk. When they saw the painting, both men hesitated for a moment; it was, Al mused, the closest either one of them would get to a million dollars. Then Regan reached into the trunk and pulled a corner of the blanket aside while Twomey shone a flashlight on the canvas, verifying the numbers on the back of the piece, just as Al had done.

With the painting's authenticity confirmed, the two men turned to face the building as instructed. When they opened their coats to put their hands in their pockets, Al couldn't help laughing. Beneath their trench coats, both Regan and Twomey were armed to the hilt. So much for promises. After a hasty count of five, the two men scuttled into the car and scrammed.

No sooner had the Buick disappeared from sight than Al did the same. Driving straight to Logan Airport, he dropped off the rented Plymouth and caught the next shuttle to JFK. By midnight he was sharing a meal with friends at Christo's in Manhattan.

At a press conference the following day David Twomey's boss, United States attorney Jim Gabriel, triumphantly announced the safe return of the Rembrandt, assuring the public that "no deal was made with any federal prisoner." Technically, at least, the statement was true. Marty Leppo's last-minute bargaining and my hasty handover to state custody made it possible for Gabriel to silence potential critics of the methods his office had used to get the painting back.

Al Dotoli got all the publicity he'd asked for, and then some. The press conference was a major media event, covered by every news outlet in the city. Saturday evening's *Boston Globe* carried a picture of Gabriel speaking to reporters. At his side, basking in the spotlight, were David Twomey and John Regan. In his room at the Waldorf, Al read about his exploits in the *New York Times*.

Conspicuously absent from the proceedings were representatives from the Boston Police Department and the local FBI office, who were not pleased by the way things had turned out. That the state police had recovered what was perhaps the single most valuable item ever stolen on the Boston PD's watch would cause a rift between the two agencies for years to come.

Especially pissed off at being deprived of his share of the glory was an up-and-coming young FBI agent named John Connolly. Connolly had come to the Boston office just two years earlier, but he was already making a name for himself. Eventually, Connolly would become infamous for his corrupt relationship with mob boss Whitey Bulger, but at the time his colleagues and the local press thought of him as merely a zealous, if somewhat unorthodox, investigator. Unfortunately, I would soon get a preview of the extremes to which Connolly was willing to go.

Twenty-Three

On January 5, 1976, my parole was formally revoked and I was returned to Walpole prison to serve out the remaining four years of my state sentence, along with the concurrent federal sentence for my role in the Wyeth thefts. No one looks forward to going to prison, and I was no exception. But I was relieved to get out of the Charles Street Jail and back to Walpole's familiar—and relatively sanitary—confines. Having mastered the prison system once before, I was confident I could do so again. A number of my friends were also doing time, including Ralph Petrozziello, so I found myself with a ready-made crew.

My first order of business was to put together a band. I was soon playing to packed houses in the prison auditorium. Thanks to the production skills of Al Dotoli, who was granted special permission by the warden to come into the prison, these concerts were much more sophisticated than the shows I'd put on during my previous stay. To listen to the recordings Al made of them is to hear the combined hopes, fears, and frustrations of the six hundred men who called Walpole prison home.

Al brought in a number of special guests to play with us, including Lenny Baker, Danny McBride, and Chico Ryan from Sha Na Na, and the blues great James Cotton. But the most memorable performers to take the stage with us were not musicians. Al came to one of our earliest shows, in 1975, accompanied by two crew members I had never seen before. Fair-skinned and slighter of build than the average roadie, the pair fairly swam in their gray coveralls and baseball caps. I soon understood why.

We were about halfway through our first set, having just starting in on a rousing rendition of the Tom Jones version of "I (Who Have Nothing)," when the two roadies rushed out onto the stage and began fiddling with one of the microphones. Then, without warning, they tore their baseball caps and coveralls off, revealing long blond hair and two sets of perfect breasts. Needless to say, the crowd went wild. Al, who was recording the concert, caught the whole thing on tape.

Despite the popularity of my shows and the relative ease with which I reentered prison society, there were serious consequences to my incarceration, the most heartbreaking of which was my separation from Martha. We both understood without question that our relationship was over. I knew firsthand the humiliations endured by the girlfriends of my fellow prisoners, the body searches and public gropings that accompanied their weekly visits to Walpole, not to mention the loneliness and ridicule they suffered on the outside. I loved Martha too much to subject her to the consequences of my actions. Fortunately, she was self-possessed enough to come to the same conclusion.

While I was looking to the future and counting the days till I would once again be a free man, there were those who could not put the past behind them. Despite John Regan's warning, I hadn't truly understood the consequences of cutting the FBI, the Boston police, and their counterparts in the Suffolk County district attorney's office out of the Rembrandt recovery. They were still pissed that Regan and Twomey had gotten all the glory, and they were determined to make me pay for snubbing them. Unfortunately for me, all three parties would soon gain some unlikely allies in their respective crusades against me.

Since his arrest earlier that winter Tommy Sperrazza had been of particular interest to both the FBI and the Suffolk County district attorney's office, who were well aware of his association with me.

Aside from being under indictment for the Roslindale shootings and a suspect in the disappearances of Karen Spinney and Susan Webster, Sperrazza was a suspect in several other crimes. One of these was the cold-blooded killing of an off-duty cop named Donald Brown during a holdup at a Roslindale shopping center.

The details of the Brown shooting were especially tragic. Brown, a twenty-nine-year veteran of the Boston Police Department who was less than a week away from retirement, was working a paid detail escorting the manager of the Purity Supreme supermarket to make a night deposit of $3,600 at a nearby bank when they were accosted by three armed men. During the course of the holdup, Brown was shot and killed.

At the time of the shooting, in May 1974, I was bound to be a prime suspect in just about any crime that was committed in the Roslindale area, and rightly so. By then my associates and I had committed numerous crimes in the area, including the bank heists and Ralph Petrozziello's contract jobs. Our reputation was such that the police had dubbed us the "Connor-Petrozziello Gang."

What the authorities failed to realize was that we were less a gang than a loose collection of independent operators who sometimes worked together. Rarely, if ever, were we all involved in any one heist. Certainly I was in no way in charge of a crew. Frequently there were jobs of which I had little or no knowledge before the fact. The Purity Supreme holdup was one of these cases.

Despite the fact that there was absolutely no evidence to suggest I'd been in any way involved with the crime, the Suffolk County DA, who had jurisdiction in the case, immediately suspected me in the robbery and shooting and began leaning hard on Sperrazza to link me to the holdup.

The lead prosecutor, Assistant District Attorney Phil Beauchesne, who had already convinced himself that I was guilty, was like a dog without a bone. Not long after I returned to Walpole he accosted my attorney, Marty Leppo, in the elevator of the Suffolk County Courthouse.

"I'm going to get your boy, Connor, on the Brown shooting," Beauchesne, who was fairly foaming at the mouth with rage, told Marty. "One way or another."

Marty tried to downplay the exchange at our next meeting. "It's just a lot of saber rattling," he told me. But I knew better than to dismiss the incident completely. And despite his assurances, Marty seemed to be taking Beauchesne's threat seriously: he'd made a formal record of the exchange for his files.

Beauchesne wasn't alone in vocalizing his feelings. One of the Boston police detectives on the case never passed up a chance to remind Marty that he had his sights set on me. "It's a long dark alley with lots of trash barrels," he used to say whenever he ran into my attorney at the courthouse. "One way or another, we're going to get him."

While the Suffolk County DA and the Boston PD were doggedly trying to conjure up a case against me in the Brown shooting, the FBI had their own agenda. The feds, who had jurisdiction in the Norfolk County Trust case because the stolen money was federally insured, had set their sights on finding a way to link me to the bank robbery. Unfortunately for me, they were about to get a significant break.

On February 28, 1976, two eleven-year-old boys were playing in the woods bordering a Norwood cemetery, looking for a place to build a fort, when they found a plastic bag, partially covered by leaves and tucked into the back of an old rock wall. Inside the bag were cloth bank bags, a number of $1,000 money bands, and a modest stash of pharmaceuticals. The boys, being the responsible young citizens they were, took their find to their parents, who immediately brought the bags to the Norwood Police Department. The police, recognizing that the cloth bags and money bands were undoubtedly the product of a bank robbery, in turn contacted the FBI.

It didn't take long for the feds to trace the bank materials to the Norfolk County Trust. Aside from the scanner Santo had left behind, and which so far had provided no solid leads, the cemetery stash was the first real evidence to turn up in the case, and the federal agents wasted no time putting it to use.

The bags had, in fact, been hidden in the cemetery by my former crew member Bobby Fitzgerald, who lived with his mother less than a block from where the stash was found. Fitzgerald's father was buried in the cemetery, and Bobby often hid drugs and other contraband in the stone wall near his grave.

During the winter of 1975 I had occasionally spent the night at Bobby's house, sometimes with Martha. In return for his hospitality I'd given Bobby some of the money from the Milton bank robbery, along with the bank bags, which he agreed to hold for me.

Fitzgerald had been arrested for heroin distribution not long before and was doing time at the lockup on Deer Island. The FBI, who already suspected me in the Norfolk County Trust heist and who knew Fitzgerald was an associate of mine, soon put two and two together and approached Bobby about a possible deal in exchange for his testimony. He snapped at the chance to reduce his sentence.

With Fitzgerald's help the federal prosecutor slowly began laying the groundwork for an indictment against me. It would prove to be a long and drawn-out process. But the feds could afford to take their time. After all, I wasn't going anywhere.

As 1976 drew to a close, the whereabouts of Susan Webster and Karen Spinney, the two young women who'd disappeared after the Roslindale bar shooting, were still unknown. Although by now almost everyone involved in the case believed they were dead and that Sperrazza and John Stokes were responsible for their murder, the Norfolk County district attorney, whose office was prosecuting the case, could not bring formal murder charges until the women's bodies were found.

To further complicate matters, Stokes, who had shown signs of being willing to cooperate with authorities, had been brutally stabbed to death the previous summer at Walpole. It was common knowledge on the inside that Sperrazza, who by then had been sentenced to life for the Cirvinale murder, was the one who'd killed his friend and former partner. People on the outside, including the staff of the Norfolk County DA's office, couldn't help drawing the same conclusion. With Stokes dead, it seemed unlikely that the girls would ever be found.

Then, early in the summer of 1977, Ralph Petrozziello pulled me aside on the yard one afternoon. "Tommy Sperrazza's got a proposal for us," he said, lowering his voice.

"Oh yeah?" I sneered, not about to do Sperrazza any favors. "Tell him he can go fuck himself."

Ralph shook his head. "Just hear me out, okay?"

"I'm listening," I said reluctantly, unable to refuse my friend.

"Sperrazza wants out of here," Ralph said. "Bad."

I laughed. "Don't we all."

"I'm serious, Myles. He wants to see his kid."

Sperrazza's wife, Deborah, had just given birth to a little girl, and Sperrazza was suddenly the proud papa, flashing pictures of the baby around his cellblock. It was hard for me to muster much sympathy for him. "He can make his case to the parole board in fifteen years."

Ralph glanced around to make sure no one was in earshot. "He wants us to bust him out," he announced.

Was he crazy? "Ignoring the fact that we're stuck in this shithole ourselves, I wouldn't help break that asshole out if he paid me a million dollars."

"He's not paying," Ralph said, "but there might be something in it for us all the same. You remember those two girls?"

How could I forget? "You mean Karen Spinney and Susan Webster?"

Ralph nodded. "Sperrazza wants you to make a deal. Like you did with the Rembrandt."

Now I was completely lost. "What the hell are you talking about?" I asked.

"Ask your buddy Regan what it'd be worth to him if he could find out where those girls are. If he can make a deal to get you and me out of here early, Sperrazza will tell us what he did with Spinney and Webster. All we have to do is promise to bust Sperrazza out."

I was right: Ralph was crazy. "Forget it," I told him, turning to go.

"Come on," he pleaded. Then, almost as an afterthought, he added, "You can do whatever you want to Sperrazza once he's back on the street."

I shook my head. "Forget it."

The matter seemed to have been resolved, but as I lay in my bunk that night I couldn't get the conversation out of my head. Losing a child is every parent's worst nightmare. At the time my own daughter, Kim, was not far in age from Karen Spinney and Susan Webster. Though I had not been the best father to her, I loved her dearly. I could only imagine what the parents of the missing women were going through. Surely, I thought, the uncertainty of not knowing what had happened must have been unbearable.

Finding out where the girls were and helping to win an early parole for Ralph at the same time wouldn't necessarily be a bad thing. But even if Ralph could get Sperrazza to tell me what he'd done with Karen Spinney and Susan Webster, I knew I could never hold up my end of the bargain. I loathed the thought of helping put Sperrazza back on the street. Unless . . .

As I drifted off to sleep, I thought back to the last thing Ralph had said to me on the yard that day: *You can do whatever you want to Sperrazza once he's back on the street.*

The next morning at breakfast I found Ralph. "I'll do it," I told him as we passed each other in the mess. "But only so I can kill the bastard myself once he's out." I wasn't kidding, and I could see in Ralph's eyes that he knew it.

Finally, I'd get a chance to do what I should have done on the way back from Northampton that night.

The next day I called Marty and asked him to come down to Walpole.

"I think I can get Sperrazza to tell me what he did with those girls," I told my attorney when we met. "But I want something in return."

"I'm not sure there's much we can do to get your sentence reduced any further," Marty said.

I shook my head. I wasn't worried about my sentence. With good behavior, I'd be eligible for parole in another couple of months. "It's Ralph I'm asking for."

"Petrozziello?" Marty asked. "What's he got to do with the girls?"

"Absolutely nothing," I told him. "Except that he's my friend and I want to help him out."

Marty looked skeptical. But he knew better than to ask too many questions.

"Just ask around," I said.

"Okay," he agreed. "I'll see what I can do." He started to go, but I stopped him.

"One more thing. If I do this, I want to work with John Regan again."

"The Norfolk County DA has jurisdiction," Marty reminded me.

"I don't care who has jurisdiction," I told him. "Regan's part of it or there's no deal."

For the next few months Marty worked diligently to win a guarantee of an early parole for Ralph in exchange for Sperrazza's information. It was no small feat bringing all the parties involved together. By the time Marty, working closely with John Regan and the Norfolk County district attorney, Bill Delahunt, finally managed to iron out a deal that satisfied everyone, summer was nearly over. In early September he came to Walpole to give me the good news: Ralph would get his parole.

It was now time for Sperrazza to make good on his promise. Several days after Marty's visit Ralph, Sperrazza, and I met on the yard.

"Swear on your mother's life you'll make good on this, Connor," Sperrazza said.

I nodded, relieved to be able to give my word in good faith. "I swear. As soon as Ralph and I are out, we'll do it."

"I've got that bank robbery trial coming up," Sperrazza suggested. "You could grab me on the way to court."

I pondered his proposal. "Not a bad idea," I said, my brain already humming with the outlines of a plan. "But first you have to tell us what you did with those girls. And don't say you put them on a goddamned train."

Sperrazza shook his head. "You remember that bank job we pulled up in Northampton?"

"Sure," I answered, thinking of the hitchhiker once again, the expression on Sperrazza's face when I'd confronted him by the side of the highway. Angry and incredulous, utterly devoid of pity.

"That's where they are," he said. "In the woods behind the VA hospital, near where we left the car that day."

At the mention of Northampton my stomach lurched. "That night at Shaw's Motel . . . ," I said, finally understanding what I'd been a party to.

Sperrazza nodded. Then, as if the news was somehow consolation, he added, "They were already dead."

On September 14, 1977, Regan, Delahunt, and I made the trip up to Northampton together. It was much earlier in the season than it had been when Sperrazza, Stokes, Ozzy, and I had robbed the bank, and the trees, which at the time had been bare, were still in full leaf. I easily found the dirt road that ran into the woods behind the hospital. But the exact spot where we'd left the car was more elusive. Sperrazza had given me a rough description of the place where he and Stokes had buried the two women. Using these shaky details and my memory of the bank robbery, I was eventually able to lead the search team to the area where Sperrazza claimed the bodies lay. Having pointed out the approximate location, I was immediately taken back to Walpole.

Excavators as well as numerous volunteers had been brought in for the grisly task of unearthing the grave, and searchers quickly set about trying to find the women. They worked all through that afternoon and night without success. Then, at 9:25 the next morning, a volunteer searcher announced that his shovel had struck something solid.

Two years and seven months after they'd last been seen alive, Karen Spinney and Susan Webster were finally found. But the discovery was cold comfort to the women's families. The bodies of Spinney and Webster had been stuffed into a green sleeping bag, along with the knife that was used to kill them, and buried one on top of the other in a shallow grave. An examination of the remains revealed that both women had been stabbed multiple times.

When the news was delivered to me at Walpole, I couldn't help thinking back to the night of the Northampton bank robbery, and how different things might have been if I had taken Ozzy's advice.

Twenty-Four

I can truthfully say that there aren't many things in this world that scare me. Having survived near drowning, multiple shootings, the horrors of the Norfolk prison hospital, and the Walpole riots, I have become familiar enough with death to have lost my fear of it. At one point or another I have been denied almost everything I value—family, friends, privacy, freedom, even control over my own body. As a result, the common phobias that plague most people seem petty to me.

Yet there is one thing of which I am terrified, and that's a good liar. I have the utmost respect for someone who can tell a lie, not out of admiration, but because I know all too well the consequences of a well-crafted falsehood, the malignant power even the smallest untruth can have.

I had witnessed that power firsthand during my rape trial, had seen just what a fragile thing the truth was and how easily it could be distorted to coincide with what people wanted to believe. My accuser in that case had been little more than a pawn, a scared child who'd been manipulated by men she had known and trusted—and perhaps even feared—into saying what they wanted her to. But I was about to confront a different kind of liar, one who knew exactly what she was doing.

The discovery of the bodies of Karen Spinney and Susan Webster was big news in Boston. When the women were found camera crews were on the scene to record all the gruesome details, including pictures of the soiled sleeping bag and bent kitchen knife that had been recovered along with the bodies. Watching the drama unfold on her television and taking a keen interest in the details of the discovery was a woman named Doreen Weeks.

I knew Weeks from the Beachcomber, where she sometimes worked as a waitress. At every rock-and-roll club there are people who are desperate to get in with the band and will do whatever it takes to secure a place with the in-crowd. Weeks was such a person. A skilled manipulator, she had learned to use her sex to remarkable advantage. At one time or another she had slept with almost every member of my band.

This fact alone made me wary of Weeks. Band politics are notoriously tricky. Keeping four or five guys happily together is never an easy task. Throw a woman into the mix and things can get dicey fast. I wasn't shy about voicing my misgivings about Weeks to my crew. Neither was Al Dotoli, who eventually had her barred from our shows. As a result, she disliked us as much as we disliked her.

Though no one knew it at the time, Doreen Weeks had good reason to be interested in the recovery of the bodies of Karen Spinney and Susan Webster. In the winter of 1975 Weeks and my sound man, Tommy Maher, had shared a basement apartment in Quincy. It was in this apartment that the women had been killed. Weeks herself was one of the last people to have seen them alive. Watching the news that night, she immediately recognized the green sleeping bag and kitchen knife as her own.

Seeing the items freshly pulled from the earth, she had to have realized that the authorities would soon link her to the case. Ever the opportunist, she also must have understood the unique bargaining position her connection to the killings could afford her. At the time, her brother was doing time in the state prison system. Looking to strike a deal for him, Weeks went to see District Attorney Delahunt.

Not having been privy to their meeting, I can only imagine what exactly they talked about. But it's easy to understand why Delahunt would not have been receptive to whatever Weeks had to offer. With the discovery of the bodies the Norfolk County DA's office had a nearly airtight case against Sperrazza. If anything, bringing a witness like Doreen Weeks on board would have served only to weaken Delahunt's case. To have made a deal with her—even one that involved merely promising not to charge her as an accessory—would have been not just unnecessary but stupid. At the end of their brief meeting Delahunt sent Weeks on her way.

Nine months later his decision to do so must have been confirmed for him when a jury found Tommy Sperrazza guilty of the murders of Karen Spinney and Susan Webster.

But unfortunately for Delahunt—and, it would turn out, even more unfortunately for me—he hadn't heard the last of Doreen Weeks.

At the end of January 1978 I was once again paroled from Walpole. Mindful, as always, of my music career, Al Dotoli immediately set to work putting together a serious working band for me. The Rebels, as we were eventually christened, consisted of Paul "PJ" Justice on bass, Joe "Ivory" Micharielli on keyboards, Tim "Stingray" Sweeney on drums, and Jim "Diamond" Baker on saxophone. Our musical director and special guest vocalist was Scott "the Cat" Anderson. The Rebels were a rock-and-roll band of the old school variety, and Al conceived a brilliant road show that highlighted our musical style. Known as Myles Connor's 1950s Rock-and-Roll Review, we were soon getting steady work all over the Northeast. In the summer we played at clubs on the Cape. In the winter we moved inland, gigging at colleges and ski resorts.

True to our name and my reputation, our shows were rowdy trips back in time and always opened with the same announcement by Arnie Ginsburg of *Night Train* fame: "Good evening and welcome to Myles Connor's 1950s Rock-and-Roll Review, starring the President of Rock and Roll, Myles Connor." The Rebels always played first. Eventually Scott would join them. When they were ready to bring me out they'd play the first few bars of "Pretty Woman." This was the crew's signal to start the smoke machine. As the stage clouded over, I'd take my place at the microphone. At last, when the moment was exactly right, Al would turn on a special fan he'd rigged, and I'd be revealed to the crowd.

The Rebels were all extremely talented musicians, and the Rock-and-Roll Review was without a doubt the best concert tour I played in. Unfortunately, it would also be the last.

My release from prison and subsequent success with the band only served to further antagonize the Suffolk County district attorney's office and the local FBI. That I was a free man again after only two years in Walpole was especially galling to them.

We've all heard the phrase "innocent until proven guilty." Most law-abiding citizens have faith in the impartiality of our country's legal system. But the truth is that justice is rarely blind. Even the most well-meaning investigator or prosecutor brings his or her preconceptions to a case. More often than not the investigation process involves con-firming already well-developed suspicions rather than searching for an unknown suspect. In many cases, prejudice against a specific suspect is an insidious thing. Those involved may not even realize it exists.

But in my case, the push to convict me was clear. By the time of my release from Walpole, state and federal prosecutors had long since accepted as fact my guilt in the Brown shooting (wrong) and the Norfolk County Trust robbery (right) and were working to prove themselves correct.

Evidence of my involvement in the bank robbery was based al-most entirely on conversations with Bobby Fitzgerald, whom the FBI had connected with the cemetery stash. The feds offered Fitzgerald immunity from prosecution along with relocation in the witness pro-tection program for himself and his wife in return for his testimony in the bank robbery case. It was an offer a rat like Fitzgerald couldn't refuse. Bobby started talking immediately, and he was telling the FBI exactly what they wanted to hear. He claimed, among other things, to have heard me planning the Norfolk County Trust robbery, and to have stored some of the cash proceeds in his house for me. He also fingered Sperrazza for the crime.

By that time Sperrazza was also a prime suspect in the Brown shooting. Knowing this, and realizing that Fitzgerald, through his connections with both Sperrazza and me, might be of use in prosecuting that case, the FBI brought Fitzgerald to the attention of the Suffolk County district attorney's office, which was prosecuting the Brown case. Assistant district attorney Phil Beauchesne immediately offered Fitzgerald total immunity from prosecution for any role he had played in the Brown shooting in exchange for any information he had to give regarding my involvement in the crime. Once again, Fitzgerald proved to be a highly cooperative source. Yet this time, having no real information to give investigators, he fabricated from scratch, telling Beauchesne that I had masterminded the Purity Supreme holdup and provided the gun that eventually killed Donald Brown.

Both were outright lies, but that didn't matter to Beauchesne. Fitzgerald's claims were the first lead the ADA had managed to unearth against me in the Brown shooting and he milked it for all it was worth.

Fitzgerald's story wasn't enough to convict me, let alone secure an indictment against me in either case. More determined than ever, investigators on both sides began kicking over rocks, hoping to find someone else willing to corroborate Fitzgerald's testimony. Leading the effort were Phil Beauchesne and several field agents from the Boston FBI office, most notable John Connolly and his colleague, John Clougherty.

It wouldn't be long before the men found what they were looking for.

By the end of 1977 Doreen Weeks, who had moved out of the Quincy apartment not long after the murders of Spinney and Webster, was shacked up with John Stokes's brother, Jimmy, in Dorchester. Jimmy was on the run at the time, wanted for his role in the shooting death of a security guard at a Hyde Park supermarket. Early in 1978, around the same time I was released from Walpole, Jimmy was finally apprehended and sent to the state prison at Norfolk.

Also at Norfolk was Joe Santo. Santo had just begun serving a lengthy sentence when Jimmy Stokes arrived at the prison. Thanks to the less than subtle efforts of investigators, both Stokes and Santo knew full well that the FBI and the Suffolk County DA's office were looking to put me away. In fact, Bobby Fitzgerald had already fingered Santo for his involvement in the Norfolk County Trust heist. The feds had been to see him about a possible deal, but Santo, a stand-up guy by nature, refused to tell them anything. Jimmy Stokes, on the other hand, wouldn't shut up.

In February 1978 Doreen Weeks went to the Boston FBI offices on Stokes's behalf. In the first of several conversations she would have with federal agents over the course of the next year and a half, Weeks offered Stokes's full cooperation in the Brown shooting and the Norfolk Trust case in return for a commutation of Stokes's life sentence.

To sweeten the pot, Weeks offered her own testimony as well. She told the agents I had used the Quincy apartment she shared with Tommy Maher to store large quantities of cocaine and heroin for distribution to Walpole inmates. She also claimed that I had "hot-shotted" my friend Ozzy DePriest, deliberately and maliciously injecting him with an overdose of heroin, then stabbing him to death in Weeks's bed while she watched. In addition, she accused me of having set fire to John Stokes's girlfriend and two-year-old child, killing them both. These were acts of pure evil. I had never been accused of anything like this before—and it was stupid of her to have made this up now. All these supposed murder victims were alive and well.

But worse than her accusations against me were those she made against Martha Ferrante. In her interviews with federal agents Doreen Weeks claimed that Martha had driven a getaway car during the Norfolk Trust robbery and that Martha and I had stopped by the Quincy apartment afterward to brag about our haul.

Thirty years after the fact, it's still a mystery to me why Weeks told investigators what she did. The Norfolk County Trust charges—of which I was, in fact, guilty—had the potential to send me away for a long time. There was no need for Weeks to lie. Not only were her claims outlandish, but most were easily disproved.

No doubt much of the insanity surrounding Weeks's testimony can be attributed to her state of mind at the time. Transcripts of her conversations with authorities show a woman who was often incoherent and almost certainly suffering from the effects of heavy drug use. In a brief October 1978 conversation with ATF agents, the record lists Weeks's answer as "unintelligible" some twenty times. At one point the interviewer remarks on the fact that Weeks is shaking uncontrollably.

Throughout 1978 and early 1979 Weeks pleaded her case, and that of Jimmy Stokes, to anyone who would listen. At the October meeting she told ATF agents, "You know, you could have murders, robberies, guns, anything you—you know." Then, bringing Santo into the mix, she added, "Joe will testify. But I'm gonna tell you right now that [he's] gonna ask for something in return."

That fall she visited Joe Santo at the Norfolk prison and told him she and Stokes were working out a deal with authorities to implicate me in the Brown shooting and the bank robbery. She wanted Santo's help. Again he refused to get involved. Undaunted, Weeks went to the Walpole police, trying to convince them of her version of events, hoping they could help her secure Stokes's release.

By the end of 1978 her efforts began to pay off. Though no one was willing to offer Stokes a deal, the feds suggested that Weeks might be eligible for the witness protection program. The offer of a new life no doubt sounded like a good deal to Weeks, who had made such a mess of her current one.

In the early spring of 1979 the FBI and federal prosecutors put all their energy into winning an indictment against me in the Norfolk County Trust case. At the end of March Doreen Weeks, their star witness, made her first appearance before the federal grand jury. Among those whom she claimed had played a direct role in the bank robbery were Joe Santo, Jimmy Stokes, Martha Ferrante, Al Dotoli, Tommy Maher, and me. She also implicated Barbara Drew, the teller who'd helped us plan the heist. Weeks testified that I had come to her apartment on the morning of the robbery asking to borrow her car, and that Martha and I had returned together immediately following the heist to show off our haul. Weeks's description of this incident was especially colorful: she told the grand jury that we'd had the bank bags in my car with us and that Martha was gleefully throwing the money up into the air. Additionally, she told the jurors that I'd been to visit her on several occasions since my release from Walpole and that I had threatened her with physical violence.

Weeks's testimony alone was not enough for an indictment against me in the case, but it helped federal prosecutors to get the ball rolling. As a reward for her cooperation, she was given a new name and a place in the Federal Witness Protection Program. Over the course of the next year she would also go on to receive over $16,000 in cash and benefits from the government.

While the feds were busy cozying up to Doreen Weeks, Ralph Petrozziello and I were focused on coming up with a plan to spring Tommy Sperrazza from Walpole. Tommy's original idea, that we break him out while he was in transit, was a good one. In fact, it was the only feasible plan. Even I knew better than to waltz into Walpole with an armed crew. The only problem was waiting for an opportunity to arise. It wasn't like Walpole was giving daily joyrides to inmates. When the three of us had discussed the idea on the inside, we'd agreed to try to grab Sperrazza during his upcoming bank robbery trial. But after nearly a year and a half of waiting, Tommy was getting impatient.

In early June of 1979, Ralph got word from Sperrazza that he was planning to speed the process along. Hoping to win a trip to the hospital, Sperrazza had stolen a pair of pliers from the shop and was going to rip one of his teeth out. It was a novel, if somewhat painful, solution to the problem.

In preparation for just such an opportunity, Ralph and I had already recruited a crew to take part in the breakout. Several days before the planned dental work, we gathered everyone together at Ralph's car wash to go over the details of the breakout. Ralph's brother Sal was there, along with a couple of relative newcomers to the crew: a kid named Billy Oikle, with whom I'd become tight during my stay at Walpole, and another kid named Mikey Donahue, who was a friend of Billy Oikle's.

At that time, anyone at Walpole in need of serious medical treatment was taken to Lemuel Shattuck Hospital in Jamaica Plain, where they had a special ward for state inmates. It was a half-hour drive from the prison to the hospital, straight up Route 1 through Norwood and Dedham. We couldn't have asked for a better setting. The busy highway provided numerous locations in which we could conceal ourselves. Ralph and I had already decided that the majority of the crew would wait in the parking lot of J. C. Hillary's, a popular restaurant in Dedham. A spotter on a motorcycle would park a mile or so south along Route 1 to watch for the transport car. This was before the days of cell phones, so someone would also have to wait at the pay phone at Hillary's for the spotter's call to come through. I appointed Mikey Donahue to this position.

We'd need three vehicles for the actual grab: one to pull up in front of the prison car and cut it off, one to trap the car from behind, and a third to pull up beside the car and take Sperrazza. As usual, Ralph graciously volunteered to provide the vehicles for the job. At the time, the Crown Victoria was our car of choice for most operations. Their V-8 engines gave them plenty of power and a fair amount of speed, making them ideal pursuit vehicles. For this same reason, they were being widely used by law enforcement. With this is mind, Ralph had managed to score a number of blue dash lights. In a pinch, we could slap these in place and pretend to be cops.

On the morning of June 13 Ralph called to tell me that he'd just gotten word from Walpole: if everything went as planned Sperrazza would be heading to Shattuck early that afternoon. Ralph and I quickly spread the news to the rest of our crew. By lunchtime we began to assemble in the J. C. Hillary's parking lot. Ralph and I arrived first, in our stolen Crown Vic, and parked next to the highway, facing traffic. Sal and Mikey Donahue pulled in not long after us.

"Where the fuck is Oikle?" Ralph wondered when Billy Oikle failed to show right away.

"He'll be here," I assured him. "He flew up from Miami last night on the champagne flight."

"He better be," Ralph remarked. "He's in charge of the weapons, isn't he?"

I nodded. We were all carrying our own pieces, but I'd asked Oikle to bring some extra firepower.

We both watched Mikey Donahue get out of the car he was sitting in and make his way toward the pay phone outside J. C. Hillary's. Moments later, Billy Oikle arrived. He parked at the far end of the parking lot and climbed out of his car, holding a large paper grocery bag, then started in Mikey's direction.

"See?" I said to Ralph. "I told you he'd show. And he's got the guns too."

"Where the fuck does he think he is?" Ralph quipped. "Palm Beach?"

Oikle, who evidently hadn't had a chance to change since he'd gotten off the plane, was wearing a bright shirt, a tropical-weight suit, and white loafers. He looked jarringly out of place among the Dedham lunch crowd.

"Hold up," Ralph said suddenly. "Who the hell is that?"

"What do you mean?" I asked, watching Mikey Donahue move away from the pay phone to meet Oikle. "It's Mikey."

"No," Ralph insisted. "In the Rambler!"

I followed his gaze to a beat-up '62 Rambler that had just pulled off Route 1 and was driving slowly in Oikle's direction. Through the windshield I could see two blond surfer types in the front seat.

"It's a fucking holdup!" Ralph said, moving to get out of the car.

It wasn't an entirely illogical conclusion—Oikle had a thriving drug business at the time, making him an excellent target—but I was pretty sure Ralph had it wrong. The two guys in the car looked more like federal agents to me, DEA or ATF. If this was the case, there was nothing we could do but watch the situation unfold and hope Oikle didn't give us away. "They're feds," I warned Ralph, putting my hand on his arm to stop him.

Hearing the car behind him, Billy Oikle glanced over his shoulder. It took him about five seconds to assess the situation and come to the same conclusion we'd reached: something was seriously wrong. Thinking on his feet, he handed Mikey the paper bag and shoved him toward the restaurant. Then he picked up his pace, walking quickly in our direction.

Suddenly the Rambler pulled to a stop. The guy in the passenger seat jumped out, running after Oikle, while the driver swerved forward, trying to cut Billy off. Realizing he was leading the pair directly to us, Oikle changed course, sprinting for an embankment on the far side of the parking lot with Blondie hot on his heels. As they neared the embankment I saw Oikle reach into his pocket and pull out something—a gun, I thought—and toss it into the bushes. The action gave his pursuer a split-second advantage. It was all the man needed. He reached out and clocked Oikle with his pistol.

Billy went down hard, but despite having been hit in the head, he had the presence of mind to put on a show. "Help!" he yelled as the man tackled him. "I'm being robbed! Somebody help!"

The Rambler skidded to a stop and the driver leaped out, brandishing handcuffs.

By now, Billy's protests had succeeded in attracting attention to his cause. Most of the customers inside J. C. Hillary's had lost interest in their lunch and were watching the scene in the parking lot. A small group of men had gathered outside the front door. Initially, they'd appeared ready to help Billy, but now they just looked confused.

I turned to Ralph. "Let's get out of here." I hated to leave my friend like that, but by now it was clear that I'd been correct in my assessment of the situation. The two guys in the Rambler were obviously cops of some kind. There was no way we could go through with our plan to grab Sperrazza now.

Ralph cautiously pulled forward and out of the lot. "What the fuck just happened?" he asked as we started down Route 1.

I glanced in the mirror to make sure no one was following us and saw two Dedham police cruisers pulling into the parking lot. "I honestly have no idea."

"You think someone dropped a dime on us?"

"Maybe," I said. "You tell anyone about Sperrazza?"

Ralph shook his head.

"Could be they were just looking for Oikle," I said. I truly hoped this was the case, but I had a bad feeling in my gut.

At the end of the summer, Sperrazza finally went to trial on the bank robbery charges, giving us the opportunity we'd been waiting for since the aborted breakout attempt in Dedham. Determined to succeed this time, we were meticulous in our preparations. I spent several weeks casing the courthouse in Lawrence where the trial was to take place, coming up with what I hoped would be a foolproof plan for springing Sperrazza.

As in Dedham, we planned to use three stolen cars from Ralph's stable to surround the transport vehicle, which at the time was usually a simple station wagon manned by two armed prison guards. As before, there would be a spotter situated somewhere along the route to alert us to the arrival of the car. With the exception of Billy Oikle, who'd been sent back to Walpole on a parole violation after his arrest at J. C. Hillary's, everyone from the Dedham attempt had signed on for the Lawrence job. Billy Irish had agreed to fill in for Oikle. Billy Hogan had volunteered to be the spotter. His position was close enough to the courthouse that we could all use walkie-talkies to communicate.

If anything, the Lawrence grab was shaping up to be easier than the Dedham attempt. After surveilling the courthouse, I'd come to the conclusion that the best course of action would be to surround the transport vehicle when it pulled up to the side door to deliver Sperrazza. There were never extra guards at the entrance, and I figured taking Sperrazza then would be far less dangerous than trying to force the moving transport vehicle off the road.

Early on the morning of Sperrazza's first scheduled court appearance, Ralph, Sal, Mikey, Billy Irish, Billy Hogan, and I met at Ralph's car wash. The day before had been unusually hot and humid, and the forecast called for more of the same. The air was saturated, the city shrouded in a sticky soup of garbage stink and diesel fumes. Even with the windows wide open, the air in the small car wash office was stifling. As was their habit, Ralph and Sal had started an informal game of gin to pass the time. The slap of their cards provided a soothing soundtrack to our last-minute preparations. Billy Irish, who was in charge of communications, handed out walkie-talkies to everyone.

Just before dawn I gathered the crew together to go over everyone's roles one last time and divvy up the three vehicles Ralph had supplied. "You're in the lead in the Impala," I told Billy Irish as I handed out black ski masks. "Mikey, you take the Lincoln. You'll be bringing up the rear. Sal, Ralph and I will be riding with you in the middle in the Crown Vic. We'll grab Sperrazza. Hogan, you take the bike. Everyone have a weapon?"

There was a collective nod; a few of the guys flashed their pistols.

"Good," I said, "Ralph and I will have the heavy ordnance." I'd brought a tommy gun for myself and an M-2 carbine rifle for Ralph. Both were already in the Crown Vic.

"Everyone feeling sharp?" I asked. Normally, I didn't like to interfere with what the guys on my crew did during their off time, but I was a stickler about sobriety on the job. I always made it clear that I expected everyone to lay off their juice of choice before any big hit.

Once again, all heads nodded.

"Okay," I announced. "Let's rock and roll."

It was light by the time we finally set out from Brockton, the day already coming to a boil. It took us a good forty-five minutes to reach Lawrence. As we got off the highway I glanced back and saw Billy Hogan veer out of sight, swinging his motorcycle into position beside the off-ramp.

The rest of us continued north, up Route 28 and across the Merrimack River, into the hulking shadows of Lawrence's failed textile mills. The courthouse itself, a modest brick building, was located just off the town common, sandwiched between two one-way streets, eastbound Common and westbound Essex. Having watched similar transports come and go, I knew the car carrying Sperrazza would come in on Common, turn south down a side alley, and park there to let him off. We would swoop in on the transport there, then hightail it back across the river.

We were all in line as we turned onto Common Street. Billy Irish, in the lead, pulled his Impala into a free spot just in front of the entrance to the alley. Sal was about to pull the Crown Vic over when I glanced up toward the roof of the courthouse and saw something move. "Keep going!" I told him, then turned to Ralph. "Look up on the roof."

Ralph peered out the window as we cruised past the courthouse. "You seeing things again?" he jibed. Then, suddenly, his expression grew serious. "Jesus," he muttered, seeing what I had seen. "It's a fucking sniper."

"Swing around the park," I told Sal.

We cruised north, then back along the far side of the town common. The northern side of the park afforded us a slightly better view. I could now see at least a dozen figures lining the rooftop, each accented by the slender silhouette of a rifle. "Radio Billy," I told Ralph. "Tell him to get the fuck out of there." I picked up my own walkie-talkie to call Mikey and heard the crackle of Billy Hogan's voice.

"Something's wrong, Myles," Hogan reported.

"What do you see?" I called back to him.

"There's a fucking caravan out here. They've got Sperrazza in an armored car with cruisers on all sides."

"Okay," I told him. "Get out of there now. Everyone, get the fuck out of here. Now!"

Sal gunned the engine, heading back to Route 28, turning south toward the river. As we started across the bridge, Ralph suddenly pointed out the front window. "There they are!"

I looked up to see a line of a vehicles coming toward us. At first glance, it looked like a cop's funeral. There were at least a dozen cruisers, all with their roof lights on. In the middle of the pack was an armored van.

There was no turning around, I thought, clutching the tommy gun, preparing to defend myself. Our best hope was to stay cool and drive right past the caravan.

"What do I do?" Sal asked.

"Keep going," I told him evenly.

As the first cruiser sped past us on its way into Lawrence, I peered through the window and was relieved to see the driver paying us no attention, his stare fixed resolutely on the road ahead. The second cruiser whipped by in similar fashion, followed by the third. Then, suddenly, the van loomed toward us.

As we passed on the bridge, I glanced over at the van, trying to see through the narrow slit windows in the back. Raising myself up in my seat, I caught a glimpse of Sperrazza. His wan face had a greenish cast to it. His dark eyes were hollow and haunted. He looked up, and for a split second our eyes met. I nodded at him, wanting him to know we were there, that we'd given it our best shot.

Given the circumstances, I wasn't expecting a pageant wave. Still, I was taken aback by Sperrazza's reaction. The look on his face when he saw me was of utter hostility. It was almost as if he knew what I had planned for him.

"Someone dropped a dime on us," I said to Sal and Ralph as Sperrazza disappeared from view. There could be no doubt this time that someone had notified the authorities about the breakout.

"Don't look at me," Ralph said. "The only person I told was Deborah."

"Sperrazza's wife? Are you fucking crazy?"

"What?" Ralph asked defensively. "She's not gonna say anything."

"Everybody knows she's banging that drug dealer over in Dorchester," I told him, certain now that Deborah had ratted us out. "Sperrazza would kill them both if he found out. The last thing she wants is for us to spring him."

"Don't worry," Ralph said, looking pleased with himself for having anticipated this. "I told her you were gonna whack him."

My gut dropped. Yes, I thought, recalling the look Sperrazza had just flashed me. He knew. What I couldn't understand was why Deborah would have told him about my intentions in the first place. Unfortunately, her reasons would soon become clear.

. . .

Earlier that summer, while the FBI and federal prosecutors were making their case against me in the Norfolk County trust robbery, Suffolk County authorities had kicked their investigation of the Brown shooting into high gear. By then, Fitzgerald had readily confessed to disposing of the rifle used in the shooting. He'd also fingered Tommy Sperrazza, Ralph Petrozziello, and a man named Paul Cook as the three individuals who'd pulled off the Purity Supreme holdup. Cook was a friend of Sperrazza's from Walpole. Big and slow-moving, with a Kewpie doll's head and the body of the Pillsbury Doughboy, Cook was known on the inside for being a mindless killer. I personally knew of at least three murders he'd committed at Walpole.

On August 29 Suffolk County ADA Phil Beauchesne and a detective from the Boston Police Department had met with Cook at the Howard Johnson's in Braintree. Their offer was simple: *Turn on your associates and we will drop all charges against you in the Purity Supreme case.* Even someone as stupid as Cook could see that it was a good deal. He agreed to testify against Sperrazza and Petrozziello. No mention was made of me at the August meeting.

But Fitzgerald was more than willing to connect me to the shooting. He had also implicated Sperrazza's wife, mother-in-law, sister-in-law, and niece with being accessories after the fact, saying Sperrazza had discussed the holdup—including the shooting of Brown—with the four women just hours after it went down, and that they had all agreed to keep their mouths shut. Seeing an opportunity to put the squeeze on Sperrazza through his family, the Suffolk County DA quickly moved to bring charges against the women. Prosecutors then told Deborah that she could avoid prosecution by getting Sperrazza to cooperate and testify against me. The strategy would soon have its desired effect.

Just days before the Lawrence breakout attempt, Deborah Sperrazza had visited Tommy in Walpole. Repeating exactly what had been told to her by the Suffolk County DA and the FBI, she pleaded with Sperrazza to implicate me in the Brown shooting. If he didn't, she warned, she and her mother would both face charges and their baby daughter would be taken into state custody.

To his credit, Sperrazza initially refused, saying Ralph and I were working on breaking him out.

That was when Deborah had repeated what Ralph Petrozziello told her. "Myles is going to kill you the first chance he gets," she'd warned her husband.

Not long after, Sperrazza flipped, telling Suffolk County authorities exactly what they wanted to hear: that I'd planned the Purity Supreme holdup and supplied the gun that had killed Donald Brown.

At the end of August, following the failed breakout attempt in Lawrence, I was picked up on a parole detainer, charged with associating with known felons, and taken first to the Charles Street Jail and then back to Walpole.

In October Bobby Fitzgerald appeared before the federal grand jury in the Norfolk County Trust case. Although less dramatic than Weeks's testimony, his version of events was, for the most part, accurate. He claimed to have been present when Joe Santo, Ozzy DePriest, and I first discussed robbing the Norfolk County Trust, and told jurors that I had given him the bank bags the two boys had later discovered in the cemetery, along with a portion of the proceeds from the robbery. Like Weeks, he fingered Barbara Drew as our accomplice.

Days after Fitzgerald's grand jury appearance, FBI agents John Clougherty and John Connolly visited Tommy Sperrazza at Walpole. Making it clear to him that they had influence over his wife's position in the Brown case, they also offered to have him transferred from Walpole's notorious Block Ten and into protective custody in a more comfortable federal facility in return for his testimony in the Norfolk County Trust case. Sperrazza readily agreed.

Less than three weeks later he made good on his end of the bargain, testifying that Joe Santo, Johnny Stokes, and I had been the main players in the bank heist. To be fair, Sperrazza's testimony was the most accurate of the three. But he failed to mention one important fact: that he himself had been inside the bank that morning. Instead, he told the jurors he had declined to participate in the robbery.

In spite of this grave omission, Sperrazza's testimony was enough to convince the grand jury that I had most likely been involved in the Norfolk County Trust heist. On November 20, 1979, they handed down their indictment in the case. Days later, Sperrazza made good on his promise to Deborah and the Suffolk County prosecutor, testifying before the grand jury in the Purity Supreme case. The next week I was indicted, along with Ralph Petrozziello, for armed robbery and the murder of Donald Brown.

Connolly and his colleagues in the Boston FBI office had finally struck back at me for cutting them out of the return of the Rembrandt. With the help of Doreen Weeks, they would soon get yet another shot at revenge.

In early 1980, while I was awaiting trial in the Norfolk County Trust robbery and the Brown shooting, Norfolk County authorities began investigating Doreen Weeks's sister, whom they suspected of forging prescription drug slips and of being involved in an extensive fraud scheme involving American Express traveler's checks. Not surprisingly, their inquiry led them to Doreen, who, police discovered, was mailing her sister the prescription slips as well as the traveler's checks. By the time the Norfolk County DA's office finally had enough evidence to charge the two women, the sisters had netted more than $22,000 in the check fraud scheme.

Weeks immediately turned to her friends at the Boston FBI office for protection. The FBI and federal prosecutor, who were not on friendly terms with the Norfolk County DA's office to begin with, were outraged. They viewed the charges against Doreen Weeks as a blatant slap in the face, an attempt by District Attorney Delahunt, who had had an amicable relationship with me in the past, to discredit their star witness in the federal case against me.

A storm was brewing, and I was at the center of it.

Weeks, no idiot, recognized an opportunity to take advantage of the chilly relations between the FBI and Delahunt's office. Recalling her initial visit to Delahunt's office after the discovery of the bodies of Susan Webster and Karen Spinney, Weeks related Delahunt's reluctance to make a deal with her to federal agents, reminding them of my prior relationship with the prosecutor.

At the mention of the Spinney-Webster case, the agents snapped to attention. That I'd had something, anything, to do with the murders was music to the men's ears. Weeks, apparently aware of this and of what it could buy her, was more than happy to oblige. After months of fingering me for the Norfolk County Trust robbery, Weeks suddenly expanded her story, telling investigators that I had also been in her apartment the night Spinney and Webster were killed and that I had personally overseen the murders.

It was a horrible, vicious lie, but it quickly took on a life of its own.

That I had been involved in the Spinney-Webster killings was exactly the kind of thing John Connolly, John Clougherty, and the other agents at the Boston FBI office had been waiting to hear. But despite their glee at the thought of putting me away for the murders, their capacity to do so was severely limited by the fact that they lacked jurisdiction in the case.

The crimes had occurred in Norfolk County, Delahunt's territory. The Norfolk County DA had already successfully prosecuted Sperrazza for the killings and officially closed the case. But the feds weren't going to let that stop them. To the contrary, they immediately recognized an opportunity to even the score with Delahunt while at the same time indicting me for the murders.

Based on Doreen Weeks's account of her original meeting with Delahunt and her claim that he had willfully disregarded her offer to give him information in the original Spinney-Webster case, the federal prosecutor, U.S. attorney Edward Harrington Jr., citing prosecutorial misconduct by Delahunt, announced that he was reopening the case. Because of the complicated question of jurisdiction and the miscon- duct claim, it was necessary to appoint a special prosecutor. The job of doing so fell, conveniently, to Harrington's friend, Massachusetts Attor- ney General Francis Bellotti, who turned to *his* friend, Suffolk County Assistant District Attorney Paul Buckley.

The appointment of Buckley to the role of special assistant attor- ney general was a brilliant and carefully conceived move. By linking the Suffolk County DA's office to the Spinney-Webster case, federal pros- ecutors were able to buy themselves a new and all-important witness: Tommy Sperrazza. Using the indictments against Sperrazza's family in the Brown case as leverage, Suffolk County authorities approached Sperrazza with yet another deal. In return for his testimony against me in both the Brown shooting and the Spinney-Webster case, the Suffolk County DA would recommend non-incarcerated sentences for his wife and mother-in-law, while the feds would guarantee the two women slots in the witness protection program.

Suddenly, Sperrazza's memories of the night of the double mur- ders changed drastically to coincide with Doreen Weeks's most recent version of events. Not only had I instructed him and John Stokes to kill the women, Sperrazza now claimed, but I had helped him bury the bodies as well.

In February 1980, the Spinney-Webster case was officially re- opened and a grand jury empaneled. Four months later, on June 26, I was indicted for the kidnapping and murder of Karen Spinney and Susan Webster, and for being an accessory after the fact to the murder of Cirvinale and the shooting of DiVingo.

Neither of the two previous indictments, in the Norfolk County Trust robbery and the Brown shooting, had come as a surprise. I was guilty of the bank robbery, after all. That the feds would eventually make a case against me was not unexpected. Likewise, the Purity Supreme case had also taken on an air of inevitability. Phil Beauchesne had been trying to pin the Brown shooting on me for years.

But the Spinney-Webster charges took me completely off guard. That I would have been involved with such a hideous crime was utterly unthinkable to me. I felt the same anger and crushing despair I'd experienced all those years earlier at the Charles Street Jail when I'd first found out about the rape accusations. Only this time, understanding the system as I did, my expectations were far less hopeful.

Things, I feared, were about to get very dark.

Twenty-Five

Because Marty Leppo represented Tommy Sperrazza and others who were going to testify as witnesses against me, he could no longer act as my attorney. Fortunately, it wasn't difficult for me to find someone else to represent me. Because of my notoriety in the Boston area, there was a media frenzy surrounding the upcoming trials. The only thing lawyers like more than money is free publicity. As a result, nearly every criminal attorney in the city was vying for the job.

My new attorney was a man named Earle Cooley. Cooley, who at the time worked for the highly respected Boston law firm of Hale and Dorr, was a brilliant criminal lawyer. His gravelly voice, no-bullshit attitude, and fringe of red hair endeared him to me immediately.

From the beginning Cooley was optimistic about my prospects for acquittals in all three trials. He had good reason to be confident. None of the witnesses against me was exactly a stand-up citizen. In order to convict me, a jury would have to believe the testimony of Tommy Sperrazza, a confessed multiple murderer, and Doreen Weeks, a thief. Still, I knew enough to prepare myself for the worst.

Not long after the indictments were handed down the trial dates for all three cases were announced. The Norfolk County Trust case was to be the first one tried, beginning in May 1980. I was relieved by this decision, as it was the one case I was most concerned about losing. At least I knew it would be over and done with quickly.

But as Cooley and I set about preparing my defense, we were confronted by an unexpected hurdle. At five-thirty in the morning on March 6 I was rousted from my cell at Walpole and whisked onto a waiting Con Air flight. I wasn't even given an opportunity to call my lawyer.

The federal agents accompanying me told me that I had been identified as the head of an inmate execution squad and that, as a result, I was being transferred to the federal prison at Marion, Illinois. This was one of the most ridiculous statements I'd ever heard. Moving prisoners around to keep them from interacting with their lawyers is a common dirty trick employed by prosecutors. I figured this was the real reason behind my transfer to Marion. But I soon realized that splitting me up from my attorney was only one of the motivating factors behind the move.

Days after my arrival at Marion, the prison library received several copies of the *Boston Globe* containing articles that claimed not only that I was involved with the execution squad but also that I had been working as an informant. The source of this information, the *Globe* claimed, was someone in the Boston FBI office. My old friends John Connolly and John Clougherty, no doubt.

My execution could not have been more certain had I been sentenced to death row. At the time the Marion facility had a reputation for being the one of the most violent prisons in the country. Informers were not tolerated. Fortunately, my fellow prisoners were not as gullible as the people who'd arranged for my transfer had taken them to be.

That night, the inmates held a prisonwide meeting in the cafeteria. I was relieved to learn that the prevailing sentiment was almost entirely in my favor.

"Do they think we're stupid?" the head of the inmate council said after opening the meeting.

An old-timer spoke up, echoing the first man's assessment of the situation. "It's the first time in twenty years I've seen the *Boston Globe* in the library."

Within minutes, the matter was settled, and everyone concurred that I was not the informer I'd been painted as.

While I was sweating it out in Marion, Earle Cooley was fighting to have me brought back to Massachusetts. Days after my transfer a federal judge ordered my immediate return, but the government continued to drag its feet. Finally, disgusted by the delay, the judge threatened to drop all charges against me if I wasn't brought back. After several days of wrangling, and with the very real possibility of a dismissal hanging over their heads, the feds reluctantly agreed to have me transferred to the state prison in Concord, New Hampshire.

It was far from a total victory for me, but at least I would be back in New England.

On May 19, 1980, the Norfolk County Trust case finally went to trial.

There have been few experiences in my life more devastating than walking into that courtroom and seeing Martha Ferrante at the defense table. There was no getting around the uncomfortable fact that she was there because of her relationship with me.

"I'm sorry," I whispered, leaning over to speak to her as I took my seat.

Martha shook her head. "It's not your fault," she said.

There's not much you can do in a situation like that except remain true to yourself and those you love. To her credit, Martha's allegiances never once wavered. She had good reason to be scared: a guilty verdict would have meant upward of ten years in federal prison for her. But if she was afraid, she never once let it show. She remained utterly calm and composed throughout the trial, even when Weeks herself was on the stand, repeating the outrageous lies she'd told FBI agents about Martha's participation in the heist.

In his opening statement Earle Cooley told jurors that the government's case was based on "a collection of murderers and other felons who have come in to lie to benefit themselves." In addition to Doreen Weeks, the felons Cooley referred to were Tommy Sperrazza, Bobby Fitzgerald, and Jimmy Stokes.

Sperrazza was the first of the bunch to testify. Still holding fast to his claim that he had refused to participate in the robbery, Sperrazza told jurors he had overheard me planning the crime on several different occasions. He also testified to Barbara Drew's involvement in the crime.

But Sperrazza wasn't exactly a stellar witness for the prosecution. By that time he was serving three life sentences, for the murders of Spinney, Webster, and Cirvinale. He had also confessed to shooting Donald Brown and to the prison murder of Johnny Stokes. Cooley was quick to point out Sperrazza's long criminal history to the jury, along with the benefits Sperrazza stood to reap in exchange for his testimony.

Fitzgerald appeared after Sperrazza, once again repeating his claim that I had given him the bank bags to hold. As with Sperrazza, Cooley immediately attacked the man's credibility.

Jimmy Stokes, who testified after Fitzgerald and who was still hoping to cut some kind of deal for himself, told the most bizarre story of all. Incredibly, he claimed that shortly after the robbery Joe Santo and I had driven up to Concord Reformatory, where Stokes was an inmate at the time, and thrown $1,700 in cash over the prison wall to him.

The story was ridiculous in every way. Why anyone in their right mind would throw that much money into a prison was inconceivable. Stokes's claim that it was to buy drugs and jewelry clearly did not go over well with jurors. From my seat at the defense table I could see the skepticism on their faces as they listened to Stokes's testimony. That he was a convicted murderer only added to their doubt.

The last of the four to testify was Doreen Weeks. She was also the only witness to link Martha Ferrante to the crime. Once again, she repeated her story of having seen Martha with me on the morning of the heist. Her tale, which as usual included the account of Martha throwing the stolen money around, was almost as unbelievable as Stokes's had been.

Martha herself took the stand to refute Weeks's testimony, saying she had been at her parents' house in Northampton with her then-boyfriend on the morning of the robbery. Her boyfriend confirmed the story, telling jurors Martha had been with him at the time the crime was committed.

By the time the trial was over, the case seemed like a slam dunk in our favor. Even so, I couldn't allow myself to hope for an acquittal until the jury finally returned their verdict. They did so on June 22, finding all three of us innocent of the charges against us. As pleased as I was to have been acquitted of the robbery, my real relief was in knowing that Martha would not be doing time for a crime I had committed.

Though Earle Cooley deserved much of the credit for winning the case, there was one other person without whom an acquittal almost certainly would not have been possible for any of us: Barbara Drew. In interview after grueling interview with federal investigators, the teller never once admitted to having been involved in the robbery. I had known from the beginning that Drew had ice in her veins. But even I could not have imagined just how cool she really was. So consistent was her story, so fervent her denials of having been a part of the holdup, that the federal prosecutor never even considered charging her as an accessory. She played no small role in discrediting both Tommy Sperrazza and Doreen Weeks.

But of all the parties involved, I think it's safe to say that the federal prosecutor bears the most responsibility for the acquittal. Had he not overreached by bringing charges against Martha, he might very well have won his case. After all, Santo and I were both guilty.

With the not-guilty decision in the bank robbery case, I naively thought the worst of my troubles were behind me.

Immediately after the verdict was announced, a *Boston Globe* reporter approached me in the courtroom.

"This was the only one we were worried about," I told him confidently, after kissing Martha and my mother.

Twenty-Six

On February 1, 1981, jury selection began in the Spinney-Webster murder trial. The proceedings were held at the old Norfolk County Courthouse in Dedham, an impressive nineteenth-century Greek Revival structure designed by renowned Massachusetts architect Solomon Willard.

Aside from its architectural provenance, the Dedham courthouse is perhaps best known for hosting the controversial murder trial of Nicola Sacco and Bartolomeo Vanzetti, two Italian-born immigrants and dedicated anarchists who were tried, convicted, and eventually executed in Dedham in 1927 for the armed robbery and murder of two pay clerks in South Braintree, Massachusetts. At the time, amid allegations of judicial and prosecutorial misconduct and accusations of anti-immigrant, anti-anarchist prejudice on the part of the jury, Sacco and Vanzetti's executions were greeted with violent protests and work stoppages in cities around the world. Significant posttrial evidence including modern ballistic tests, revelations of mishandled evidence, recanted testimony, and a jailhouse confession to the crime suggest that the men were, in fact, railroaded to their deaths.

I was well aware of the history of the Sacco-Vanzetti trial. That my contempt for authority had brought me to the same place as the two anarchists was a coincidence not lost on me as I entered the courthouse on the first morning of the trial. I could only hope the outcome of my trial would be more favorable than that half a century earlier.

Earle Cooley was as meticulous about jury selection as he was about every other aspect of the trial. There was controversy surrounding the selection process even before it began. Rumors of a feud involving Regan, Delahunt, Belotti, and Harrington had been making the rounds of the Boston media since the previous winter. Then, in October, WCVB, one of the local television stations, had aired an investigative news piece titled "Witnesses for Hire." Doreen Weeks and Tommy Sperrazza were both featured prominently in the program, which focused on abuses in the Federal Witness Protection Program.

Paul Buckley, the special prosecutor in the reopened Spinney-Webster case, had fought to have the program kept off the air, arguing that it would make it nearly impossible for him to seat an impartial jury. A judge eventually allowed WCBV to air the program, but only after recommending that the judge in the Spinney-Webster case allow for extra challenges during the jury selection process. Both Buckley and Earle Cooley took full advantage of the allowance, painstakingly vetting each prospective juror. By the time the actual trial began, we had already been in the courtroom for nearly two weeks.

In his opening statement Paul Buckley outlined the state's case against me. The prosecution wasn't even going to attempt to prove that I had wielded the weapons that killed either of the two women. Instead, Buckley contended that I had ordered Sperrazza and Stokes to kill Spinney and Webster, giving the men exact instructions as to how to do so.

The motive Buckley outlined for the jury was shaky at best. After shooting DiVingo and Cirvinale, the prosecutor claimed, Sperrazza and Stokes panicked and brought the two women, both witnesses, to Doreen Weeks and Tommy Maher's apartment in Quincy with the intention of killing them. But when their original attempts to stab the women to death failed to yield the lethal results that had hoped for, Sperrazza called me for advice. Afraid the women would be able to identify my voice, I ordered Stokes and Sperrazza to kill Karen Spinney and Susan Webster by stabbing them both in the head with a screwdriver. I then came to the apartment, helped transport the bodies to Northampton, and oversaw their burial.

The prosecution's theory had several obvious flaws, the most problematic of which was the motive. In order to buy into Buckley's version of events, the jury would have to believe that either Karen Spinney or Susan Webster could have recognized my voice over the telephone receiver. It seemed ridiculous to me, but I'd known jurors to overlook similar improbabilities. It would be my attorney's job to make sure they didn't.

In his initial remarks to the jury Earle Cooley focused on the credibility of the state's main witnesses and the large number of inconsistencies in their various statements about the night of the murder. "This case," Cooley told them, "will hinge on who you believe." After the verdict in the Norfolk County Trust case, I was hopeful the Spinney-Webster jury would follow in the footsteps of their predecessors and choose not to believe Doreen Weeks and Tommy Sperrazza.

One of the first prosecution witnesses to testify was an old friend of mine from Milton named Clifford Kast. Cliffy and I had known each other since the sixth grade. He wasn't the brightest guy, but he was sweet and likable. Like David Houghton, Cliffy was a legitimate working guy and only a peripheral member of my crew. He occasionally did small favors for me or my friends. Often this involved registering a vehicle—most likely a stolen one—in his name.

As it turned out, the 1967 Cadillac Stokes and Sperrazza were driving the night of the of the Spinney-Webster murders was registered and insured in Cliffy Kast's name. Though Cliffy had registered a number of cars for me in the past, the Cadillac was not one of them. In fact, it was Sperrazza who had asked Cliffy to help him with the Caddy. Both Stokes and Sperrazza had accompanied Cliffy to get the car insured. Cliffy had told this to the police when they first questioned him about the vehicle, but it was not what they wanted to hear. By the time Cliffy testified before the grand jury he had changed his story, saying that he had registered the Cadillac at my behest and that I had accompanied him to do so.

That Cliffy had agreed to testify against me came as no surprise. He had always been an easy mark for bullies. Knowing what he'd most likely gone through with investigators, I felt sorry for him more than anything. But it wasn't until he took the witness stand in the Dedham courtroom that I understood exactly what had happened.

As Cliffy settled into the dock on the morning of February 14, Paul Buckley looked on confidently. The prosecutor had no reason to expect any surprises. None of us did. All friendly witness are thoroughly vetted before testifying, and Kast was no exception. He and Buckley would have painstakingly reviewed his testimony the day before.

Buckley waited for Cliffy to finish taking his oath, then rose from his seat and approached the witness stand. "State your full name please," the prosecutor said.

"Clifford T. Kast," Cliffy replied.

"Where do you currently reside, Mr. Kast?" Buckley asked. It was a routine question, as were those to come.

"Emerson Road, Milton," Cliffy answered.

"What is your relationship with the defendant, Myles Connor?" Buckley said, motioning in my direction.

Cliffy swallowed nervously. "Myles is a friend of mine."

"And how long have you known Mr. Connor?"

"A long time. Since we were both twelve years old."

Buckley nodded approvingly, then took a few steps back, like a pitcher preparing his windup. Clearly, all was going as planned. "In February of 1975, did Mr. Connor ask you to register a red 1967 Cadillac in your name as a favor to him?"

Cliffy swallowed hard, then glanced in my direction. He looked scared, really scared, like the kid I'd known in junior high.

"Please answer the question, Mr. Kast," Buckley admonished him.

Cliffy ducked his head slightly, leaning toward the microphone in front of him. "No," he said. His voice was barely audible.

This could not have been the answer Buckley was expecting, and for a moment he appeared not to have heard it. He turned to the jury with a satisfied look on his face. Then, finally understanding what Cliffy had said, he whipped his head around and stared incredulously at the witness stand. "Do you need me to repeat the question, Mr. Kast?" he asked.

Cliffy shook his head vigorously, his act of defiance making him suddenly brave. "No," he said. "I heard you the first time. Myles didn't ask me to register the Cadillac for him. Tommy Sperrazza and John Stokes were there. But not Myles."

I could see Buckley struggling to control himself. "May I remind you of your testimony to the grand jury on this matter?"

"I remember exactly what I told the grand jury: that Myles asked me to register the car. That was what Clougherty told me to say," Cliffy said, referring to John Clougherty, one of the FBI agents who'd investigated the case. "He gave me a form and said, 'Read it, this is what I want you to say,' quote, unquote. He said I'd be charged as an accomplice if I didn't."

Buckley's face was red. "Are you saying you lied to the grand jury?"

Cliffy nodded. "Yes, sir."

Perjury in a capital case is a serious crime. With Cliffy's admission, the judge immediately ordered Kast's testimony stopped so that he could retain a lawyer. He also ordered Cliffy held at the Charles Street Jail pending his reappearance in court. Within minutes, Cliffy was handcuffed and hauled out of the courtroom.

Unfortunately for Cliffy, all of this took place on a Friday, which meant he would be spending the entire weekend behind bars. Two days and three nights in the Charles Street Jail could make even the most hardened criminal do desperate things, and I fully expected Cliffy to change his mind over the weekend. But much to my surprise, he didn't budge.

Buckley was cleary infuriated by Cliffy's change of heart, but there was absolutely nothing he could do about it. Even after repeated badgering by the prosecutor, Cliffy continued to insist that it was Sperrazza, not me, who'd gone with him to register the Cadillac.

During Earle Cooley's cross-examination, Cliffy told jurors that he had been pressured to implicate me by Boston police officers, and later by Suffolk County ADA Philip Beauchesne who, Cliffy claimed, warned him, "If you don't cooperate with us, I have enough evidence to indict you for being an accessory to murder."

Recounting his meeting with the ADA, Cliffy admitted, "It scared the hell out of me."

He also repeated his claim that FBI agent John Clougherty had told him exactly what to say to the grand jury.

As Cliffy left the stand I allowed myself to glance over at the jurors. I wasn't expecting sympathy from them; considering the brutal nature of the murders, sympathy was too much to ask for, especially so early in the trial. But I was looking for something that would give me hope—distaste for Buckley, or at the very least skepticism about his methods. Much to my dismay, I saw neither. It was going to be a long trial, I thought.

N ext on the prosecution's witness list was Doreen Weeks. Weeks gave a wrenching account of seeing Susan Webster and Karen Spinney with Stokes and Sperrazza on the night of the murders. As she and Tommy Maher were leaving their apartment to go to the Beachcomber, Weeks recalled, she met Stokes, Sperrazza, and the two women coming down the stairs to her apartment. The men told Weeks and Maher that they needed to use the apartment for a few hours.

'The girls were handcuffed and they were trying to get away," Weeks testified. "The girl Tommy Sperrazza was with was holding on to the banister, trying to get away from him."

Instead of attempting to help the women, Weeks and Maher continued on their way to the bar. But after spending some time at the Beachcomber, Weeks recalled, she felt sick and wanted to go back to the apartment. She called once, she told the jury, and spoke to Stokes, who told her to call back later. When she called the second time, she claimed, I answered the phone.

"Connor picked up the phone and started arguing with me,"

Weeks testified, "that Tommy Maher was supposed to make the calls every hour to the apartment and I was not to make any."

When she finally returned to the apartment several hours later, she said, there was blood spattered on the walls and on the bathroom sink and mirror, the sheets had been stripped from her bed and the mattress stained with blood, and the telephone was broken and bloody as well.

Weeks's testimony, especially her claim that I had answered the phone at her apartment, was absolutely essential to the prosecution. In his cross-examination Earle Cooley set out to discredit Weeks by pointing out to the jury the many inconsistencies in her interviews with investigators. Key to Cooley's defense strategy were taped recordings of conversations Weeks had with federal agents regarding my involvement in a number of crimes. It was during one of these interviews that Weeks told investigators that she had seen me kill my old friend Ozzy DePriest with an overdose of heroin and that I had set fire to the apartment of John Stokes's girlfriend, killing her and her child. The recordings hurt Doreen Weeks's credibility and made it absolutely clear that the federal agents interviewing Weeks knew full well that all three of my purported victims were alive and well and that Weeks was lying.

"Buckley's going to fight tooth and nail to have those tapes excluded," Earle Cooley warned me.

As Cooley predicted, the prosecutor objected vigorously to the recordings being played for the jury. Incredibly, the presiding judge agreed with him. The tapes, he ruled, would not be allowed into evidence. Additionally, the judge ruled to severely limit my attorney's questioning of Doreen Weeks in regard to the benefits she'd received and the money she'd stolen while in the Federal Witness Protection Program.

The judge's decisions were a huge blow to my defense. But Cooley pressed on as best he could with his strategy of discrediting Doreen Weeks, grilling her on her efforts to win a commutation of her then-boyfriend Jimmy Stokes's life sentence and on the numerous inconsistencies in her interviews with various investigators, including contradictory statements she'd made concerning whom she'd seen bringing the girls into the apartment and what exactly she had told Norfolk County District Attorney Delahunt during their first meeting.

An article in the next morning's *Boston Globe* remarked on Weeks's testimony, saying Cooley "frequently drew the same response, 'I don't remember.'"

Earle Cooley had made his point, but whether Weeks's foggy memory and the inconsistencies in her story were enough to sway the jury in my favor was anyone's guess.

The last of the major prosecution witnesses to testify was Tommy Sperrazza. By then Sperrazza had been convicted of killing both Susan Webster and Karen Spinney, and he freely confessed on the stand to having done so. He had also admitted to the prison murder of John Stokes and to fatally shooting Donald Brown.

As Sperrazza recalled in gruesome detail the events of the night of the murder and the subsequent burial of the women's bodies, the entire courtroom—spectators, jurors, and court officers alike—listened in rapt silence. Many kept their heads down while Sperrazza testified, unable to look at him. Others could not look away.

He spoke calmly and quietly, recounting the shooting outside the Roslindale bar and his subsequent decision to take the two young women to Doreen Weeks's basement apartment. Once there, Sperrazza told jurors, he handcuffed Susan Webster in the bedroom and Karen Spinney in the bathroom. It was at this point, Sperrazza claimed, that he and Stokes then called me for advice. Supposedly afraid the women would recognize my voice, I ordered Stokes and Sperrazza to kill them, telling them that I was on my way to the apartment.

Sperrazza's description of what happened next was chilling:

"We had weapons—guns—which we couldn't use in the apartment," he testified, "so we decided on stabbing them to death. . . . I got a steak knife. . . . Stokes had the screwdriver. I went in the bedroom where Susan Webster was and sat down beside her. She was lying down. . . . I put the pillow over her face and stabbed her repeatedly.

"I walked out of the bedroom. . . . I seen Miss Spinney stumbling from the bathroom to the kitchen–living room area. She was bleeding. She was mumbling. I took Miss Spinney, laid her on the kitchen floor, and stabbed her. Myles," Sperrazza added, "was right there. Then I went in and took Miss Webster off the bed, put her on the kitchen floor, beside Karen. They were both alive. I was instructed how to kill them."

Here he put his hand to his temple, pointing to the spot on his own head where, he claimed, I'd indicated the women should be stabbed. It was a dramatic gesture, especially coming as it did on the heels of such shocking testimony. Not a person in the courtroom could have failed to imagine the impact of the screwdriver on each woman's temple. More than one of the jurors winced. Several glanced in my direction.

Earle Cooley did his best to discredit Sperrazza, questioning him about his cooperation with federal prosecutors, eventually getting Sperrazza to admit that he'd agreed to become a witness in order to keep his wife and mother-in-law from being prosecuted in connection with the Brown murder and that he himself had been transferred to a federal prison and into the witness protection program. Cooley also reminded jurors that Sperrazza had never once mentioned my name during his own murder trial. But Sperrazza had clearly been expecting this question and was quick with a response, claiming he had made a deal to keep my name out of the original trial and that in exchange I had promised to help him escape from prison once I was out on parole.

That I had overseen the burial of the bodies of Susan Webster and Karen Spinney was essential to the prosecution's case against me. Earle Cooley and I both knew that this was also where Buckley had the best chance of winning over the jury. The fact that I had led Delahunt to the grave did not look good for me, especially since I was certain Sperrazza would never admit to the actual deal he and I had made with each other.

But by far the most damning piece of evidence to suggest that I might have had a hand in disposing of the bodies was the entry I'd made in the register book at Shaw's Motel clearly stating my name and my mother's Milton address. The entry and signature, penned in green ink and dated February 22, the night after the Roslindale shooting, provided definitive proof that I had been in Northampton around the time the bodies were buried. Sperrazza even went so far as to say that I had transported the bodies to Northampton and that my mother had come along, not knowing that the dead women were in the trunk of the car she was riding in.

There was one major flaw in Buckley's theory: according to Sperrazza, the actual burial of the bodies had taken place the following night, around midnight on February 23. In fact, my band had backed up James Cotton in front of a full house at the Beachcomber that night. But Sperrazza and Buckley had constructed an answer for this as well. When confronted with my alibi by Earle Cooley, Sperrazza claimed that I had driven to Northampton immediately following my gig to help him and Stokes dispose of the bodies, a trip that at the time took nearly three hours to make.

There's no way the jury'll buy that bullshit," Earle Cooley assured me when the prosecution had rested its case.

Indeed, the number of logical flaws in the prosecution's version of events seemed overwhelming. But I was still worried. I'd been in enough courtrooms to understand the power of emotion in swaying jurors. Few crimes were more emotionally charged than the murders of Karen Spinney and Susan Webster.

Cooley wasn't going to let my pessimism bring him down. A fighter to the core, he wasted no time in attacking the prosecution's case and the testimony of their witnesses. The first person to take the stand in my defense was Joe Santo. Santo recalled Doreen Weeks's visit to the Norfolk Correctional Institution in the summer of 1978 and her attempt to involve him in whatever deal she was making with authorities. Santo also disputed an earlier claim made by Sperrazza that I had borrowed his car in order to transport the bodies of Karen Spinney and Susan Webster to Northampton, saying he had been in Texas at the time, visiting his godchild.

Next to testify on my behalf were Larry Faherty, a sound man and audio engineer at the Beachcomber, and my band manager, Al Dotoli. Both men told the jury that I had been onstage at the club performing with James Cotton on the night Sperrazza claimed to have buried the bodies of Susan Webster and Karen Spinney.

Next, Cooley called on Boston police detective Robert Hudson. Hudson had interviewed both Sperrazza and Weeks regarding my participation in the murders. Under questioning by Cooley the detective recalled that both witnesses had made statements to him that were different from their sworn testimony in the case. According to Hudson, Doreen Weeks had an especially difficult time remembering the events of the night of the murder, making varying claims about who exactly had appeared at her apartment and at what time. Two other Boston detectives, as well as two FBI agents, also testified to inconsistencies in the statements made to them by both Weeks and Sperrazza.

Finally, Earle Cooley called four Walpole inmates, all of whom had spent time with Sperrazza on the prison's Block Ten, to the stand. All four men testified to having discussed the murders of Susan Webster and Karen Spinney with Sperrazza, three of them before the bodies had even been discovered. All testified that although Sperrazza had bragged openly about killing the women, he never once mentioned my name in connection with the murders.

I desperately wanted to take the stand in my own defense; in particular, I was eager to explain to the jury how my name came to be in the register at Shaw's Motel. But Earle Cooley was adamant that I not testify. His opinion was not unprecedented. Defense attorneys often resist putting their clients on the stand, knowing the risks involved in opening them up to cross-examination. In the end, Cooley's arguments won me over and I agreed not to testify.

By the time the seven-week trial concluded, sixty-five witnesses had taken the stand, many of them giving contradictory evidence. It was an incredible amount of information for a jury to absorb.

"It's insane," Earle Cooley told the jury in his final argument. "The logic of the situation, as alleged by the government, has to come right up to you and scream, 'It can't be!'" He urged the panel not to convict me on the word of "a five-time killer who's been paid for his testimony" and that of a "proven liar."

"Myles Connor should not be whipsawed in a vicious, knock-down, dragged-out battle between law enforcement agencies," Cooley concluded.

For his part, Paul Buckley was determined to paint me as a criminal mastermind and skilled manipulator—albeit one who recorded his name in a motel register while on a trip to dispose of two dead bodies.

"Who's the schemer here?" he asked the jury. "Who's the one putting it all together? Myles J. Connor, the leader of the band."

Though I had my suspicions throughout the trial that most of the jurors were not exactly fond of me, my first real confirmation of this fact didn't come until after the trial itself had concluded. On Thursday night, March 19, after thirteen hours of deliberations, one of the jurors, a college student from Quincy named Charles Graham, asked to be excused from the case. Earlier in the proceedings Graham had complained to the judge that his fellow jurors were discussing the case as the evidence was presented, something that is strictly forbidden under the rules of the court. In requesting to be excused, Graham once again stated that this was the case, saying he found it "impossible to work with this jury and that this jury was acting emotionally and not on the basis of reason and was not following the judge's instructions."

Graham's petition was granted and a new juror chosen from among the alternates. At the judge's instruction, the panel began their deliberations anew. Within hours they had reached a unanimous decision.

There is nothing as nerve-wracking as waiting for a jury to return their verdict, especially when you suspect, as I did, that the decision will not be a favorable one. As I waited out the hours in my holding cell on the second floor of the courthouse I thought about the two anarchists, Sacco and Vanzetti, who must have known what awaited them long before the jury returned. At least, I reminded myself, I did not face the noose, as they had—though at the time death seemed in many ways preferable to a guilty verdict.

It was not the idea of spending my life behind bars that terrified me, but the knowledge that, if convicted, I would never be able to overcome the monstrous reputation Paul Buckley had so carefully constructed for me. Everyone, including many of those who loved me, would believe me capable of ordering the violent deaths of two young women, of callously leaving their bodies to rot in an unmarked grave, and of forcing my own mother to ride along with the bloody corpses. These were the thoughts that kept me from sleeping that last night in Dedham.

They were the same thoughts that accompanied me to the courtroom on the morning of March 20, 1981, when the judge finally called us back.

I have little memory of the actual moment when the guilty verdict was announced, but those who were there that day, including the *Boston Globe* reporter who covered the case, noted that I appeared deeply shaken. I do recall the hush that descended over the courtroom when the foreman opened his mouth to speak, and the sound of choked sobs coming from the front row of the spectators' section, where the parents of Karen Spinney were sitting. There is nothing that can mitigate that kind of pain, and I certainly do not begrudge the Spinneys their grief.

Immediately after the verdict was read, the judge sentenced me to life in the state prison for the murder of Susan Webster, announcing that my sentences in the second murder and the kidnappings would be imposed at a later date. With that, I was handcuffed, taken from the courtroom, and driven under heavy guard to Walpole prison.

Twenty-Seven

The Spinney-Webster convictions devastated me. I returned to Walpole in a fog of anger, raging against everyone who'd had a hand in putting me away. I can tell you right now, being pissed off is no way to do time. Prison is full of angry men, each dragged down by the weight of his rage. Those who survive being on the inside with any semblance of their humanity intact are those who learn to let go of the resentments that plague them. I had succeeded in doing this during my previous stays at Walpole, making the best of my situation, focusing on the future. But now with no future to look forward to, I was sick with anger.

Earle Cooley was angry too. He was a man who hated to lose, and the fact that he had underestimated Buckley bothered him immensely. Cooley and I had talked about the possibility of an appeal even before the jury announced their verdict. He had good reason to believe he might eventually win a new trial for me. The dismissal of Charles Graham from the jury was grounds enough for a review of the case by the Massachusetts Supreme Court. The fact that the presiding judge in the trial had limited Cooley's cross-examination of Doreen Weeks was yet another strike in our favor.

But for the time being an appeal in the Spinney-Webster case would have to wait. The Brown shooting was scheduled to go to trial in November, giving Earle Cooley and me just a few months to prepare my defense. The prosecution's claims in the Brown case were no less ridiculous than those made by Paul Buckley in the Spinney-Webster case, but Cooley and I had learned our lessons the first time around and were taking no chances. We both worked doggedly, hunting down friendly witnesses, looking for holes in the prosecution's case. By the time the trial began we were as prepared as we could possibly be.

Considering the fact that Phil Beauchesne had spent nearly six years building a case against me in connection with the Brown shooting, the hand he showed the jury in his opening statement was surprisingly weak. Like Paul Buckley before him, Beauchesne had no intention of trying to prove I had actually committed the murder of which I stood accused.

All three of the state's main witnesses, Tommy Sperrazza, Paul Cook, and Bobby Fitzgerald, readily attested to the fact that I had not been anywhere near the Purity Supreme Supermarket on the night of the holdup. Sperrazza himself admitted to having shot Brown, and Cook to having played the role of bagman. Only Ralph Petrozziello, who had driven the getaway car, had yet to admit to his role in the robbery, and he was on the run, having escaped from prison in Concord several months earlier.

The only charges against me Beauchesne had been able to make stick were those of accessory before the fact to robbery and murder. And in order to gather enough evidence to win an indictment, he'd had to grant full immunity from prosecution to Sperrazza, Cook, and Fitzgerald.

It was an untenable position on the part of the prosecution, to say the least.

Fitzgerald was the first witness to testify. He told the jury that in March 1974 I'd asked him to keep two handguns and a British-made Lee-Enfield .303 rifle, the same gun that was used to kill Paul Brown, at his apartment for me, and that I then returned a week before the Purity Supreme holdup to retrieve the weapons. Fitzgerald also claimed that he had disposed of the Lee-Enfield rifle after the robbery by throwing it into the Cambridge Reservoir.

Cook and Sperrazza reiterated Fitzgerald's testimony, saying I had provided the guns that were used in the holdup. Both men also claimed that I had planned the robbery, giving them specific instructions at a meeting at Ralph Petrozziello's house the night beforehand. According to Sperrazza, I had even gone so far as to tell him that he should be the one to carry the rifle, and had instructed him to shoot the guard who would be accompanying the supermarket manager to make the deposit if he so much as reached for his gun.

In his cross-examinations Earle Cooley skillfully attacked the credibility of all three witnesses, reminding jurors of Bobby Fitzgerald's participation in the witness protection program and of the fact that all of the men—and Sperrazza's family—had been given blanket immunity in exchange for their testimony.

But Cooley didn't stop there. He had a number of witnesses lined up to testify in my defense, including a man named Warren Dougan. Dougan was serving a life sentence in Walpole at the time of the trial. But in the spring of 1974, when the Purity Supreme holdup took place, Dougan had been the leader of a Hyde Park motorcycle club. He was also a major supplier of illegal weapons. Dougan testified to having sold Sperrazza a Lee-Enfield rifle in early May 1974 in exchange for two pounds of Mexican marijuana.

Perhaps the most important defense witness was the Boston cop who'd originally interviewed Sperrazza and Fitzgerald regarding the shooting. Not only had he been a lifelong friend of Brown's, but he had been one of the first cops to arrive at the scene on the night of the shooting and had held the dying Brown in his arms.

I was slightly uneasy when Earle Cooley told me that he would be taking the stand in my defense. Watching the reactions of John Clougherty and John Connolly when Earle Cooley called his witness to the stand, I could tell that FBI men were incredulous. No doubt they assumed the man would turn on me during his testimony. But nothing could have been further from the truth.

"When did you suspect Myles Connor was involved in the Purity Supreme holdup?" Cooley asked the officer.

"Never," he replied.

Out of the corner of my eye, I saw the two G-men flinch.

"Mr. Connor's name didn't come up in a single interview I conducted," the officer elaborated.

Earle Cooley was silent for a moment, letting the jury ponder this information. "Not long after you began your investigation," Earle began at last, "you were taken off the case. Is that correct?"

"Yes."

"Can you tell us why that happened?"

"Sure," the officer replied eagerly. "The DA wanted me to frame Myles. I wouldn't go along with it, so they booted me off the case."

This time, Connolly and Clougherty did more than flinch. When I looked over I could see their mouths hanging open in disbelief.

Without a doubt the most memorable twist in the Brown case took place outside of the courtroom. Because of my reputation the trial was fairly big news in Boston. One afternoon a local AM talk radio host was discussing the trial on his call-in show when he suddenly announced that he had Ralph Petrozziello on the line. Ralph, who was still on the run and very much a wanted man, had called in to defend me. On live radio he announced that he, Cook, and Sperrazza had planned and executed the holdup and that I'd had nothing to do with it.

By the end of the trial I knew my chances for an acquittal were good. Even so, as the jury filed out of the courtroom to begin their deliberations I reminded myself to prepare for the worst. Fortunately, I didn't have long to dwell on my possible fate. After less than an hour and a half of deliberations, the jury announced that they had reached their verdict.

Most people like to believe that a quick verdict bodes well for the defense, as any reasonable juror would want to take his or her time sending even the most obviously guilty man to prison. Having known my share of unreasonable jurors over the years, I wasn't sure what to think. But I needn't have worried. In one of the shortest deliberations in a murder case in Massachusetts history, the jury of eight women and four men had unanimously voted in favor of an acquittal.

When the verdict was read I glanced over at Phil Beauchesne. The prosecutor was slumped in his chair, staring at the jury. He looked like a boxer who'd just taken a knockout punch.

Vindication is a sweet thing, and the memory of Beauchesne's face when the jury foreman announced the not-guilty verdict in the Brown case carried me through many a long night at Walpole. The jury's decision also gave me hope that I might eventually be acquitted of the Spinney-Webster murders as well. With the Brown case behind him, Earle Cooley began working to bring an appeal before the state Supreme Court.

The Spinney-Webster convictions cost me dearly, but they took their heaviest toll on my father, who was unable to come to terms with the fact that his eldest son had been found guilty of such a horrible crime. I can't say he lost his faith in me, but he was a man with a deep and abiding respect for the law, and I'm sure he was torn between his love for me and his trust in the justice system.

Not long after I was sentenced for the murders and returned to Walpole, my father passed away. That he died without seeing me vindicated has been the greatest tragedy of my life.

In the years immediately following the trial I had few visitors at Walpole. My mother, who was in poor health, continued to make the grueling trip on a regular basis, along with my sister, Patsy. I had another regular visitor as well: a young woman named Suzanne King.

Susie and I had been introduced to each other by a mutual friend during my previous parole. An Audrey Hepburn look-alike, Susie had been a huge fan of mine and a Beachcomber regular for some time. Like many of the young women who came to my shows, she had a stagefront crush on me. Susie was still a teenager when we first met, far too young for me to be interested in her romantically. But drawn to each other by our mutual love of animals and by a shared interest in martial arts, we quickly became friends.

Susie adored all creatures, but she especially loved horses. She'd started working at a stable near her house in South Boston in return for riding privileges at the age of eight. By nine she was walking the streets of Southie selling pony rides. Her dream, one I shared with her, was to one day own a small piece of property on which she could keep horses and other animals. Despite the age difference, I eventually found myself falling for her.

After the Spinney-Webster indictments were handed down I fully expected Susie to abandon our friendship. I certainly would not have blamed her for doing so. Yet she was fearless and fiercely loyal, a force to be reckoned with. She eventually became one of my most vocal defenders, showing up in court every day during all three of my trials, often accompanying my mother, to whom she was devoted.

Susie was equally religious about coming to see me in Walpole. She was there six days a week, every week, for five long years. In those days, prison policy was much more lax than it is now. On nice days inmates and visitors were allowed to sit outside together on the prison lawn. We could touch each other, and even hug and kiss. Susie never came to see me empty-handed. Generally, she brought food of some kind or another, sometimes cases of it.

It's difficult to imagine what those years would have been like without Susie. That I survived them with my sanity intact is due in no small part to her love and unwavering support.

Twenty-Eight

In late August 1984 Earle Cooley came to see me in Walpole with good news: the Massachusetts Supreme Court had set aside my convictions in the Spinney-Webster case, citing the dismissal of Charles Graham from the jury and the limitations placed by the presiding judge on my attorney's cross-examination of Doreen Weeks.

Cooley was elated. "We're going to win this one this time around," he assured me. "I promise."

"I'll believe it when I see it," I told him.

With the verdict overturned, my life sentence was vacated as well. In October, pending a new trial, I was released from prison on $25,000 cash bail. There was little time for celebrating. The retrial was scheduled to begin in early February, giving us less than four months to prepare my defense. This time around, Cooley wouldn't be pulling any punches.

Paul Buckley, the special prosecutor assigned to the original case, had been replaced by an assistant United States attorney Paul Healy Jr. The state's case remained unchanged, relying heavily, as it had in the original trial, on the testimonies of Doreen Weeks and Tommy Sperrazza.

On February 3, 1984, the Spinney-Webster retrial got under way. Doreen Weeks was one of the first prosecution witnesses to take the stand. The four years since her last court appearance had not been kind to her. Her skin was ashen, her hair disheveled. She slumped in her chair, struggling to keep her eyes open, while Healy questioned her about the night of the murders. Watching her fight to keep herself together on the stand, I almost felt sorry for her. Almost.

Earle Cooley's brutal cross-examination of her began on February 14. I couldn't have asked for a better Valentine's Day present. Confronted with the recording of her 1979 interview with federal agents, Weeks had no choice but to acknowledge having told them that I had murdered Ozzy DePriest and set fire to the apartment where John Stokes's girlfriend and baby were living. She also admitted to the theft of $22,000 in American Express traveler's checks while in the witness protection program, to having voluntarily lived with John Stokes while he was on the run in 1977, and to later having approached law enforcement officials with the intention of winning Stokes's freedom.

Sperrazza testified after Doreen Weeks, repeating the story he'd told jurors in the original trial. Earle Cooley once again hammered at Sperrazza's credibility, questioning him on the various deals he'd made with state and federal prosecutors. This time around, Cooley also paid close attention to the issue of my motive, grilling Sperrazza on his claim that I had ordered the women killed out of fear that they would recognize my voice, forcing him to acknowledge that I had never actually met either of the victims.

Having learned his lesson the first time around, Earle Cooley was taking nothing for granted in the second trial. Cooley had assembled a huge list of defense witnesses, many of whom testified to the glaring inconsistencies in the various statements Doreen Weeks had made regarding my involvement in the murders. Norfolk County Assistant District Attorney Robert Banks told jurors that it had taken nearly a year of questioning for Weeks to use my name in connection with what had happened in her apartment on the night of the killings. Assistant Massachusetts Attorney General Stephen Delinsky testified that Weeks had admitted lying to him in July 1978 when she told him she had mentioned my involvement in the murders to Bill Delahunt.

Joe Santo again told the jury that Weeks had come to see him at Norfolk prison to ask for his help in implicating me.

"She told me, 'The agents I've been talking to want him bad and they'll do anything to get him,'" Santo testified.

In addition, Cooley produced numerous transcripts of conversations Weeks had had with authorities, all of which were riddled with inconsistencies. In one, a July 1979 interview at Boston police headquarters at which two detectives and the police commissioner were present, Weeks insisted that in the weeks before the murders I was "constantly making up plans for the murder of the girls," an allegation that not only was ridiculous considering the fact that I didn't even know who Karen Spinney or Susan Webster were at the time, but also completely undermined the state's case against me by suggesting that the killings had somehow been premeditated. Another transcript recorded Weeks's response to being informed by federal agents that three of my purported victims, Ozzy DePriest and John Stokes's girlfriend and child, were all alive and well: "That's weird," was all Weeks could think to say.

To refute Sperrazza's claim that I had been with him and Stokes in Northampton on the night the women were buried, Cooley called a number of witnesses, including Al Dotoli, Lenny Baker, blues singer James Cotton, and Beachcomber owner James McGettrick, to testify that I had been onstage at the Beachcomber in Quincy, nearly three hours' drive from the grave site, from 11:45 P.M. on February 23 to 2:00 A.M. on the twenty-fourth. Two employees from Maison Robert, the Boston restaurant where I'd taken my mother to dinner on the night in question, also testified to my whereabouts.

Another witness, Richard Duarte, a librarian and unofficial legal adviser at Walpole prison, testified that Sperrazza had come to him in the days before the bodies of Susan Webster and Karen Spinney were found, seeking advice. Duarte told the jury that Sperrazza, who said he'd been talking to police about the case, had been especially concerned about what would happen to him if he were found out to be lying. "He told me, 'Connor was not there, he had nothing to do with the murders,'" Duarte testified.

One of the final defense witnesses to testify was Ozzy DePriest. Determined to leave no doubt in the jury's mind as to Doreen Weeks's ability to fabricate, Earle Cooley had decided to bring Ozzy into the courtroom to prove the obvious: that I had not murdered him, as Weeks claimed I had. Ozzy, who was working on a lobster boat out of New Bedford at the time, was none too pleased to have been hauled away from his paying job and into court, and he wasn't shy about voicing his feelings on the matter.

In fact, when confronted with the gruesome details of his murder as described by Weeks, he was downright belligerent.

"Is it true," Earle Cooley asked, "that in the winter of 1978 the defendant, Myles Connor, injected you with a fatal dose of heroin while you were in Ms. Weeks's apartment in Quincy?"

Ozzy snorted. "Absolutely not."

"And is it true," my attorney continued, "that he stabbed you and then wrapped your body in a sheet?"

"Of course not!" Ozzy barked. "And I don't appreciate being dragged all the way up here just to state the obvious."

Earle Cooley had convinced me not to take the stand in the first trial, but I was determined to plead my case this time around. It's hard to say how much weight, if any, my testimony carried with the jury. That I was innocent was what they expected me to say, no matter what. But I felt compelled to testify, if only for myself. When I first took the oath I was literally shaking with pent-up frustration. Looking the jury in the eyes and telling them I had had nothing to do with the murders of Karen Spinney and Susan Webster was one of the most emotionally charged moments of my life.

Cooley had warned me that Paul Healy's cross-examination would be grueling, and it was: the prosecutor questioned me for over four hours. But I had waited so long for the opportunity to defend myself that, far from being intimidated, I was relieved to be able to set the record straight, especially where the register book from Shaw's Motel was concerned.

"Do you really think I would have signed my name in bright green ink if I'd known what Stokes and Sperrazza were doing up there?" I countered when Healy asked me about the register.

When he had finished with his interrogation, Healy turned to face me one last time. "Sir, you wouldn't lie to this jury to avoid being convicted of two first-degree murders, would you?"

It was the question I had been hoping he would ask, and I responded forcefully. "Sir, I wouldn't take this oath and lie for anybody."

In his closing argument Earle Cooley once again attacked the logic behind the prosecution's case, saying, "The motive ascribed to Connor is so ridiculous as to require that this whole case be thrown out on that alone."

Paul Healy's assessment of his case was perhaps even less optimistic than that of my attorney. In fact, an observer walking into the courtroom for the first time during closing arguments would have had trouble telling whether Healy was working for the prosecution or the defense. Referring to Tommy Sperrazza, Healy called his star witness "the lowest form of human trash." Refuting the claim that my signature in the motel register indicated that I had not been trying to hide anything, Healy declared, "The burden on the commonwealth is to prove him guilty, not to prove he's smart."

"As nonsensical as it might be," the prosecutor concluded, summing up his case for the jury, "that's the way it happened."

"Not exactly a ringing endorsement for a guilty verdict," my attorney gleefully remarked as Healy made his way back to the defense table.

"No," I commented, scanning the faces of the jurors, trying to read the panel's mood. "But we were surprised once before."

Despite Earle Cooley's repeated assurances, I was not at all confident that the outcome of the second trial would be any different than that of the first. After the jury left the courtroom on March 2 to begin their deliberations, I went back to my mother's house in Milton to do some deliberating of my own.

My mother, who had been suffering from emphysema for some time, had gone into the hospital just a few days earlier, and the place was disconcertingly quiet without her. Her prognosis was not good, and the thought that she might die while I was in prison and that I could be denied the opportunity to say my good-byes to her only added to my fear that I would be convicted once again.

Determined not to leave my fate in the jury's hands, I made up my mind to skip out on my final court appearance. If the jury voted to acquit, I'd be looking at a month or two for bail-jumping charges. On the other hand, if they found me guilty once again, I'd be going back to prison for the rest of my life. It was a gamble I was willing to take.

With my decision made, I drove to the hospital to see my mother. I had never before involved her in any of my illegal activities. But as sick as she was, I felt I had to tell her about my plan to jump bail.

"How are you feeling?" I asked, pulling a chair up next to her bed, laying my hand on her frail arm.

"Not so good," she replied, laboring over each word.

"You look good," I told her. It was a lie, and we both knew it.

"No, I don't," she corrected me.

I hesitated for a moment, listening to the mechanical ebb and flow of air going in and out of her lungs. "I'm not going back to Walpole," I told her at last.

"Of course not," she wheezed. "Everyone can see you didn't kill those girls."

"Maybe," I offered. "But I'm not waiting around to find out."

She shook her head, then opened her mouth to speak.

"Don't try to talk me out of this," I told her.

To her credit, she knew me well enough not to. But I could tell she wasn't happy with my decision.

"I'll come see you," I promised her. "No matter what."

The very next day, on March 3, 1985, after only eight hours of deliberation, the jury of six men and six women found me not guilty of all the charges against me, including the murders and kidnapping of Susan Webster and Karen Spinney, and two counts of accessory after the fact to the shootings of Ralph Cirvinale and Anthony DiVingo.

The verdict was read at 1:13 P.M. in Norfolk Superior Court at the Dedham Court House, but by then I was over sixty miles away. The night before, after leaving the hospital, I'd driven down to a friend's house in Dartmouth, just south of New Bedford. It wasn't until that evening that the news first reached me.

Any reasonable man would have turned himself in at that point, and I suppose that's what I should have done. But I truly couldn't help myself. By then running was second nature to me. I knew skipping out like that made me look guilty. But I also knew my actions made little difference one way or another. I would never be able to shake the fact that I'd been convicted of the murders the first time around, no matter what I did.

My plan was to leave Massachusetts, and perhaps even the country, but for the moment I was reluctant to stray too far from Boston. My mother was getting worse by the day, and my sister, Patsy, and I both knew she didn't have long to live. Still, we were both taken off guard when, just nine days after the Spinney-Webster verdict was announced, she passed away.

"She's at Malloy's," Patsy told me when I called her to find out the details of the funeral and visitation. "I won't expect you to come, given the circumstances."

"Don't worry," I told my sister. "I'll be there." I had given my word that I would visit my mother, and it was a promise I was determined to keep, no matter what the circumstances.

"The cops'll be watching the place," Patsy warned me. "They've had a couple of guys on our house since you took off, and a couple more over at Oak Road."

"I'm coming to see her," I said.

When I was growing up Milton was the kind of town where everyone, at least within their social stratum, knew everyone else. This was especially true for the Irish community, where the average number of children per family virtually guaranteed a connection to someone in the clan. The Malloys, who owned the funeral home, were such a family. As chance would have it, I had gone to school with one of their sons.

Tommy Malloy was a good kid, and I knew I'd be able to trust him. I called him as soon as I hung up with Patsy.

"Sorry about your ma," he said. "You know we'll take good care of her."

"I'm sure you will," I agreed. "But here's the thing: I don't think I'll be able to come to the service tomorrow. I was wondering if we could arrange a private viewing."

Morticians are on par with priests and psychiatrists when it comes being privy to people's dirty little secrets. I'm sure mine wasn't the first request of this sort Tommy had received. "Sure, Myles," he said, without batting an eye. "You have something in mind?"

"As a matter of fact," I told him, "I do."

The next evening Tommy and I met behind Giuliani's Garage in Quincy. With the cops watching the funeral home, I figured there was only one way for me to get inside without being seen: the way all of us eventually make our final trip to the mortuary, in the back of a hearse.

Tommy had gone all out for me. He'd brought his father's brand-new Cadillac Superior, the best car in their fleet. In the back of the hearse was a magnificent mahogany casket, the wood polished to a high sheen. I highly doubt I'll get that rich a send-off the next time around.

"Ready?" he asked, hopping out of the driver's seat, opening the Cadillac's rear doors.

I nodded, then climbed up into the back of the hearse. It had been my idea to make the trip into the funeral home inside the coffin. But now, faced with the reality of getting into the casket, I involuntarily balked.

"Don't worry," Tommy said, seeing me hesitate. "I won't close it all the way."

It was a meager consolation, but his reassurance gave me the confidence I needed. I slid into the casket and felt myself enveloped by the soft satin lining. Suddenly an unsettling thought occurred to me. "This isn't hers, is it?" I asked.

Tommy leaned into the hearse and put his hand on the lid. "Whose?"

"My mother's," I said, swallowing hard.

Tommy shook his head. "Nah. This one's for tomorrow's burial," he said. Then he lowered the lid, leaving me in utter darkness.

It wasn't far from Giuliani's to the funeral home, a ten minute drive at most, but they were some of the longest ten minutes of my life. Despite their plush appearance, coffins are surprisingly uncomfortable. By the time we reached Malloy's I had come to the conclusion that cremation was the best option for me. As we turned into the driveway I lifted my head slightly and peered out through the narrow opening Tommy had left for me, catching a glimpse of the unmarked car parked across the street and the two plainclothesmen in the front seat.

We pulled to a stop by the morgue doors and Tommy cut the engine. Lifting the coffin's lid myself, I clambered out at last.

"Visitation ended half an hour ago," Tommy told me, glancing at his watch as he hastily ushered me inside the home and through the embalming room. "You should have the place to yourself by now." We paused at the swinging doors that led to the viewing room. "Take as much time as you need," he said, leaving me on my own.

I waited a moment, listening to Tommy's fading footsteps as he disappeared back into the bowels of the building, readying myself in some small way for what I was about to do. Then I put my hand on the double doors and pushed through.

I was prepared to encounter death on the other side; what I had not expected was the living. The sight of a man standing on the far side of the viewing room caught me entirely off guard. For a moment, seeing the blue uniform I'd watched my father put on so many times, I thought he was a ghost.

"Hello, Myles," he said, raising his hand, tipping his hat slightly.

"Hugh?" I said, recognizing one of my father's old friends from the Milton Police Force.

Hugh glanced at my mother's open casket. "You go on and say your good-byes," he said, moving toward the door. "As far as I'm concerned, you were never here."

He was gone before I had a chance to thank him.

Finally alone, I made my way to my mother's side. Physically, my mother had never been a large person, but now, robbed of her indomitable personality, she seemed unnaturally small and frail. I bent down and slipped my arms around her tiny body, feeling the two sharp wings of her shoulder blades against my palms, cradling her for a moment, as she had no doubt cradled me on countless occasions.

It was without question the darkest moment of my life. Even so, I took some small comfort in the fact that my mother had lived to see me acquitted of the murders. If she had not, I might not have been able to live with myself.

On July 10, 1985, I was at the house on Oak Road with my daughter, Kim, and my son, Myles III. The house, which had been up for sale since my mother's death, had finally sold, and we were there clearing out the last of her furnishings, including my vast collection, which I was taking to the house of another family member.

To tell you the truth, I was half expecting the cops to show up. Just the day before, one of the neighbors had walked by while I was sitting on the porch. I had a good four months' growth of beard at the time. But though the shock of red facial hair hid my features, it knew it did little to disguise my identity.

I was inside when the cruisers pulled up, and I got a glimpse of them through the front window: at least a dozen marked cars blocking the street; and a phalanx of cops, some wearing state police uniforms, others in Boston PD blues.

As the men moved to surround the house I bolted for the back door, flying out the steps and into the yard. With little time and few options, I headed for the tool shed at the back of the garden, wriggling into the cramped crawl space beneath the shed's floorboards. It was an uncomfortable spot, and not only because it was small and damp. Years earlier, after the Tijuana incident, I'd stored several leftover bundles of dynamite under the shed. Now I found myself literally nose to nose with the explosives.

Holding my breath, I peered out through one of the narrow openings in the shed's cinder-block foundation. I could see at least a dozen pairs of boots fanning across the yard.

"The shed!" someone called. "I saw him heading for the shed."

Within seconds I was surrounded. I heard the click of a safety and turned my head to see a state trooper peering in through the foundation gap, his gun pointing right at me.

"Just like old times, isn't it, Myles?" the man said, grinning slightly.

That October, with Marty Leppo once again representing me, I pled guilty to the bail-jumping charge in Norfolk Superior Court. Like Earle Cooley, Marty was optimistic about my sentence. Arguing that I had already spent over four years in prison for the Spinney-Webster murder, Marty urged the judge to be lenient. But his pleas fell on deaf ears.

On Halloween I was sentenced to a year in the Norfolk County Jail, the maximum term allowable.

Twenty-Nine

Throughout both murder trials, the intervening four and a half years in prison, and the months I'd spent on the run, Suzanne King had remained unflinchingly loyal to me. She was a welcome constant in my otherwise tumultuous life, and I had come to love her deeply. But life in Boston and her association with me had taken its toll on Susie.

Desperate to get out of Massachusetts, she moved to Louisville, Kentucky, to take a job working as a horse trainer and groomer at Churchill Downs. It was a dream job for Susie. But it was a hardscrabble existence, especially for a young woman. During her first year there she bunked in the tack room at the track. Eventually she was able to rent a small house in the country.

In the summer of 1986, after serving nine months of my year-long sentenced, I was paroled from the Norfolk County Jail. I was a free man, but I had little to return to. Despite the fact that a jury had found me not guilty of the murders, my original conviction in the Spinney-Webster case still dogged me. The family of Karen Spinney, especially her father, had been vocal in their anger over the second verdict. And the local media eagerly fanned the flames of their rage. One *Boston Herald* columnist had gone so far as to dub the panel of twelve men and women who'd found me not guilty "the World's Dumbest Jury."

Boston, the city that had once embraced me as its prodigal son, that had seen in me its own restless image, no longer wanted anything to do with me. The bank robberies and art thefts had been one thing; if anything, my outlaw reputation had only added to my allure as a rock and roller. But the murders were another matter altogether. My music career was finished.

With little to keep me in Boston, I decided to join Susie. In the fall of 1986 I moved to Kentucky, taking my son, Myles III, with me. I brought along a few of my more impressive pieces, including a number of Japanese swords of which I was especially fond and one of the Simon Willard clocks I'd taken from the Woolworth mansion over a decade earlier, but my collection was far too large to transport in its entirety. Most of it remained behind at the home of a family member.

I won't lie to you: I hadn't abandoned my life of crime entirely. Using some of my old connections and some I'd made in prison, I set myself up with a small import business, bringing wholesale quantities of cocaine from suppliers in Miami to dealers in Boston. Compared to Susie's work at the stables, it was ridiculously easy money: two or three times a month I'd drive down to Florida, load the trunk of my car with kilo bags, and head north to Massachusetts.

All in all, our life in Kentucky was very good. We quickly acquired a small menagerie, including a mare named Candy Girl that Susie boarded at a neighboring farm. The horse world being what it was, most of the people we associated with had had their own brushes with the law or knew people who had. No one seemed overly concerned by my past. In fact, I made a number of friends who shared my criminal history.

One of these was a man named Dave Grant, who was the manager of the farm where Susie kept her horse. Grant had done time in the federal prison in Leavenworth, Kansas, on drug charges. After his release he'd spent several years in Alaska, eventually moving to Kentucky when, he claimed, he got tired of the long arctic winters.

That Grant had lived in Alaska after his prison stint should have been a red flag. I've since found out that the state is a popular destination for people in the witness protection program. I guess the feds figure no one will know who they are up there. Whatever the case, the idea of a hornet's nest of informants freezing their asses off in the arctic gives me no small amount of satisfaction. At the time, however, I was unaware of this fact, and believed Grant when he said he had gone up to Alaska to work on the oil pipeline.

Grant was particularly interested in my collection, frequently dropping by the house, professing an interest in art and antiques, asking me questions about individual pieces. Always a sucker for anyone who shared my passion for antiquities, I happily obliged his curiosity.

Grant also took a liking to Myles III, eventually hiring him to work in his barn. Myles was not always easy to get along with—we would eventually learn that he suffered from an emotional problem, but at the time, though we had our suspicions, none of us knew how serious the condition was—and I was grateful for the kindness Grant showed him.

One day in the summer of 1988 Grant came to me for a favor. He had a friend, he said, who was looking to buy a small quantity of cocaine for personal use. By this time it was no secret that I was in the business. Thinking nothing of Grant's request, I readily agreed, giving him the drugs that very night. He left my house with it and returned several days later with his friend's payment.

What I didn't know at the time was that Grant's "friend" was actually a federal agent. A decade after their humiliation at my hands over the theft and subsequent return of the Rembrandt, the FBI had finally found a way to get to me.

Several months after the cocaine incident Grant again approached me, this time with a more lucrative proposal.

"I've got a friend who might be interested in that clock of yours," Grant told me one night.

"The Simon Willard?" I asked, taken off guard by his unexpected proposal. Grant had asked me about the clock numerous times. Though I hadn't told him exactly how I'd come by the piece, I'd given him a brief tutorial on its provenance and approximate worth. He had seemed duly impressed at the time.

Grant nodded. "We met up in Leavenworth. Guy's a collector, like you. Very discreet, if you know what I mean. A family man."

"He's connected?" I asked, thinking it sure sounded like Grant was trying to tell me the guy was mobbed up.

"You could say that."

"He's in Louisville?"

Grant shook his head. "He lives up in Bloomington, Illinois."

"What's his name?" I asked.

"Tony Graziano," Grant said. "But everyone calls him Big Tony."

"Graziano, huh?" It wasn't a name I recognized.

"His family's big in Indianapolis," Grant explained.

"Sounds interesting," I mused.

Though I'd known Grant for some time, I didn't yet trust him enough to enter into business with his so-called friend. But neither was I entirely uninterested in his proposition. I let the subject go, confident Grant would bring it up again.

It didn't take long for him to do so.

"I just talked to my buddy up in Illinois," Grant said when I went to pick up Myles III at his farm one afternoon. "You know, that guy I was telling you about: Big Tony. I told him about your clock. He's willing to give you ten grand for it."

The amount was much less than the clock was actually worth. But then, because of its size and history, the Simon Willard was an awkward piece to fence. All things considered, $10,000 was a fair offer. Still, it was a small payoff for what could be an awful lot of trouble. On the other hand, I had a number of big-ticket items I was looking to unload. If Grant's friend turned out to be the real deal, I stood to make a lot more than ten grand off him.

"Maybe you could get us together sometime," I told Grant.

A fter several weeks of back-and-forth Grant finally arranged a meeting. On December 5, 1988, I drove to Illinois with the clock in the back of my van. The next day Tony and I met at the Ramada Inn in Bloomington.

It was a fairly straightforward exchange. Tony gave me the $10,000 we'd agreed upon. In return I gave him the Simon Willard grandfather clock Bobby Donati and I had stolen all those years earlier from the Woolworth estate.

"There's lots more where that came from," I told him as we transferred the clock from my van to his.

"Oh yeah?" he remarked. "Dave said you've got quite a collection of Japanese swords."

"Among other things."

Tony nodded appreciatively. "I'll be in touch."

Not long after I returned to Kentucky, Grant once again approached me on his friend's behalf. "It looks like you two have a lot more in common than your love of antiques," Grant said. "Big Tony's got a nice side business going with the college kids up there. Very lucrative, from what he says. He's always looking for reliable suppliers."

I know what you're thinking: I should have smelled a rat. In hindsight, even I have trouble understanding why I took Grant's bait. The truth is that I didn't entirely trust him. But despite the not-so-subtle stench of rodent in the air I managed to convince myself that Grant wouldn't double-cross me.

There comes a point when you have to take it on faith that your friends are who they claim to be; if you don't eventually trust people, you'll have a long, lonely life ahead of you. I'm the first to admit that this way of thinking has gotten me into trouble on more than one occasion. Still, I have few regrets.

Of these, my association with Stokes and Sperrazza is by far the greatest. In terms of the repercussions it had on my own life, my reply to Grant's request is not far behind.

"Tell Tony I can get him whatever he wants," I said.

Over the next several weeks, using Dave Grant as our intermediary,

Big Tony and I laid the groundwork for what promised to be a highly lucrative business arrangement but was in fact an elaborate setup. Not content to simply bust me for the sale of the Simon Willard clock, Grant's handlers at the FBI were determined to up the ante. Tony wanted drugs, Grant told me. Cocaine, mostly, in large quantities. But he made it clear that he would buy pretty much anything I brought him.

Getting my hands on the drugs was no problem. But the quantities Tony was talking about—several kilos at a time—represented a significant investment on my part, $24,000 for the first kilo alone. It was money I didn't have. But while I was cash-poor, I had a small fortune tied up in my collection.

Learning this, Grant conveniently stepped forward with a solution: if I could offer Tony sufficient collateral, Grant suggested, he might loan me the cash I needed for my initial purchase. If Tony liked the pieces enough, he might even consider purchasing them.

On January 11, 1989, with the preliminary details of my partnership with Tony agreed upon, I set out for Illinois. I'd managed to procure a modest supply of pharmaceuticals—100 hits of LSD and a similar number of oxycodone pills—which I intended to sell to Tony. I had also brought along the two paintings I'd stolen years earlier from the Meade gallery at Amherst college: Pieter Lastman's "St. John the Baptist," which at the time was worth well over $150,000, and Hendrick Cornelisz van Vliet's "Interior of the Nieuwe Kerk, Delft," which was valued at a quarter of a million dollars. They were two of the more impressive pieces in my collection, and by far the most difficult to sell. If Tony had been able to fence the Simon Willard clock, I figured he might also be able to find a buyer for the paintings.

The following day Tony and I met at the Eastland Suites Lodge, an ugly, neo-Elizabethan faux-brick compound near the Bloomington airport, to negotiate the final terms of our arrangement. Much to my chagrin, Tony wasn't interested in buying the paintings. But he agreed to loan me the cash for my initial purchase, on the condition that he hold on to the paintings until I repaid him, preferably in cocaine. Along with the loan, Tony also paid me $1,700 for the LSD and oxycodone.

On March 1, with $24,000 cash in hand, I flew to Ft. Lauderdale, Florida, to pick up the kilo of cocaine I'd promised Tony. Less than a week later I was back in Illinois with the drugs. On March 7 Tony and I again met at the Eastland Suites. Only this time he hadn't come alone. No sooner had I produced the kilo bag than my hotel room was swarmed by federal agents. "Big Tony" flashed his badge, and I was immediately placed under arrest.

Grant had been right about one thing: the deal had turned out to be profitable, just not for me. For his role in setting me up, Dave Grant was paid over $60,000 by the FBI. Though I knew Grant had orchestrated the Bloomington sting, it wasn't until several weeks later that I realized the full extent of his betrayal. In an attempt to cover up the fact that he had brutalized his own wife, Grant told his handlers that Myles III had assaulted and attempted to rape her. It was a bald-faced lie. Grant's wife and another witness eventually signed sworn affidavits saying it was Grant, not Myles III, who had assaulted her. But the accusation had been made, and it stuck.

It was a good thing I was in jail when I found out about the allegations. Had I not been locked up, I have no doubt I would have hunted down Grant and killed him for involving my son in his sordid dealings.

In November 1989, eight months after my arrest in Bloomington, I pleaded guilty to all the charges against me, which included possession of cocaine with intent to distribute and conspiracy to distribute. My adventure, begun all those years earlier on the high bank of the Union River, was drawing to a close. But my old life in Boston wasn't finished with me quite yet.

In March 1990, while I was awaiting sentencing in the Bloomington case, federal agents came to see me at the Sangamon County Jail in Springfield, Illinois. Days earlier thieves had robbed the Isabella Stewart Gardner Museum in Boston, and the FBI was convinced I knew who had done it. I had my suspicions, but I wasn't about to share them with the feds.

I'd read about the heist in the paper, taking special note of the list of items taken, which included a bronze flagpole finial in the shape of an eagle. The finial was a piece that particularly puzzled investigators, given its relatively modest value and the time and energy it had taken to get it in the first place.

But it wasn't a mystery to me. I knew exactly who'd stolen the finial: Bobby Donati. It had taken him nearly two decades since our initial visit to the Gardner Museum to make good on his plan to rob the place. But he had left his calling card, as promised: *the eagle had landed.*

Several weeks later my suspicions about Bobby's involvement in the Gardner heist were confirmed when I received an unexpected visitor. David Houghton, my old friend from Milton, had flown out to see me, and he had some very interesting news. David had always remained close to my family, especially my mother. During my last stint in Walpole he'd cared for her as if she'd been his own flesh and blood. But I hadn't seen much of him since my mother died.

"Did you hear what we did?" David asked excitedly. He was a big man, three hundred pounds on a good day, with a mechanic's grease-stained hands, but the expression on his face was that of a young boy who'd just landed his first fish.

He glanced around the visiting room, then, confident that we were out of earshot of the guards and other prisoners, leaned across the table that separated us. "The Gardner," he whispered. "That was us."

"What the hell are you talking about?" I asked. That Bobby had something to do with the theft came as no surprise to me, but it had not even crossed my mind that David might have been involved as well.

"We're gonna get you out of here, Myles," he said. "Just like you did with the Rembrandt."

As much as I appreciated my friends' plan to once again bargain me out of prison, I found David's visit unsettling. I couldn't speak for Bobby, but David, at least, seemed entirely unaware of the difficulties involved in such a negotiation. The months I'd spent haggling with

Regan and Twomey had been a delicate affair. Neither Bobby nor David had the connections or the savvy necessary to make a deal of such magnitude.

Holding the single Rembrandt had been one thing, but the Gardner haul was another matter altogether. The pieces Bobby had chosen were the kind of things people kill for. If rumor got out that Bobby or David knew anything about the whereabouts of the art, they'd be in real danger.

Unfortunately, my misgivings proved to be warranted. David's visit was the last time I heard from either man.

The following summer U.S. District Judge Richard Mills sentenced me to twenty years in prison, more than double the sentence requested by the prosecutor in the case.

"You're obviously a smart man," Judge Mills told me. "Someone could write a book about you someday, but no one would believe it."

In the fall of 1990 I was transferred to the federal penitentiary in Lompoc, California. Not long after, Bobby Donati was found stabbed to death in an automobile trunk, in what was obviously a mob hit. A year later, David Houghton died of a heart attack, leaving nothing behind but his 1988 Oldsmobile Delta and roach-infested house in Malden.

What happened to the Gardner art is a question that remains unanswered.

I have not been inside the Gardner Museum since the afternoon I spent there with Bobby Donati. For obvious reasons, I would not be welcome. But I know that, thanks to a clause in Isabella Gardner's will stipulating absolutely no changes to the museum's collection, the empty frames from which the paintings were cut that foggy March night still hang on the walls, mute witnesses to a crime that will, in all likelihood, never be solved.

In the Dutch room Rembrandt himself, captured in a self-portrait at the age of twenty-three, seems unable to look away from the blank space where his magnificent seascape once hung. His painted gaze is drawn to it, as are those of the thousands of visitors who shuffle past this spot each year. Among the 2,500 pieces of priceless art housed in the Gardner Museum, this is what they most want to see. Not the painting itself, but the puzzle of it, the thing that begs to be understood.

I, on the other hand, have a clear memory of the canvas as I saw it. The boat brimming with disciples riding the dark sea. The enormous white wave that threatens to engulf them all. The men trying desperately to wrangle the craft.

In the end, I suspect, this is how Bobby Donati and David Houghton must have felt, foundering in a storm of their own creation.

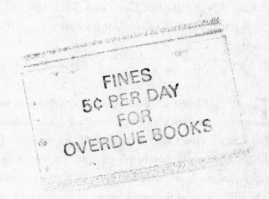

Epilogue

It's difficult to put an exact value on a collection like mine. So many of the pieces I accumulated over the years—hundreds of Japanese swords; dozens of paintings; countless ceramics, bronzes, ivory carvings, Japanese netsukes, and Chinese watercolors; and arms and armor of various provenance—were priceless. But it's safe to say that by the time I entered Lompoc I had accumulated several million dollars' worth of art and antiques. It was a fortune I intended to make good use of upon my release. In an interview from my prison cell I once said that I planned to retire to my own private island off the coast of Japan. Unfortunately, I spoke prematurely.

A lot can happen while a man is in prison: people move or pass away, loyalties shift, desperation rears its ugly head. The family member with whom I'd originally stored my things moved to Florida several years before I was paroled, leaving the bulk of my collection with a former prison associate of mine. It seemed like a good idea at the time. Unfortunately, my associate developed a nasty heroin addiction almost immediately after his release. Over the course of the next several years he sold nearly everything to pay for his habit. By the time I was paroled most of my collection was gone. Forget the island; I couldn't have afforded a tea house.

With nothing left, I went home. Susie, who remained devoted to me throughout my decade in prison, had returned to Massachusetts not long after my arrest, and I joined her there.

I won't lie to you: there are times when I've wondered about all the other lives I might have led. The possibilities are inescapable. And though I try to console myself with the fact that I wouldn't have been comfortable in any other skin, I suspect that this is not actually the case. I would have been good at any number of things, and may very well have found a great deal of satisfaction in being a doctor or a lawyer. Still, I wouldn't trade the life I have lived for anything.

In speaking of the Divine, Hindus tell a parable about three blind beggars who come upon an elephant. The first one grabs the elephant's tusk and says: "An elephant is long and smooth and hard with a sharp point—like the strongest smoothest stick I have ever come across." The second beggar grabs the elephant's leg. "No," he says. "An elephant is rough-textured and immovable, like the trunk of a tree." "You are both wrong," says the third beggar as he grabs the elephant's tail. "It is thin, flexible and swings about like a rope tied to a tree."

Of course they're all wrong.

No man's life is merely a sum of its parts. Taken as such, mine would read as pure tragedy, the occasional moments of triumph poor recompense for three decades spent in prison. Yet this is not the case. There is no scale on which to set the thrill of holding a Rembrandt in one's hands. No stick by which to measure the cheers of six hundred men in the Walpole prison auditorium.

They say most people lead lives of quiet desperation. Mine, at least, has been anything but.

Acknowledgments

For their invaluable help with the completion of this project, the writers wish to thank Suzanne King, Charlie Moore, Martha Ferrante, Billy Oikle, Earle Cooley, Marty Leppo, and Dan Conaway. Thanks also to Bruce Nichols, Adam Rosen, superhero copy chief Amy Vreeland, and everyone else at HarperCollins who helped turn this manuscript into a book. The writers are especially grateful to Al Dotoli, a true friend and a terrific manager, whose contributions to this book and Myles's career in general cannot be overstated. Al knows Myles better than anyone, and without his help this story could not have been told.

The episodes depicted in this book cover a specific and relatively brief time period. As a result, many of Myles's closest friends and family members were not mentioned. Additionally, certain individuals were purposefully excluded, either because they could not be located for permission, or because they asked that their names not be used. Myles wishes to express his personal gratitude to the following people: Vicky, Kim, and Myles III; Patsy and Steve Harrington, their son, Bobby, and their daughter, Kelly; Myles's half brothers, Father Sean Connor and Jamie Connor (one of the finest men to ever wear the badge), and his half sisters, Erin and Katy; Robert and Joan Paton; Chris and Doug Connors; Billy Roach; Billy Libby; Joe Rego; Matthew Norris; Peter Walsh; Bean; Lenny "The Mechanic" Biondi and Jimmy "The Fixer" Biondi;

Jimmy McGettrick, owner of the Beachcomber; Pat Nee; Dr. Anthony Von Vought; Jimmy Martorano; Tommy Cass (you'll always be my pal); Moya Kinneally; Katherine Pederson (the nicest person I've ever met); Phillip and Dorothy Senna; J. D. Mix; Rocco Ellis; Arnie "Woo Woo" Ginsburg; Warren and Kaye Dougan; the Petrozziello family; the King family; Emmy Lou Dunbar Pinkham; Tim and Richard Steinmetz; Philip Demerzia; Ruth Engles; Anthony "the Animal" Felela; Jimmy "the Rooster" Reagon; Donnie "the Detailer"; Tom Mashberg; and the many others who prefer to remain unnamed. Myles would also like to acknowledge all those doing time, as well as the men and women of the badge, the vast majority of whom are decent and honorable people. Finally, to Ozzy DePriest, Ralph Petrozziello, and all those who have passed on: may you rest in peace.

Index